"I highly recommend this very valuable resource for both practitioners and academics interested in orality. The whole collection is informative, making it a go-to book on the subject for both novices and experts. The authors share thought-provoking and engaging insights that will surely invite readers to reflect deeply on their practice and thinking."

—**Edwardneil A. Benavidez**, Adjunct Faculty, Asian Seminary of Christian Ministry

New and Old Horizons in the Orality Movement

Evangelical Missiological Society Monograph Series

Anthony Casey, Allen Yeh, Mark Kreitzer, and Edward L. Smither
SERIES EDITORS

———————————

A Project of the Evangelical Missiological Society
www.emsweb.org

New and Old Horizons in the Orality Movement

Expanding the Firm Foundations

EDITED BY
Tom Steffen
AND
Cameron D. Armstrong

FOREWORD BY
Romerlito Macalinao

◥PICKWICK *Publications* • Eugene, Oregon

NEW AND OLD HORIZONS IN THE ORALITY MOVEMENT
Expanding the Firm Foundations

Evangelical Missiological Society Monograph Series 14

Copyright © 2022 Wipf and Stock Publishers. All rights reserved. Except for brief quotations in critical publications or reviews, no part of this book may be reproduced in any manner without prior written permission from the publisher. Write: Permissions, Wipf and Stock Publishers, 199 W. 8th Ave., Suite 3, Eugene, OR 97401.

Pickwick Publications
An Imprint of Wipf and Stock Publishers
199 W. 8th Ave., Suite 3
Eugene, OR 97401

www.wipfandstock.com

PAPERBACK ISBN: 978-1-6667-3080-7
HARDCOVER ISBN: 978-1-6667-2274-1
EBOOK ISBN: 978-1-6667-2276-5

Cataloguing-in-Publication data:

Names: Steffen, Tom, editor. | Armstrong, Cameron D., editor. | Macalinao, Romerlito, foreword.

Title: New and old horizons in the orality movement : expanding the firm foundations / edited by Tom Steffen and Cameron D. Armstrong ; foreword by Romerlito Macalinao.

Description: Eugene, OR: Pickwick Publications, 2022 | Evangelical Missiological Society Monograph Series 14 | Includes bibliographical references.

Identifiers: ISBN 978-1-6667-3080-7 (paperback) | ISBN 978-1-6667-2274-1 (hardcover) | ISBN 978-1-6667-2276-5 (ebook)

Subjects: LCSH: Intercultural communication—Religious aspects—Christianity. | Storytelling—Religious aspects—Christianity. | Literacy. | Oral communication.

Classification: BV2082.I57 N49 2022 (print) | BV2082.I57 (ebook)

01/06/22

Contents

List of Illustrations: Figures and Tables | vii

Book Dedication | ix
    Tom Steffen

Foreword | xiii
    Romerlito Macalinao

Setting the Stage | xvii
    Tom Steffen

Abbreviations | xx

Part 1: Measuring the Horizons

1. An Orality Learning Journey | 3
    Jerry Wiles

2. Deconstructing Oral Learning: The Latest Research | 15
    Lynn Thigpen

3. The Metanarrative of Scripture: A Critical Factor in Cross-Cultural Ministry | 46
    Wiley Scot Keen

Part 2: Horizon: The Classroom

4. Theological Institutions and Orality: Paying Attention to Non-readers at Home and Abroad | 65
    Larry Caldwell

5. Storying in Seminary: Romanian Theology Students Using Oral-based Teaching Methods | 83
CAMERON D. ARMSTRONG

6. For a Time Such as This: Oral Bible Schools Take Root in Sub-Saharan Africa | 106
A. STEVEN EVANS

7. Mining the Biblical Narratives for Individual and Communal Transformation: Bible Storytelling that Moves Beyond Proclamation to Deep Level Discipleship | 132
JENNIFER JAGERSON

Part 3: Horizon: Bible Translation

8. What can We Expect from Oral Bible Translation? | 151
JOHN E. STARK

9. Are We Telling Faithful Stories? The Need for Evaluating Bible Storying | 171
DON BARGER

Part 4: Expanding the Horizons

10. Is it Time for the Return of Oral Hermeneutics? | 201
TOM STEFFEN

11. New Hope: A Theo-dramatic Approach to Trauma Healing | 232
TRICIA STRINGER AND STEPHEN STRINGER

12. What's Patronage Got to Do with It? Beyond Storying in Oral Learning | 251
LYNN THIGPEN

Concluding Thoughts | 275
CAMERON D. ARMSTRONG

List of Contributors | 279

Lists of Illustrations

Figures

Figure 2.1	Important Elements in Deconstructing Orality	22
Figure 2.2	Learning Quadrants	32
Figure 2.3	Reconstructing Oral Learning based on Research	34
Figure 5.1	Literature Review Intersections	85
Figure 5.2	Central Understanding	94
Figure 6.1	Oral Bible Schools Spectrum in Sub-Saharan Africa	107
Figure 8.1	Key Elements of Oral Bible Translation	152
Figure 8.2	The Basic Elements of Translation	157
Figure 8.3	Partial Incarnation	167
Figure 8.4	Full Incarnation	167
Figure 8.5	Literate vs. Oral Fuel Gauge	170
Figure 9.1	Transcripted Back Translation	193
Figure 10.1	The Oral Hermeneutic Wheel	196
Figure 12.1	Frankena's Reasoning in Evaluating a Philosophy of Education	253
Figure 12.2	The World of Connected Clients	261
Figure 13.1	Approaches to Orality Research	277

Tables

Table 9.1	Summary of Tests with Testing Goals	193
Table 10.1	Oral-Textual Hermeneutic Continuum	196

Celebrating J.O. Terry's Role in Bible Storying

Book Dedication

THE YEAR WAS 2000. The place was Chiang Mai, Thailand. The occasion was the grand opening of a graduate extension center for the Cook School of Intercultural Studies, Biola University. To welcome incoming students, a celebration dinner was held before classes began. The dean of the school, Doug Pennoyer, and I were busy setting up equipment. I turned and saw an unfamiliar, smiling face headed towards me. Then I heard: "Hi, Tom. I'm J.O. Terry."

That was my first face-to-face encounter with J.O., although we had previously exchanged emails on numerous occasions. He was not there for classes; he was there because he had heard I was in town and teaching a class on narrative. What a great time getting caught up to date with this quintessential Bible storyteller affiliated with the Southern Baptist Foreign Mission Board (IMB)!

Not only do I consider J.O. a close friend and a "go-to person" for information on the orality movement because of his extensive global knowledge, practice, materials and influence, I believe God has used J.O. in a formable way to advance the modern-day orality movement. This movement began in the Philippines with Trevor McIlwain of New Tribes Mission (now Ethnos360). The movement's waves first traveled beyond Philippine shores in 1981. Some backstory follows.

Jim Slack, an IMB church growth researcher in the Philippines and a good friend of Dell Schulze, then President of New Tribes Mission of the Philippines, heard about McIlwain's teaching on "Chronological Bible Teaching" and wanted it introduced to IMB. McIlwain taught the first IMB seminar in Baguio, Philippines, in 1983. The rest is history. IMB, with willing personnel, ample funding, and the prolific production of Bible storying sets, books, journals, newsletters, training materials and seminars would eventually propel McIlwain's Bible Storying model designed for evangelism, discipleship and long-term church planting/multiplication into a global movement far beyond New Tribes Mission.

Now retired, J.O. misses being on the field. He wishes he was younger and able to be out there testing new models in various cultural and religious settings. That does not, however, stop Bible Storyers from around the globe from seeking his advice on multiple issues related to Bible Storying. He gets numerous questions like, "How do you know which stories to tell?" "I've tried these stories, but the people don't seem interested or are not responding. What should I do?"

Ask J.O. a question and expect to receive an answer, resources, and a long email. I found his lengthy emails so resource-rich regarding personnel, philosophy, and practice in relation to Bible Storying that I began a file with dates and yellow highlights of all J.O.'s emails.

Familiar with market research from his background in radio broadcasting, J.O. understood the importance of knowing your audience. Never claiming his materials were the beginning and end all, J.O. asked recipients to craft the stories for their specific audiences and let him know what changes they made so these ideas could be passed on to others.

Having not finished seminary and therefore having no credentials that mattered in the formal educational world, J.O. always co-taught with a professor-of-record who could post the grades, even if the class was basically his. The graduates, once spread around the world, continued to email him asking for input. Besides answering their emails, J.O. initiated and continues to edit the "Bible Storying Newsletter" that addresses orality issues with storying examples from around the world, alerts readers to the latest relevant publications in orality and Bible Storying, and so forth. Now in his mid-eighties, people often address him, deservingly, as Dr. Terry.

Besides teaching Bible Storying classes in the seminaries and universities and starting a periodical newsletter, J.O. changed accepted nomenclature early in the game. After listening to McIlwain teach a seminar on Chronological Bible Teaching in Chiang Mai, Thailand, he concluded there was way too much emphasis given to teaching by the Bible storyteller. To show his trust in the power of story to convey its own message, J.O. replaced "Chronological Bible Teaching" with "Chronological Bible Storying." J.O. believed theology should evolve through relationally based narrative.

J.O. also started the use of the term "storying," (which he saw in a book titled *Management by Storying Around*) preferring it over "storytelling," as it described more accurately what they were attempting to do. He always capitalizes "Bible Storying," considering it an oral methodology.

Often finding himself in social settings where he had only a few minutes or hours to tell the gospel, J.O. realized it was impossible to present anywhere from twelve to sixty-eight evangelistic Bible stories from creation to Christ. So to accommodate an abbreviated aggregate of Bible stories he coined a new term—"fast tracking". Rather than celebrating his nomenclature creativity, J.O. felt he was guilty of inventing terms to describe activities or methods because he was not aware of the existing terms in academia.

J.O. also challenged Bible Storyers to learn the worldview of their audience (recall his radio broadcasting background) before beginning to tell the Bible stories, providing a chart to aid in the process. J.O. believes that anyone who had a defined list of Bible stories to be used anywhere in the world assumed a generic worldview and would therefore be ineffective. He was disappointed and distressed when IMB leadership dismissed learning the worldview of the host culture because it took too much time away from planting/multiplying churches.

Here's a few more of J.O.'s contributions that include books and story sets:

Basic Bible Storying;

Hope Stories from the Bible (thirty-two stories);

Food Stories from the Bible (forty-four stories);

Death Stories from the Bible (forty-two stories;

Water Stories from the Bible (twenty-two);

Grief Stories from the Bible (thirty-nine);

Bible Storying Handbook for Short-Term Mission Teams, Mission Volunteers (thirty-two stories);

Oralizing Bible Stories for Telling;

The Holy Rosary Gospel Stories of Jesus (twenty meditations);

Heaven is for Women;

God's Gift of Forgiveness;

Peace for Hindu Women;

Ebenezer Stories;

HIV Hope;

Let's Just Talk.

If EMS could do it, the Society would award an honorary doctorate to J.O. for his foundational and far-reaching contributions to the modern-day orality movement that changed ministry models not just abroad, but later in the USA as well. Since this is impossible, something else is necessary: Dr. Terry, because of your dedicated life's work in honoring the King and the Sacred Storybook through practice-based philosophical theories in Bible Storying that resulted in clearer understanding of Bible stories for peoples of all the major world religions, EMS dedicates this book to you! Congratulations and thank you for your lifetime of dedicated sacrifice and service for Bible Storyers.

Tom Steffen

Professor emeritus of intercultural studies
Cook School of Intercultural Studies, Biola University

Foreword

Romerlito Macalinao

The majority of the remaining Bibleless people groups are predominantly oral. Because oral cultures neither read nor write, their access to God's Word is not based on the printed text. I clearly heard that message in a presentation at a global gathering of Wycliffe/SIL in Singapore in 2010. That message impacted me immeasurably.

At the time, I served as executive of a newly recognized Wycliffe member organization. If that was the fact of the century, how does the Bible translation enterprise respond? Is there not a program that could prepare people to be able to reach the world's oral peoples? Speaking as an educator that has been in the field of theological/ministerial education for decades, both formally and non-formally, I decided a training program to address that need must be developed. I never realized this event would trigger my journey in learning about orality in missions, understanding oral cultures, and developing strategies to enable oral Bibleless people groups to have access to God's Word in all available oral formats. God did something to strengthen my heart that day. A passion was born. A personal meta-narrative was unfolding. I was never the same again. I now hold a firm conviction to advance the Great Commission among the oral Bibleless and unreached people groups of the world by employing Oral strategies.

This book is a tribute to J.O. Terry, a man who surpassed the lack of academic credentials to become a model and mentor in the theory and practice of reaching Oral cultures; an Oralist *par excellence*. The journey to this point of seeing these contributions from reflective practitioners in one volume took decades. Each in their own right, these writers tried to make sense of what it means to engage non-reading cultures in various stages and realities of life. Armed with empirical research and a heart for the mission of God, each author embarked on documenting, immersing, analyzing, interpreting, formulating, and integrating a way of understanding oral cultures in order to effectively communicate the Gospel of our Lord and Savior Jesus Christ. Now experts in their own field as academics, mission leaders, and practitioners, these men and women present to us their own learning journey.

I also underwent my own journey in orality praxis, both as an advocate in theological education and a practitioner in Bible translation. In those days, I had to self-educate, complete a training in "One Story," read, study, and connect with practitioners. This journey led to developing an orality-focused missionary training program for Bible translators. Consequently, divine appointments led me to the International Orality Network, for which I was later invited to be part of the regional leadership and global executive team. That advocacy involved orality papers written, South East Asia orality initiatives mobilized, and speaking at local, regional, and international conferences. Those years bore good and lasting fruit. Many former students and colleagues now serve on the mission field. Some are specialists in storying, ethnoarts, and oral Bible translation.

This compendium is a Living Library of oralists, modeling the way for orality praxis. Jerry Wiles illustrates the application of storying in various fronts, whether in the urban setting of the business world or in the rural corners of Africa by providing Living Water. Lynn Thigpen offers the latest research with a deconstruction Orality and a reconstruction of the brand name into Connected Learning, based on twenty years of ministry among the animistic Buddhists of Cambodia. Wiley Scot Keen asserts that every culture has their own defining unique story, a metanarrative, noting that it is imperative for cross-cultural workers to make that discovery so that every culture can find itself in the meta narrative of Scriptures. Larry Caldwell introduces the term "theological quotient" to refer to oral learners in the seminary, showcasing how a theological institution shifted their bachelor to doctoral degrees to incorporate orality. Cameron D. Armstrong teaches in a seminary in Romania and presents his research on how orality and andragogy intersect in implementing orality-framed teaching strategies among highly literate Romanian students. A. Steven Evans narrates the development of Oral Bible Schools in Sub-Saharan Africa and the successes of the program, recognizing the foundational work of Grant Lovejoy. Jennifer Jagerson develops the idea of Narrative Psychology in deep-level disciple-making and the utilization of Simply The Story methodology. John E. Stark offers a consultant's perspective on oral Bible translation as an incarnational ministry that necessitate coaching and mentoring of consultants-in-training. Don Barger explains his research and suggests a process in developing storying consultants and checking story sets. Tom Steffen explains oral hermeneutics and shows the way of communicating, processing, and applying Scriptures among oral cultures, drawn from ministry among the Ifugao of Northern Philippines. Tricia and Stephen Stringer introduce the concept of theodrama which utilizes the power of biblical narratives and the process of oral hermeneutics in trauma healing. Lynn Thigpen demonstrates how pedagogies of information are transcended by pedagogies of transformation and socialization so that disciple-making takes place among oral cultures, specifically among adults with limited formal education.

The roots of the Orality Movement began in the Philippines as early as 1975 with Trevor McIlwain of New Tribes Mission. Literate workers among non-reading and writing cultures questioned how to convey the message of the Gospel and the full counsel of God's Word in a way that is understandable and produces transformation. The answer gave birth to the Orality Movement with all the unique initiatives that capture the multidimensional character of oral cultures. The new horizons of orality continue to build on the foundations of the old horizons and the cornerstone of the Great Commission.

The work of championing, collaborating, and showcasing orality initiatives never stops until all have heard the Gospel and come to the saving knowledge of our Lord and Savior Jesus Christ. With the expanding reservoir of human knowledge, new information technologies, stewarding kingdom currencies, and a cornucopia of best practices by oralists at the disposal of the Global Church,[1] there is no reason why Bible translation cannot be completed in this decade and see every oral Bibleless unreached people groups impacted by the Great Commission. The Lord Jesus said in Matthew 24:14 (NASB), *"This gospel of the kingdom shall be preached to the whole world as a witness to the nations and then the end shall come."* I firmly

---

1. Perseverance paid off. Advocating for Orality for eight years finally bore fruit. In partnership with ION and members of the Orality Movement, the Asia Graduate School of Theology—Philippines will offer a ThM/PhD in Orality Studies in 2022. Preparations are under way to formalize the Memorandum of Agreement between the two parties. This program will be the first of its kind in the region and the intention is to extend this program in the region and elsewhere requested. Another advocacy that bore fruit is with Barclay Bible College in the USA. In partnership with Wycliffe Associates, this seminary will be offering an Orality track in the MA program in Bible Translation.

believe that we have in our lifetime the ability to fulfill our responsibility. This book is a great starting point to that end. May the love of the Father unite His people in Christ so that by the power of the Holy Spirit we shall see the discipling of the nations.

Rev. Romerlito C. Macalinao, EdD

Dean, Asia Graduate School of Theology—Philippines
Director of Global Networks, Wycliffe Associates

Setting the Stage

Tom Steffen

Orality formed us. Orality forms us. Orality will forever form us. Orality is a central theme of our lives.

In this fast-paced world, few Christian workers take the time to look back to learn and build on the lessons of the past. Wise Christian workers, however, do not forge ahead into new horizons without first investigating past horizons. They understand in this complex world there are too many strong shoulders of the past to be overlooked.

What you are about to read builds on the past to advance the modern-day orality movement to new heights. These chapters represent papers presented in the Orality Track at the virtual Evangelical Missiological Society annual meeting held October 9–10, 2020, hosted by Dallas International University. In this groundbreaking volume that centers on the modern-day orality movement—now 40 years young,[1] having done much to advance the gospel and mature and multiply churches globally—twelve authors build on a strong past as they make informed future advancements. The reader is in for a real treat as past horizons extend to enlightened future horizons, all well-versed in scholarship baked in practice.

The editors divided the book into four parts. Part 1 measures the horizons. Here Jerry Wiles reflects on his decades-long orality journey in "An Orality Learning Journey." Lynn Thigpen follows by questioning the accepted definition of orality in "Deconstructing Oral Learning: The Latest Research." She then redefines oral learning in a landmark way. Wiley Scot Keen closes this horizon with "The Metanarrative of Scripture: A Critical Factor in Cross-Cultural Ministry." To influence people of competing worldviews, he argues, it is necessary to not only know your metanarrative

---

1. Steffen, *Worldview-Based Storying*, 34.

and that of the host audience, but also Scripture's metanarrative, and how it intersects with the other two.

Part 2 considers the horizon of orality in the classroom. In "Theological Institutes and Orality: Paying Attention to Non-readers at Home and Abroad," Larry Caldwell offers concrete ways Bible schools and seminaries can incorporate oral-based pedagogy in both teaching and learning. In "Storying in Seminary: Romanian Theology Students Using Oral-based Teaching Methods," Cameron D. Armstrong offers an instructive case study from two classes he taught at Bucharest Baptist Theological Institute using oral-based methods. He identifies four themes that emerged. A. Steven Evans then explores oral Bible schools as they moved from a novelty to a necessity in "For a Time Such as This: Oral Bible Schools Take Root in Sub-Saharan Africa." Evaluating seven schools in six countries, Evans investigates the levels of oral methodologies used and their implications. Jennifer Jagerson concludes this horizon with "Mining the Biblical Narratives for Individual and Communal Transformation: Bible Storytelling that Moves Beyond Proclamation to Deep Level Discipleship." Through qualitative research, Jagerson discovered the dynamic effectiveness of Simply the Story, resulting in significant implications for theological education at home and abroad.

The horizon of Bible translation is considered in Part 3. John Stark begins with "What can We Expect from Oral Bible Translation?" Here he considers where, when and why an oral Bible translation should happen, and identifies key factors to its success. Don Barger concludes with "Are We Telling Faithful Stories? The Need for Evaluating Bible Storying." He explores the factors involved in testing stories and consultants checking Bible translations, offering a model for checking Bible stories and story sets.

Part 4 expands present horizons. I begin by asking the question: "Is it Time for the Return of Oral Hermeneutics?" Here I make the case that oral hermeneutics provides a more robust means to explain and interpret the narrative sections of Scripture than does textual (grammatical-historical) hermeneutics. Tricia and Stephen Stringer follow with "New Hope: A Theo-dramatic Approach to Trauma Healing." Here the couple shows how the theo-drama approach creates a structure through which God's Word can reframe and reshape traumatic experiences, and how narratives used within this framework significantly contribute to the development of a living, healing community participating in God's theo-drama. Lynn Thigpen concludes this horizon with "What's Patronage Got to Do with It? Beyond Storying in Oral Learning." Built on extensive research and experience in Cambodia, she explores how oral / connected learning and spiritual patronage (animism) merge in bringing soul transformation and spiritual maturity.

Written to be read, this scholarly researched volume based on extensive ministry experience is designed to be applied globally with adaptation. The editors believe this volume offers readers new horizons built on strong past horizons. And we expect these contributions will be built upon. We hope you will be one of those contributors.

Bibliography

Steffen, Tom. *Worldview-Based Storying: The Integration of Symbol, Story, and Ritual in the Orality Movement.* Richmond, VA: Orality Resources International, 2018.

Abbreviations

ACT	Artist in Christian Testimony
AIM	Africa Inland Mission
ALFE	Adults with Limited Formal Education
ASM	American Society of Missiology
CBS	Chronological Bible Storying
CBT	Chronological Bible Teaching
CBTE	Competency-based theological education
DMM	Disciple-Making Movements
DRC	Democratic Republic of the Congo
ECC	*Église* du Christ au Congo
ESL	English as a Second Language
EMS	Evangelical Missiological Society
EQ	Emotional Intelligence
FCH	Faith Comes by Hearing Bible recordings
FOBAI	Forum of Bible Agencies International
IMB	International Mission Board
ION	International Orality Network
JAM	Journal of Asian Mission
JBTM	Journal for Baptist Theology & Ministry
JETS	Journal of the Evangelical Theological Society
JFP	The Jesus Film Project
LCWE	Lausanne Committee for World Evangelization
LWI	Living Water International
MALP	Mutually Adaptive Learning Paradigm
OBS	Oral Bible School
OBT	Oral Bible Translation

OH	Oral hermeneutics
OT4T	Orality Training for Trainers
PIAAC	Program for the international assessment of adult competencies
PIER	People as informal, extended resources for learning
SFS	Sioux Falls Seminary
SIL	Summer Institute of Linguists
SLIFE	Students with Limited or Interrupted Formal Education
STS	Simply the Story
S-T4T	Storying Training for Trainers
SWBTS	Southwestern Baptist Theological Seminary
T4T	Training for Trainers
TAs	Training Advisors
TE	Theological education
TH	Textual hermeneutics
TQ	Theological Intelligence
ULD	Undiagnosed Learning Disabilities
WASH	Water Access Sanitation and Hygiene
WEC	Worldwide Evangelization for Christ

Bible Versions

ESV	English Standard Version
HCSB	Holman Christian Standard Bible
NIV	New International Version
NLT	New Living Translation
VOICE	The Voice

Part 1
Measuring the Horizons

I

An Orality Learning Journey
Lessons from More Than Three Decades in the Orality Movement

JERRY WILES

IT WAS IN THE early 1980s that I came across Herbert Klem's book, *Oral Communication of the Scripture: Insights from African Oral Art*.[1] I was working with an international publishing and broadcasting organization at the time. It was a time of recognizing that what I was doing was effective with only about 20–30 percent of the world's population. I then began to get connected with a few mission leaders who had some experience with or interest in orality, oral cultures, and reaching oral learners and unreached people groups. Those years put me on a new path of discovery and understanding about what it will take to reach the whole world and complete the Great Commission.

In collaboration with others during the 1980s and 1990s about the use of Oral Methods for sharing the gospel and making disciples, I found a few who were interested and some with practical experience. At an Evangelism Roundtable Conference in Washington D.C. a church growth leader took interest and invited me to present a workshop on "Oral Discipleship" at a major conference in the summer of 1988, called "Chicago '88." The conference was attended by several thousand pastors, evangelists, missionaries and church/mission leaders.

Oral Disciple Making

The workshop I led at the Chicago '88 event was based on my personal experimentation, research, and a concept paper I had written in 1983, titled,

1. Klem, *Oral Communication of the Scriptures*.

"Oral Discipleship: A Strategy of Evangelism and Discipleship Designed to Reach Primarily the Non-Reading People of the World, Using Oral (Verbal) Methods." (The term orality was not commonly being used at that time). Just a few years ago I discovered that my workshop at that conference had been archived at the Billy Graham Center at Wheaton College. Samuel Chiang, former executive director of the International Orality Network, credits me with coining the term "Oral Discipleship" (although I now prefer the term Disciple-Making, rather than Discipleship).

Since those years, I have been on an ongoing learning journey and have connected with many others on the way. My research and experimentation during the 1980s and 1990s provided a good foundation for my work in launching our Contextual Bible Storying, and Orality Training Programs with Living Water International (LWI). We began with Bible Storying training and practices in 2006, then followed up by launching our first Orality Training Workshops in 2009, in Liberia and Honduras. The first rendition we called "An Introduction to Contextual Bible Storying." Following those early days of experimentation and refining, we took the training to all our program countries throughout Africa, Central and South America and Asia.

Bible Storying: An on Ramp to the Orality Movement

What we call Contextual Bible Storying has come about from a considerable amount of research and gleaning from many other models of Bible Storying and Orality-based methods. Chronological Bible Storying was the most commonly used method at that time. However, we also gleaned concepts and principles from Relational Bible Storying, Thematic Bible Storying, Topical Bible Storying, Panoramic Bible Storying, and Conversational Bible Storying, to name a few. Another important feature of this model is emphasizing the appropriate biblical and cultural context.

A Growing Interest in Orality

Over time, we began to experience a growing interest in orality from LWI's short-term mission trips and supporting churches. In 2010 we began conducting Bible Storying / Orality Training Workshops for churches, mission organizations, and with academic institutions throughout the United States. Initially, pastors and mission leaders became interested in training for those going on short-term mission trips. Then, as they saw its effectiveness and impact, they began to discover applications in their local churches and communities. In the process of time, a good number of US-based churches began conducting their own orality training events. Some are finding the training effective with various outreaches, including assisted living facilities, prison ministries, refugee and immigrant communities, and international students, to name a few. Churches are also experiencing very positive results from conducting orality training events with pastors in Southeast Asia, Africa, and on mission trips to Central America and elsewhere.

Back to the Basics

A major lesson that seems to be so transformational is learning more about the power of the collective memory in training and practice. The more relational, communal, oral cultures in the Global South are providing many lessons for those of us in the Global North. We recognize that the rapidly reproducing disciple-making and church planting movements are primarily in those regions. Small, simple, and reproducible systems and structures are concepts we need more of here in North America and the Western world. In many ways the Orality Movement is creating greater awareness that there may be better ways of advancing the gospel than what have been the common practices over the past 500 years. Back to basics seems to be a common theme we are hearing these days.

Contextual Bible Storying

LWI's basic Orality Training (An Introduction to Contextual Bible Storying) is based on using a five-story set. It was not designed to be a comprehensive training, but to be a sample, to get people on the journey. It is an easy on ramp, or low barrier entry, to the Orality Movement. In our experience, with the five stories from the gospels, with the appropriate pre- and post-story discussion and dialogue, we can give a village, a community or tribal group a simple, biblical theology of what is means to have a relationship with the Lord and become reproducing followers of Jesus. Part of that process is to move away from an exclusively modern Western, Post-Reformation perspective, to a more biblical, Early Church and Global South mental model.

Significant Influences

Some of the helpful resources and influences in the formative stages of our Orality Training programs and strategies would include the works of Trevor McIlwain, Mark Naylor, James Slack, Mark Snowden, Tom Steffen, J.O. Terry,

Avery Willis, Thomas Winger, and a good number of others.[2] As was mentioned earlier, Herbert Klem's doctoral dissertation on *Oral Communication of the Scriptures* was a catalyst and inspiration to many of us on the Orality journey. Amsterdam 2000, Table 71, and formation of the Oral Bible Task Force (forerunner of the International Orality Network) have all been significant influences that have accelerated the Orality Movement.

One of the concepts that has made the LWI model so effective is focusing on learning a little, practicing a lot, and sharing the stories often. We often say it is better to know a little and share a lot, than to know a lot that we keep to ourselves. We have this saying, "Keep the faith, just don't keep it to yourself." There are many examples of how these principles are being worked out. A lady in a West African country told about telling one of the stories to three Muslim women in the marketplace that she had just learned that day in the training. After hearing and discussing the story, all three of the women wanted to follow Jesus. One of them also showed up in the next day's training in their community.

Living Water Case Studies

In an orality training in Honduras, a legally blind lady learned the story of the blind beggar receiving his sight, from Mark 10. During her prayer time at home the evening after the first day of training, she was meditating on that story. With closed eyes, she said to the Lord, "Lord, I believe, Lord, I believe." When she opened her eyes, she could see. With great joy, she shared that testimony with the group in the training the next morning. After hearing the story of the Gerasene man with the evil spirits, from Mark 5, a woman in the training in Nicaragua approached one of the pastors and said, "I'm like that man, I need help." It turned out that she had been involved with sorcery. After a time of prayer and deliverance that evening, the next day she was calm and learning with the group. There are so many compelling stories and testimonies like these that could fill several books.

After observing the impact of the basic orality training within LWI's program areas, we moved to a new level of training trainers. The Orality Training for Trainers (OT4T) took us to a new level of more accelerated and multiplying impact. This concept of training is based on training teams, to train as teams. Through collaboration with the International Orality Network, and other mission networks and associations, we now have access to a wealth of knowledge and experience about the many aspects and

2. Naylor, "Towards Contextualized Bible Storying"; Steffen, *Reconnecting God's Story to Ministry*; Willis and Snowden, *Truth that Sticks*.

applications of orality. It is also from our collective experience and lessons learned with LWI, as well as our affiliates and partners, that our global community of learning and practice continues to grow.

Metrics to Measure Impact

One of the big challenges with LWI and other mission groups is tracking and reporting the results of orality training and practices. However, with the story-impact tool and the most significant change model, we have a much better way of tracking, reporting and evaluating. The monitoring and evaluation programs of LWI have provided a much better way of documenting and demonstrating the impact of our orality strategies. Other groups have been good resources for determining the metrics to measure impact and spiritual metrics. There is no shortage of anecdotal examples and stories. Since most of our training experiences are in oral cultures, many do not have the capacity or resources to report results. However, when we return to those areas and interview some of the trainees, the stories and numbers are quite impressive.

Multiplying Impact of Orality

Two years after training more than 1,000 individuals in a West African country, I had the opportunity of conducting our Orality Training for Trainers. We heard many testimonies and verbal reports of the results from the earlier trainings. With the assistance of a missionary and a local translator, we requested more detailed explanations of how they were using the stories and methods. Out of 15 individuals we interviewed, collectively they reported that more than 795 people had come to the Lord over those two years. We could assume that the other 985 or so individuals could have had experienced similar results.

A senior leader with the Evangelical Fellowship of Zimbabwe participated in Living Water's Orality Training for Trainers (OT4T) in 2013. During an ION Africa Consultation in South Africa in 2018, he reported that since that time, he had trained more than 4,000 pastors with that basic model. Furthermore, according to the reporting of EFZ, those 4,000 pastors had trained more than 400,000 others. In Burkina Faso, we have received reports of how Orality Training has greatly accelerated their church planting movement. The churches meet under trees, and pastors have had little or no theological training. They are an example of how orality can be used for rapidly spreading the gospel and enhancing disciple making movements.

Orality for Leadership Development

Over the past few years, with LWI and other partner and affiliate groups, we have expanded orality methods and strategies into several other areas of application. Communicating the gospel and making disciples are the most basic focal points. However, principles of orality are amazingly effective with hygiene education, public health and community development. In 2017 we launched what we called Contextualized Leadership Development for Oral Cultures. It has since been simplified to Orality Leadership Workshops. The idea is to equip pastors and other leaders with the best leadership skills from contemporary, historical, and biblical resources. Of course, our best model for effective leadership is the life, Spirit, and teaching of Jesus. While knowledge and skill are important, the primary focus is on character development. Guided discovery, action learning, and participatory models of learning are also extremely valuable in this arena.

Collaboration and Shared Learning

The collaboration and shared learning within ION and other mission and ministry groups is continuing to enhance our global community of learning and practice. We are also experiencing many opportunities of bringing our orality methods and strategies into the veins of other networks, alliances, and associations. A few of those include the Global Alliance for Church Multiplication, the Christian Leadership Alliance, the Global CHE Network (sponsor of the annual International Wholistic Mission Conference), Missio Nexus, Mission ConneXion conferences, the Accord Network, the Millennial Water Alliance, Church Planting Networks and others. Obviously, ION's affiliation with the Lausanne Movement and the World Evangelical Alliance are fruitful collaboration opportunities.

Strategic Resource Leveraging

All these developments are leading to greater opportunities for strategic leveraging of impact for kingdom advancements. According to Steve Douglass, president of Cru, orality is a game changer for global mission strategies for unreached people groups, but also for local ministries and reaching the nations among us.[3] Increasing numbers of mission and church leaders are recognizing that orality methods and strategies are transformational and

---

3. Douglass, "Keynote Address."

changing the face of missions around the world. As the movement gains visibility, there is obviously increased interest among educators and in the academic communities. In fact, we are continually identifying valuable scholarly work that has been around for many years, but not very visible, and has not been implemented into contemporary mission/ministry strategies.

Orality Missiology Collaboration

Still in its early stages, the Orality Missiology Collaboration Group consists of a growing number of practitioners, trainers, researchers, and scholars. Now, it also includes several doctoral candidates doing dissertations on orality and related topics. In our research efforts, we are discovering seminaries, universities, and other institutions of higher education with excellent programs that fit within the orality domain. Some of those include areas such as ethnomusicology, ethno-doxology, ethno-dramatology, and theological aesthetics. Other disciplines or fields of study related to orality include narratology, oral traditions, Early Church history, linguistics, cross-cultural studies, oral literature, and worldview issues. There is growing recognition within the orality mission community and educational institutions that there are many resources available to enable one to gain understanding of this important field of learning and practice.

Orality in Business

Progressively, we are experiencing a growing interest and recognition of the multiple applications of the principles of orality. An example would be our networking and collaboration with the Business as Mission Movements. Orality is being effectively used in the areas of team building and improving corporate culture. Howard Partridge is one who has participated in LWI's orality training and applied it to his coaching and consulting businesses. He is well known for his expertise through his work with Phenomenal Products and with the Zig Zigler organization. Among several books he has authored, it is in *The Power of Community* that he addresses the use of his orality training.[4] Concepts of orality can enhance developing skills of communication, sales, marketing, organizational change, leadership, and management.

---

4. Partridge, *Power of Community*.

Networking and Cross-Pollination

Through networking and cross-pollination, we continue to discover additional applications of orality. Some of those would include trauma therapy, racial reconciliation, solving tribal conflict, and promoting unity and cooperation, to name a few. A businessman with a long history of mission work, locally and globally, participated in multiple orality training events. He has been involved with training in the areas of stewardship, financial management and planning. After receiving the basic orality training and Orality Training for Trainers (OT4T), he adapted his model to a more oral learner friendly approach. He first tested it in Africa, where they saw a more rapid reproduction of the training in several other countries. Then, he began implementing that simplified model in the USA as well, with improved results. Some of the key changes and lessons learned included reducing the content, more repetition, more engagement, focus on communal participatory learning, and less dependency on written materials.

Relational Unity

One of the aspects we have observed conducting orality training in East Africa is how pastors and church leaders find common ground and ways of working together. A church in Texas hosted an orality training workshop among some of their most senior members. By the middle of the afternoon, many in the group were in tears as they shared their stories and testimonies. Even though many of them had been attending church together for 25–30 years, they realized how much they did *not* know about each other. They shared testimonies about their personal storms of life, answered prayer, and their born-again experiences. The biblical stories provided a platform for them to share at a heart level they had never done before. Greater relational unity is another benefit businesses, churches, and organizations can receive through orality training.

The Value of Gatherings

ION conferences and consultations over the past few years has brought attention also to various other disciplines and applications. Honor and Shame was the focus of a Consultation on Orality in Theological Education, hosted by Houston Baptist University in 2014. Daystar University in Nairobi, Kenya hosted a similar consultation in 2015 with more a focus on practitioners and trainers. A number of other such consultations have taken place in Hong

Kong, Wheaton, Asbury, Oklahoma, Oxford, England, Manila, Philippines, Togo, West Africa, Johannesburg, South Africa and others. In the North America Regional context, annual conferences have been in Houston, Colorado Springs, Orlando, Toronto, Dallas, Saint Louis, Asheville, and other major cities. Each gathering enriches participants with greater awareness, networking, learning, collaboration, and partnership opportunities.

Church and Community Mobilization

Over the past decade, orality strategies have increasingly become a significant part of Living Water International and their many affiliates and partner's programs around the world. In the water sector, WASH (Water Access, Sanitation and Hygiene) has become the important focus. WASH program areas are also focused on community development and spiritual transformation. In partnership with the Church, locally and globally, LWI's strategy is known as Flourish: Mobilizing Churches and Communities for WASH-Focused Transformation. That program, which also includes Bible Storying and other Orality Training, is not only about sharing the gospel, disciple making, and church planting, but has been instrumental for influencing national policy on child marriage in Southern Africa. Orality principles were very effectively used by LWI workers in Liberia and other West African countries addressing the Ebola crisis a few years ago.

Focus on the Great Commission

The theme of the Orlando conference in 2018 was "Orality: Many Applications–One Mandate." The one mandate, of course, is the Great Commission. While there are many different aspects to the orality domain and a wide variety of special interests, we like to maintain a focus on communicating the gospel and making disciples as foundational to everything else. In relation to the arts, Artists in Christian Testimony (ACT International) is a key network that specializes in that area. The 2019 Toronto conference emphasized indigenous arts, women's issues, reaching first nations, and young leaders. Toronto, being the most ethnically diverse city in the world, was an excellent place for those discussions. Houston, now the most ethnically diverse city in the USA, is scheduled to host the 2021 ION North America Regional Conference. All that to say, orality is becoming even more important for North America and the Western World.

Orality for Relief and Development

Several relief and development organizations have taken an interest in orality methods and strategies. Some missionaries and mission executives are requesting assistance in implementing oral strategies and methods for areas such as agriculture, cooking, and nutrition programs. Engineering ministries are recognizing that orality-based strategies are effective, not only in their disciple making efforts, but also for training practical skills in a cross-cultural context. Through connections and relationships with the National Religious Broadcasters, program producers and others are realizing the benefits of orality methods and strategies. A few recent articles, seminars and webinars have addressed areas such as: Arts and Orality for Wholistic Missions, Orality in Business, The Place of Orality in Church Planting, Oral Strategies for Rapid Multiplication, The Importance of Orality in the Church, Missions and the Academy, Orality in Education, Orality and Missions, Short-term Missions, and Orality in the Academy and Beyond.[5]

New and Encouraging Developments

There are several encouraging developments that have occurred over the past few years. The increased interest in orality by youth and young leaders is growing and spreading. One example is the ION Youth initiative which emerged from the ION Africa Consultation in Johannesburg in 2018. From that gathering, young people in Zambia began conducting their own orality-focused outreaches and training events. That has also spread to other countries throughout the region.

Tools of the Age–Tools of the Ages

Digital storytelling and online collaboration and training are providing new opportunities for engaging younger leaders. Zoom calls, webinars and other online orality training workshops are taking on new expressions. Our new foci in the North America regional context are arts, media, and young leaders. A common theme is about using the most effective tools of the age, and the tools of the ages. That is, using all the modern technological resources, but also the ancient methods we learn from Jesus, the Early Church, and from the rapidly reproducing disciple making and church

---

5. Wiles, "Orality in the Academy and Beyond"; Wiles, "Place of Orality in Church Planting"; Wiles, "Importance of Orality in the Church, Missions and Academy"; Partridge, "Power of a Story: Orality in Business"; Wiles, "Oral Strategies for Rapid Multiplication"; Walters, "Orality in Education"; Wiles, "Orality and Missions Webinar"; Walters, "Orality in Short-Term Missions."

planting movements, primarily in the Global South. We like to emphasize that principles of orality are the most effective ways that people have learned and communicated from the beginning of time.

Impact of Children

Another strategic opportunity in the orality movement is connecting with and supporting children's ministries. Child Evangelism Fellowship, AWANA, and others are beginning to implement story and orality-based methods. The 4 to 14 Window Movement, and its many member organizations, is another example of the expanding and multiplying impact of the orality movement.

What we have observed is that when children learn stories, they tend to tell stories. In our orality training in Central America, we often have children as young as five or six years old participate. They often learn and retell the stories, sometimes to groups of several hundred participants. Adults are encouraged when they see how children can learn the stories so well. A pastor in one of the trainings made the comment, "I see now how I can equip, train, and mobilize storytelling evangelists at every level of education and economic status."

Prayer Networks and Movements

Connecting with prayer networks and prayer movements are also channels for introducing and injecting orality concepts and principles for accelerating impact. Children's prayer movements in South Asia are growing, and obviously have tremendous potential for long-term impact for the kingdom. Integrating orality methods into women's prayer movements, especially in creative access countries in the Middle East and North Africa, is an area for expanding impact.

Concluding Reflections

In the Orality Movement, it is a never-ending learning journey. We often emphasize that Orality is better experienced, than explained. There is so much more to be learned as practitioners, trainers, researchers, scholars and mobilizers. Thankfully, the opportunities to learn and collaborate with others on the journey are accelerating tremendously. We can fully expect the depth and breadth of the movement to continue to grow exponentially in future years and decades. The increasing volume of research and scholarly work becoming available should also enhance and enrich the momentum of the Orality Movement.

Bibliography

Douglass, Steve. "Keynote Address." September 19, 2018, ION North America Regional Conference, Orlando, FL.

Klem, Herbert V. *Oral Communication of the Scriptures: Insights from African Oral Art*. Pasadena, CA: William Carey Library, 1982.

Naylor, Mark. "Toward Contextualized Bible Storying." MA thesis, University of South Africa, 2004.

Partridge, Howard. "The Power of a Story." *Business as Mission*, January 27, 2017. https://businessasmission.com/orality-in-business/.

———. *The Power of Community*. New York: McGraw-Hill, 2018.

Steffen, Tom A. *Reconnecting God's Story to Ministry*. Waynesboro, GA: Authentic Media, 2005.

Spradlin, Byron. *Arts and Orality for Wholistic Missions*. Nashville: ACT International, 2019.

Walters, Jayne. "Orality in Education." International Orality Network. https://orality.net/content/orality-in-education/.

———. "Orality in Short-Term Missions." International Orality Network. https://orality.net/content/orality-in-short-term-missions/.

Walton, John H., and Brent D. Sandy. *The Lost World of Scripture: Ancient Literary Culture and Biblical Authority*. Downers Grove, IL: InterVarsity, 2013.

Wiles, Jerry. "The Importance of Orality in the Church, Missions and the Academy." *Anthology: Equipping Global Thought Leaders* 6 (2018) 19–21.

———. "Networking for Influence and Impact: International Orality Network." *Evangelical Missions Quarterly* 56 (2020) 24–25.

———. *No Greater Joy: Power of Sharing Your Faith through Stories and Questions*. New Kensington, PA: Whitaker House, 2010.

———. "Orality and Missions Webinar." Sixteen: Fifteen: Church Missions Coaching. https://1615.org/project/orality-missions/.

———. "Orality in the Academy and Beyond: Practical Resources for Advancing the Great Commission." *Lausanne Global Analysis* 7 (2018). https://www.lausanne.org/content/lga/2018-05/orality-in-the-academy-and-beyond.

———. "*Orality Missiology*" series and related topics. Lake Forest, CA: Assist News Service, 2010–2020.

———. "Oral Strategies for Church Multiplication." GACX: A Global Alliance for Church Multiplication, January 25, 2018. https://gacx.io/resources/oral-strategies-rapid-multiplication.

———. "The Place of Orality in Church Planting." *Evangelical Missions Quarterly* 55 (2019) 26–29.

———. "A Practitioner/Trainer Perspective on Orality." *Missio Nexus*, July 1, 2015. https://missionexus.org/a-practitioner-trainer-perspective-on-orality/.

Willis, Avery T., and Mark Snowden. *Truth That Sticks: How to Communicate Velcro Truth in a Teflon World*. Colorado Springs, CO: NavPress, 2010.

2

Deconstructing Oral Learning
The Latest Research[1]

Lynn Thigpen

Foley lamented, "orality alone is a 'distinction' badly in need of deconstruction, a typology that unfairly homogenizes much more than it can hope to distinguish; it is by itself a false and very misleading category."[2] Sterne joined him: "As a concept, orality has something of a vexed and uncharted intellectual history."[3] Some see orality as communication, some as learning preference, others as involving storying or mostly oral tradition. So, what exactly is orality? I struggled for some time with the term and the methods associated with orality. Having worked with so-called oral learners in Cambodia for many years, I found them also relying on visual cues and their powers of observation, immersed in embodied modes of learning that included taste, touch, and smell. So, how do oral learners truly prefer to learn? How can we deconstruct oral learning and better understand the distinction?

Smith called the gap between orality and literacy "a yawning chasm into which no one is more likely to tumble than the scholar who ventures into the realm of orality without first shedding the bundle of literate preconceptions he habitually carries about with him."[4] Watson likewise discussed "interpreting across the abyss."[5] Very few have bothered to cross the divide and climb to the other side in exploration. Unlike the folks Smith

---

1. This chapter is a summary or precis of my dissertation and subsequent American Society of Missiology monograph book entitled *Connected Learning*.
2. Foley, "Word in Tradition," 170.
3. Sterne, "Theology of Sound: A Critique of Orality," 209.
4. Smith, "Worlds Apart," 6.
5. Watson, "Interpreting Across the Abyss," 1.

and Watson mention, I knew I needed to make the journey and learn more about my oral friends.

The Background

Having lived in Cambodia for over 15 years when I began doctoral studies, I finally started to ask the right questions. I had observed my oral friends and knew they learned by means other than just hearing. Pictures assisted them, so we added that resource to The Oral Bible School,[6] but I continued to wonder, how did they truly learn best? When they needed to know something or learn to do something, how did they accomplish the task? Or did they just avoid learning altogether? What I learned from that quest redefined orality for me.

In total, I spent 20 years working in Cambodia, a war-torn nation whose now older population experienced great atrocities and an interruption in their lives and education. When I explored their folklore and common stories, I found they could not recount any narratives told by their parents and extended family. Why? They were too busy trying to survive to garner a formal or an informal education. Those same survivors living in the capital of Phnom Penh now have grandchildren attending international schools and studying English. These grandparents, many of whom cannot read or write, can scarcely communicate with their grandchildren in their native tongue. Education passed them by, and they lament their current situation.

That leads me to the appropriate name for my friends. I cringe at the term "illiterate," defining someone by what they do not possess. Some call them "oral preference learners."[7] My colleague Russell West denounced that term, stating orality is not "a preference (as if an insider cultural participant could choose or not choose oral style), but . . . an identity."[8] He dubbed non-readers as "oralists," whose learning was "experiential, gestural, actional, and holistic in nature over those *habitus*-shaping effects that literacy-contingent models produce, e.g., 'compartmentalized, passive, cerebral, isolationistic, elitist, and professionalization-based.'"[9] Finkelstein agreed: "As for the tribal society, it was not 'oral' and 'auditory.' The tribesmen had keen, observant

---

6. Thigpen, "Oral Bible School."

7. Moon, "Discipling Through the Eyes of Oral Learners"; Moon, "Understanding Oral Learners."

8. West, "Re-Eventing of Theological Education," 1.

9. West, "Re-Eventing of Theological Education," 1.

eyes and skillful hands as well as sensitive ears."[10] Orality does not seem to be the polar opposite of literacy as Ong's classic might suggest.[11]

Some call oral learners "preliterate"[12] or "nonliterate," terms also which seem ethnocentric and promote the hegemony of literacy. Brod used the term "non-readers,"[13] and Colter "low literates."[14] In 2005, a symposium for "Low Educated Second Language and Literacy Acquisition" began.[15] Indeed, those in the field of teaching English met my friends when arriving as refugees or immigrants. Studying English in new lands, they were called SLIFE or "Students with Limited or Interrupted Formal Education."[16]

My friends, however, were a hodge-podge of folks. I knew older ladies who survived the Khmer Rouge and said they could not study in their youth because their parents feared they might write love letters. Most of the older population lacked a great deal of formal education; and most of the non-readers I knew were too busy surviving to learn something new. Since my friends in their native environment were not students, I adapted the SLIFE term and called them "Adults with Limited Formal Education" or ALFE (al-phee). The term is still short of endearing, but I found it more descriptive than any other choice until the conclusion of my research.

Before focusing on deconstructing oral learning, I must delineate a few more terms. "*Learning* is the complex, often ubiquitous, cognitive/psychomotor/social/affective process of gaining knowledge, skills, values, and beliefs which includes interaction between what is known and what is yet to be acquired."[17] Watkins and Mortimore define *pedagogy* as "any conscious activity by one person designed to enhance learning in another."[18] Botha stated *orality* "as an analytic concept, involves a mindset, a whole attitude towards reality and experience."[19]

Various forms of orality dot the literature. *Primary orality* "is the condition of persons never schooled in writing. Primary oral cultures have no

---

10. Finkelstein, *Sense and Nonsense of McLuhan*, 37.
11. Ong, *Orality and Literacy*.
12. Thompson, "Perceptions of Teaching Nonliterate Adults in Oral Cultures."
13. Brod, *What Nonreaders and Beginning Readers Need to Know*.
14. Colter, "Audience You Didn't Know You Had."
15. van de Craats et al., "Research on Low-Educated and Second Language Acquisition."
16. DeCapua and Marshall, "Students with Limited or Interrupted Formal Education in US Classrooms," 160.
17. Thigpen, *Connected Learning*, 9.
18. Watkins and Mortimore, "Pedagogy," 3.
19. Botha, "Letter Writing and Oral Communication in Antiquity," 24.

written language."[20] *Secondary orality* is "the literate orality of popular culture" or communication delivered orally but based on text, such as news broadcasts.[21] Finally, *traditional orality* "is the situation of persons who may know how to read and write but prefer oral learning in daily life."[22]

Government statistics in Cambodia listed the mean years of education in 2013 as 5.8;[23] but at the time of my research a few years later, that statistic declined to 4.4 years.[24] I, along with other colleagues, found ALFE to be a majority in Cambodia. Smith-Hefner, working with Cambodian refugees, also found "most rural Khmer women over the age of 40" were non-readers.[25]

Orality dominates the scene in Cambodia, but what about the world? According to the experts, 4 billion people over 15, "two-thirds of the world's population are oral communicators."[26] This global majority does not turn to books for their learning needs. For some, non-reading seems to be a sort of "liminal state on the path to literacy,"[27] a disability, or a danger to society. These kinds of views make literacy a goal and "disguises the cultural and ideological assumptions that underpin it so that it can then be presented as though they are neutral and universal."[28] He continued, "The Western concept of 'illiteracy' creates stigma."[29] Fingeret lamented that "definitions of literacy are used to sort people into categories of 'literate' or 'illiterate.' As such, they are normative; 'literacy' represents an ideal state. The sorting process occurs in the dominant class, and the criteria, therefore, represent dominant-class norms."[30] The problems with the oral-literate dichotomy promoted by some writers definitely involve issues of ethnocentricity.[31]

Global institutions function as if oral communicators were not the majority, as if reading were the norm. It is not—not in the United States and not in many countries across the globe. In the last PIAAC (Program for the

20. Thigpen, *Connected Learning*, 10.
21. Ong, *Rhetoric, Romance, and Technology*.
22. Thigpen, *Connected Learning*, 11.
23. United Nations Development Program (UNDP), "About Cambodia 2013."
24. United Nations Development Program (UNDP), "About Cambodia, 2016."
25. Smith-Hefner, "Education, Gender, and Generational Conflict among Khmer Refugees," 137.
26. International Orality Netwok and Lausanne Committee for World Evangelization, *Making Disciples of Oral Learners*, 3.
27. Thigpen, *Connected Learning*, 50.
28. Street, *Autonomous and Ideological Models of Literacy*, 1.
29. Street, *Social Literacies*, 14.
30. Fingeret, "Illiterate Underclass," 83.
31. Swearingen, "Oral Hermeneutics during the Transition to Literacy."

International Assessment of Adult Competencies) study nearly half of the Western population operated at a Level 2 proficiency out of six levels (Below Level 1, Level 1, Level 2, Level 3, Level 4, and Level 5).[32] Highly proficient readers number a scant two percent (Goodman et al. 2013, 3).[33] Why is two percent of the population steering the education of the ALFE majority? Why are more people not exploring the chasm and examining ALFE learning needs? This grave inequity must be addressed.

The Literature[34]

Turning to deconstructing oral learning from the literature, the classic work in the field is Ong's *Orality and Literacy*.[35] Sterne declared "Ong's conceptualization of orality" as "the most influential," but "deductively derived from a set of binary oppositions between hearing and seeing."[36] Regarding the major contributors to the field during the time of Ong, Cruikshank commented: "I recall reading Ong, Havelock, and Innis years ago, intrigued by their arguments but troubled that none of these theoretical giants had actually spent much time talking with oral storytellers."[37] Ong's work was not primary research into the lives of oral learners, but a conceptual study done by an English professor. De Vries stated, "Qualifications as a rule did not emerge from empirical study of specific primary oral societies in their historical unicity but seem to result from universalistic projections on these societies, of pictures from various academic debates such as the Homeric debate, the debate of written versus oral style in English, and the anthropological debate on cognitive dichotomies."[38] Unfortunately, many writings in applied orality quote Ong extensively without knowing these facts.

Writing long before Ong's *Orality and Literacy*, Finnegan maintained orality was a "huge and complicated subject—far too complex to be reduced to trite classifications or the categorization implied when we facilely define

---

32. Goodman et al., *Literacy, Numeracy, and Problem Solving in Technology-Rich Environments*, 3.

33. Goodman et al., *Literacy, Numeracy, and Problem Solving in Technology-Rich Environments*, 3.

34. For a more complete literature review with charts, please consult Thigpen, *Connected Learning*. It is impossible in this brief chapter to discuss all the literature on orality.

35. Ong, *Orality and Literacy*.

36. Sterne, "Theology of Sound," 211.

37. Cruikshank, "Orality and Literacy," 712.

38. de Vries, "New Guinea Communities without Writing and Views of Primary Orality," 397.

certain groups as 'nonliterate' and unthinkingly go on to assume consequences from this for the nature of their thought."[39] A number of other writers and researchers had written about traditional cultures, media, and orality well before *Orality and Literacy*. For a more thorough discussion in this regard, see *Connected Learning* and a chart of influences on Ong's work.[40]

Since this chapter focuses on deconstructing orality and not the rise of the field, I turn to examine other literature according a conceptual framework exploring ways of knowing or storing information (epistemology), ways of being (ontology), ways of transmitting knowledge (communication/teaching), and ways of taking knowledge from the environment (learning). Exploring epistemology and ontology, Hiebert found: "In oral societies, knowledge is stored in the forms of stories, parables, songs, aphorism, proverbs, riddles, poems, creeds, and catechisms that can be easily remembered. It is also stored in rituals that are living reenactments of primordial events."[41] Bradt proclaimed story (an element of orality) "a way of knowing,"[42] while Bruner delineated paradigmatic and narrative modes of thought.[43] These experts saw narrative as more than a pedagogical device, but also as a way of knowing or storing information. Likewise, Arrington found hymns to be a "storage language" for "biblical abstractions."[44] Foster agreed, proclaiming African songs carried oral theology.[45] Others also found storage avenues in the form of proverbs, ceremonies, rituals, drama.[46] Knowledge storage in oral learning is varied and complex.

What about communication, teaching, and learning? Lovejoy insisted, "What sets orality apart is *reliance* on spoken language. To the extent that people rely on spoken communication instead of written communication, they are characterized by 'orality.'"[47] Is this true? Opposed to binary descriptions, Finnegan deemed orality "multiplex" and "multimodal,"[48] full of nonverbal cues and gestures, as did Jousse.[49] Orality is not merely speech versus

39. Finnegan, "Literacy vs. Non-Literacy," 112.
40. Thigpen, *Connected Learning*, 36.
41. Hiebert, *Transforming Worldviews*, 116.
42. Bradt, *Story as a Way of Knowing*.
43. Bruner, *Actual Minds, Possible Worlds*.
44. Arrington, "Hymns as Theological Mediator," 157.
45. Foster, "Oral Theology in Lomwe Songs."
46. Avoseh, "Proverbs as Theoretical Frameworks"; Keysser, *People Reborn*; McIntyre, "Using Ceremonies to Disciple Oral Learners"; Moon, "Using Rituals"; Moon, "Using Proverbs"; Moon, "Rituals and Symbols in Community Development."
47. Lovejoy, "Extent of Orality," 12.
48. Finnegan, "Orality and Literacy," 9.
49. Jousse, *Oral Style*.

text, ear versus eye, or orality versus literacy. Deconstructing oral learning means considering all the ways AFLE learn.

A significant body of literature exists among those teaching English as a second or foreign language. They receive students from the global community, including ALFE, and recognize the need to reconceptualize their education because of different learning needs.[50] Ramirez-Esparza opined, "The socio-interactive practices required in formal classrooms limit their ability to learn."[51] DeCapua recognized this "cultural dissonance" and felt the situation should be viewed "as a *mismatch* and not a *deficit*," that their needs are "different rather than deficient . . . one's culture and one's learning paradigm are inextricably linked . . . Culture influences the learning process, with respect to both how people learn and what they value as part of learning," thus they proposed a mutually adaptive learning paradigm (MALP) as a solution to SLIFE learning needs.[52] Watson also recognized learners needed "a pragmatic approach" and relevance in learning.[53] Deconstructing oral learning means examining and employing appropriate pedagogies and honoring those.

True research not focused on storying with oral learners is scant. Conducting actual field studies, Shuter found Hmong refugees retain "oral stylistic patterns" or "residual orality" even if they became literate.[54] Aikman studied the Arakmbut and found they gained information from the elders, dreams, and experience.[55] Diouf, Sheckley, and Keharhahn studied "what, when, why, how, and from whom do adults in African villages learn" and found farmers preferred experiential learning with demonstrations and hands-on involvement.[56] In Thompson's study in West Africa, learners preferred rituals, mentoring, observation, use of every sense, and experiential learning, among other concrete methods.[57] Vautrot studied in Appalachia and found learners there also espoused "experientially-based approaches."[58] Hvitfeldt found relationships primary, while practical and relevant learning

---

50. DeCapua and Marshall, "Serving ELLs," 51.

51. Ramirez-Esparza et al., "Socio-Interactive Practices and Personality," 542.

52. DeCapua and Marshall, "Students with Limited or Interrupted Formal Education in US Classrooms," 159, 163–64.

53. Watson, "Interpreting Across the Abyss," 239.

54. Shuter, "Hmong of Laos," 106.

55. Aikman, *Intercultural Education and Literacy*.

56. Diouf et al., "Adult Learning in a Non-Western Context," 32, 42.

57. Thompson, "Nonliterate and the Transfer of Knowledge in West Africa."

58. Vautrot, "'Why Don't They Come?'"

reigned in the Hmong ESL classroom.[59] Fanta-Vagenshtein explored learning channels and how illiterate people learn but only touched on illiteracy.[60] In Botswana, Merriam and Ntseane found spirituality and community greatly impacted learning.[61] Probing ways of learning in an ESL class, Lado complained those "programs are mismatched to the needs of the lowest level illiterate immigrant."[62] Likewise, Parker's dissertation gave perspective to the lives of illiterate adults in the United States by noting their shame and the coping skills they use to navigate a heavily literate world.[63]

In conclusion, Figure 2.1 depicts the major elements in this discussion. All important considerations in oral learning—nature of thought, communication style, the self, information storage, poverty, teaching and learning, oral tradition, and Ong's binary contrast with literacy—are depicted in this deconstruction.

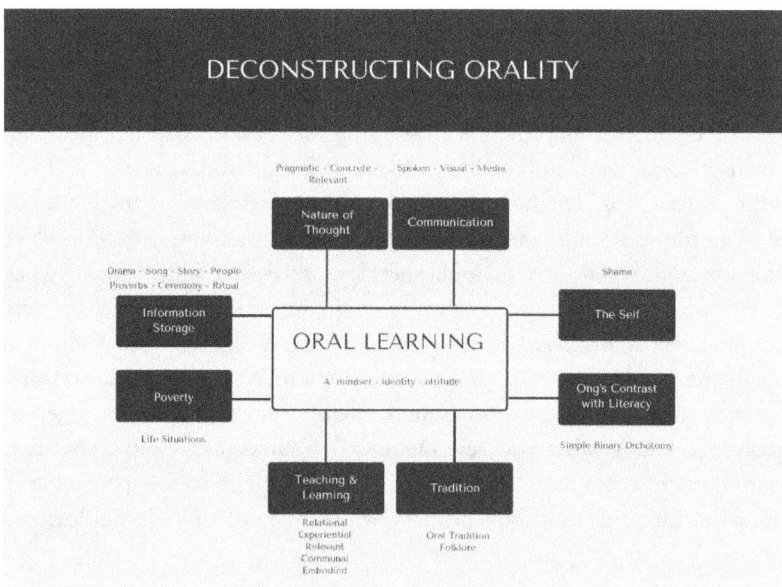

Figure 2.1. Important Elements in Deconstructing Orality

59. Hvitfeldt, "Traditional Culture, Perceptual Style, and Learning."
60. Fanta-Vagenshtein, "How Illiterate People Learn."
61. Merriam and Ntseane, "Transformational Learning in Botswana."
62. Lado, "Ways in which Spanish-Speaking Illiterates Differ from Literates in ESL Classrooms," 24.
63. Parker, "Adults' Perspectives on the Impact of Low-Level Literacy/Functional/Illiteracy on their Lives."

The Quest: Researching Oral Learning

"Interpreting across the abyss"[64] sent me asking questions to understand how "oral Cambodian adults with limited formal education (ALFE) learn or acquire new knowledge, beliefs, values, and skills."[65] I explored the roles people, context/environment/setting/time, self, media, and religion play in this enterprise. As we all know, adults usually continue to learn throughout their lifetimes. But without reading, how did my friends learn? If we know the answer to this question, we know how to teach in more effective ways. In this section, I discuss my research journey and a bit of the results.

The Research Journey

Even though I worked with ALFE daily, I entered the abyss in three stages. During the first stage, and identification stage, I lived five intolerable days as a non-reader. This literate could not endure the humbling state and difficulties of asking someone else for help, depending on others to decipher letters in print. I experienced boredom, powerlessness, anger, and frustration.[66] "Without connection to living, breathing people, life was difficult, if not impossible."[67] I found myself wondering how ALFE could possibly function on a day-to-day basis.

The next stages involved participant observation and interviews. I was Simmel's "stranger who stays,"[68] having a privileged outsider perspective changed by many years of immersion in the culture, but I still chose to spend time observing learning situations prior to interviews. The combination of observation and identification provided me with an acute sensitivity to the learning needs of ALFE prior to the interviews.

Conducting an ethnographic grounded theory study with a wisdom focus, I interviewed participants until no new information emerged (theoretical saturation). I explored how ALFE acquire skills, knowledge, values, and beliefs and what role people, context, media, self, and religion play in their learning.[69] In the end, 38 Cambodians who had studied six or fewer grades in school shared their learning journeys with me. From ages 19 to

---

64. Watson, "Interpreting Across the Abyss," 1.
65. Thigpen, *Connected Learning*, 9.
66. To learn more, read my autoethnographic chapter, "Conversing with Orality: My Experience as a Non-Reader," in Appendix B of *Connected Learning*.
67. Thigpen, "Connected Learning," 103.
68. Simmel, "Sociological Significance of the 'Stranger.'"
69. Thigpen, *Connected Learning*.

83, 25 were female and 14 were male. 18 were Buddhist, 15 Christian, and 5 not claiming any particular religion. I interviewed throughout the country, in both rural and urban settings. Beyond those interviews, I conversed with many additional Cambodians who were not suitable candidates for the study based on their education levels.

Three groups emerged from the participants–incidental learners, maintenance learners, and purposeful learners. The incidental learners seemed to have no hope and no aspiration to learn. The maintenance learners seemed to struggle through life but attempted to make the most of their situations. The last group, however, found success in spite of their life situations, learned to read, and turned to assist those in the other two groups. Most of them found hope from their spirituality.

The Results

Despite living long term in Cambodia, the interviews surprised me. Ashamed I had never bothered to explore ALFE learning before, I still thought the journey was a cognitive quest. Instead, I encountered a constant lament with tears—for me and my interviewees. I researched in a monocultural environment, among ethnic Cambodians with a common language; but othering, shaming, and marginalizing filled the space. My friends introduced me to the "dark side of orality."[70] In fact, one young man told me how he felt going to a place that used printed materials, to church where everyone else seemed able to read. Because of the shame, he confessed he felt like killing himself. In deconstructing oral learning, shame must factor into the equation.

Before I discuss the results, I must introduce you to the life of my ALFE friends. During my research, I had a trusted companion, Ms. Sona, who introduced me to some participants and who made sure I understood them completely. One day we walked to an interview in her village, a setting on the banks of the Mekong. As we arrived at the concrete areas for processing fish and smelled the odor, I watched an older lady rummage through the trash. Ms. Amie washed useable bags in the muddy Mekong water, then spread yellow, green, and pink plastic on a wire. Hoisting the hundreds of sopping wet bags took great strength, but this widow in ill-health managed to lift the mass and tie the wire so her wares could waft in the wind. Her daily efforts usually garnered about 5000 riel or $1.25 US dollars.

Why was this difficult operation her occupation? Ms. Amie took me to her tall house on wooden stilts, a patchwork dwelling of reclaimed wood, to

---

70. See Thigpen, "Dark Side of Orality."

tell me her story. In her two-room dwelling high above the floodwaters lived a family of five. Her main room contained an altar, high-hung pictures, a few plastic flowers, some mats for sitting and sleeping, and a television, and here she told me her story. When her husband lived, their life was good. Widowhood and caring for six children, including one with mental issues due to a fall, was challenging. What else could she do? She had only studied a few grades when the Khmer Rouge came through Cambodia, so further study was impossible. Her skills were limited, as were her options. Deconstructing oral learning involves considering life circumstances.

Another friend told me about her failure to learn to read. All the while her younger sister sat by and did something common in the culture. Thinking it might help, she shamed her older sister, called her names, and berated her. A typical American, I could not bear the weight of her words. That day I met the poison of shame in oral learning and I hated it. I turned to big sister and lathered on an antidote—grace and honor. I touched her arm and told her I thought she looked like a beautiful and capable lady. She had given birth to children and worked hard. She was not incapable, lazy, or inept.

Not a special education teacher, I finally realized this friend and others I interviewed must have learning disabilities, perhaps dyslexia. In the midst of that shaming session, I continued affirming my friend and introduced her to a "disease" of mixing up letters, one millions of people have. At that time there was no word for dyslexia in the Khmer language and very few avenues for addressing learning disabilities. No, she was not *l'ngong*, or stupid. Others used the same words or said they were not so *poo-kie-ee* (clever).[71] A smaller group described learning to read in school as *ree-un aht jole* (the learning would not enter their minds). Tanner spoke of the "conundrum of failure" among dyslexics, especially among those with undiagnosed learning disabilities or ULD.[72] Learning disabilities must figure into deconstructing oral learning.

Not everyone I interviewed had learning disabilities. Some did not learn to read because of lack of opportunity, war, or poverty. War stole childhoods, educations, relationships, and generational stories. All of them keenly felt the sting of shame. Living in a culture with a written language and formal schooling, they had dashed dreams, a dignity deficit, and disregarded learning needs, and herein lies an inequity to be rectified. Poverty, war, and inequitable life situations must also figure into deconstructing oral learning.

---

71. Thigpen, *Connected Learning*, 83.
72. Tanner, "Adult Dyslexia and the 'Conundrum of Failure,'" 785.

Examining the social aspects of ALFE learning, I found people played a primary role. When I inquired about learning a skill, the oft-cited phrase was, "*Ree-un pee gay*" ("to learn from others"). To my surprise, this was the key. Some had to sneak to observe a process they wanted to emulate or ask others for information or knowledge.

As for time, context, environment, I learned my ALFE friends lacked margin for learning. Living in poverty, work and life's difficulties consumed time. So many friends lost schooling options because of family needs, being forced to work instead.

In regard to media and its influence on ALFE learning, I thought technology might be greatly used. Instead, I found barriers. What should offer easy information presented obstacles in language and heavy use of text. Other media use, such as radio and television, required precious time. Most listening or watching was relegated to just before bed.

The affective, or the self, played a dominant role in ALFE learning. For some, there were feelings of being ashamed, "incomprehensibly flawed"[73] or having "global inadequacy."[74] Ignorant (*l'ngong*) was already stamped on every ALFE forehead, a seeming pronouncement of their status and worth. ALFE needed hope, agency, and self-efficacy in order to learn.

Beyond the emotional self, the physical also played a role in ALFE learning. "One characteristic that is missing from Ong's inventory of orality's psychodynamics is the aesthetic nature."[75] Jousse saw all oral learning as gesture,[76] and West concurred, redefining an oral learner as "a person whose socialization and identity is immersive in a concrete, relational, gestured and actional way."[77] Much of the work ALFE do involved all their senses and physical, hands-on effort.

Finally, in considering spirituality, I found many ALFE who learned to read did so for religious reasons, whether they were Buddhist or Christian. Christians prayed for assistance to learn; Buddhists learned chanting bit by bit. In this area especially, spirituality opened the door for aspirational hope.[78]

---

73. Orenstein, "Picking Up the Clues," 36.
74. Flanders, *About Face*.
75. Hadisi, "Exploring the Performance," 450.
76. Jousse, *Oral Style*, 8.
77. West, "Re-eventing of Theological Education."
78. Wydick and Lybbert, "Poverty, Aspirations, and the Economics of Hope."

Concluding Reflections

Through this experience, I learned limited education is a qualifier, but orality is a social identity. My friends preferred to learn by means of people instead of print. They trusted not in texts, but in time-tested relationships. Motty agreed with this research, stating "to be oral is to be relational and people-oriented."[79] Ong felt language was paramount for oral learners,[80] but I found connection paramount. The difference was not just epistemological, but also ontological. Turning to reconstruct oral learning in this section, I consider the possibility of renaming orality in light of the research, a resultant learning quadrant diagram, and final recommendations.

The Renaming

In researching "how oral Cambodian adults with limited formal education (ALFE) learn or acquire new knowledge, beliefs/values, and skills?"[81] I found the central understanding and majority reply centered around the word *connection*. ALFE preferred to *ree-un pee gay* (to learn from others), so "the central theme that emerged was one of connected or relational learning or learning by socialization."[82] I found connected learning to be

- A relational or social process, with a preference for observing and learning from known, trusted, and/or successful people. ALFE preferred learning from people instead of learning from print.
- A reflexive process in regard to one's self as learner. This kind of learning was connected to self and self-image in all of life's dimensions—cognitive, affective, and physical (psycho-motor). Connected learning depended heavily on self-efficacy and honor or dignity. Any resulting relational and cultural shame due to failure, therefore, was a definite deterrent to successful learning.
- A redemptive process, learning that was highly connected to one's faith or spirituality as a source of aspirational hope, purpose, and assistance.
- A relevant process. This kind of learning was highly related to one's context and culture and was experience based and practical.

---

79. Motty, "Contextualizing Theological Education in Africa," 155.
80. Ong, *Orality and Literacy*, 6.
81. Thigpen, *Connected Learning*, 100.
82. Thigpen, *Connected Learning*, 100.

- Repackaged learning or packaged differently from print learning. This kind of learning included connection with accessible technologies and other portable vehicles of connection, such as stories, parables, metaphors, drama, art, and the like.[83]

The term *connected learning* was already being used for a political learning approach for youth.[84] However, a study of nurses also unearthed a relational learning theme, much like this research.[85] Resembling social learning or "learning by observing and interacting with others,"[86] researchers also found the process in Thailand, where "the Thai have a tradition of learning from people rather than from books."[87] Other researchers found relationship paramount in training and in development. Studying in Somalia, Bigelow found, "Orality does not just denote communicating through listening, speaking, orating, and reading poetry; in the deepest sense, it refers to a way of life entirely organically fashioned on face-to-face human relations."[88] Rhoads discovered life in oral cultures to be "relational and social—face to face."[89] Shuter agreed: "The Hmong culture relies strictly on people and groups to transmit information."[90] Merrifield and Bingman found Appalachian learners also had "other-oriented learning strategies," plus visual strategies (watching others, having someone model a skill), oral strategies (dialogue), and cooperative learning.[91]

ALFE see people as a kind of fund of knowledge and store their knowledge in others.[92] Hardman, working with Cambodians learning English in the US, found they also considered their colleagues as "knowledge holders" and "funds of knowledge."[93] Hiebert explained:

> We who are literate tend to think only in terms of storing and communicating the gospel in spoken and written forms. We fail to realize that oral societies are not 'illiterate.' They have, in fact, a rich supply of cultural knowledge and many different ways of

---

83. Thigpen, *Connected Learning*, 100.
84. Ito et al., *Connected Learning*, 4.
85. Ryan et al., "Wise Women," 183.
86. Bentely and O'Brien, "Tipping Points among Social Learners," 298.
87. Taylor, "Study," 118.
88. Bigelow, "Orality and Literacy within the Somali Diaspora," 55.
89. Rhoads, "Biblical Performance Criticism," 157.
90. Shuter, "Hmong of Laos," 104.
91. Merrifield and Bingman, "Living and Learning," 181.
92. See Moll et al., "Funds of Knowledge for Teaching"; Rodriguez, "Power and Agency in Education;" Valez-Ibanez and Greenberg, "Formation and Transformation."
93. Hardman, "Community of Learners," 145–66.

storing it. In such societies we must use these media to present the gospel in concrete ways that the people will recall.[94]

Oughton asked, "Whose knowledge counts?"[95] Before experiencing my brief experience as a non-reader, my chosen fund of knowledge was text. ALFE choose people: "You know a person who holds a specific knowledge that you want to get, and you start a process of letting him know that you are interesting learning what he holds if he is willing to transmit it to you."[96]

As an academic, I value research and "the literature." For connected learners, most books are unnecessary. People are the key—not someone to be heard, but a more holistic, organic, and relational type of learning event. Einstein explained, "Knowledge exists in two forms—lifeless, stored in books, and alive in the consciousness of men. The second form of existence is after all the essential one; the first, indispensable as it may be, occupies only an inferior position."[97] "Oral society has faith in one type of text. Literate society in another."[98]

The Learning Quadrants

When you rely on people for learning needs, trust becomes crucial. In the eyes of connected learners, who then is trustworthy? Bogale learned participants preferred the advice of female friends to that of male doctors.[99] Studying in Malaysia, Merriam and Mohamad, found learning "intertwined with family relationships."[100] I quickly learned my credentials were unimportant in Cambodia. As a laboratory scientist, I often offered advice but found it rarely taken. Only the advice of trusted friends and family was honored. Blankstein also wrote about "relational trust as foundation for the learning community."[101] This "prior question of trust" (PQT) becomes important for connected learners[102] and needs to be considered in reconstructing orality.

---

94. Hiebert, *Transforming Worldviews*, 162.
95. Oughton, "Funds of Knowledge."
96. Diouf et al., "Adult Learning in a Non-Western Context," 40.
97. Einstein and Calaprice, *The Ultiimate Quotable Einstein*, 439.
98. Stock, *Listening for the Text*, 146.
99. Bogale et al., "Reaching the Hearts and Minds of the Illiterate Women," 2.
100. Merriam and Mohamad, "How Cultural Values Shape Learning in Older Adulthood," 52.
101 Blankstein, *Failure is Not an Option*, 62.
102. Mayers, *Christianity Confronts Culture*, 7.

If you create a diagram with the horizontal aspect depicting learning from people versus learning from print and the vertical axis focused on trust–either in academic experts or in valued relationships, you can see the various possibilities that arise in the resulting quadrants. No longer is orality a dichotomy juxtaposed with literacy (see Figure 2.2). The possibilities are endless.

Learners in the top right quadrant acquire "knowledge and skills through learning agents and other channels that bypass literacy-based learning."[103] This natural learning begins at birth and is organic, involves observation, and continues throughout our lives. It is our default learning process, a "panhuman phenomenon."[104]

Along this path of never-ending socialization, some of us are whisked away from our family cocoons and taken to buildings with teachers, books, and other students. We are schooled to recognize scribbles on paper. Not everyone across the globe follows this trajectory, so I purposefully did not place orality on the left and literacy on the right as some future goal. Learning from people is lifelong. Literacy takes us in a different direction, for different purposes. Mazamiza called this trajectory into "textuality" "resocialization."[105] Diamond deemed formal education in primary oral cultures "as strange and repugnant as jails."[106] Even Father Ong called orality "the 'primary modeling system'—as an anachronistic deviant from the 'secondary modeling system' that followed it."[107] Reading is not a natural process and learning to read changes the brain.[108] Researchers found the brain area used for reading is the same area used for face perception, and when learning to read "face perception suffered in proportion to reading skills."[109]

In the bottom left quadrant lies academia, with an emphasis on reading and trusted literature and research. Those who prefer to "learn through connecting with knowledge holders via technology"[110] or secondary learners, can be found in the bottom right quadrant. They rely on social media and the internet, a "digital orality."[111] Schrage called digital orality a "rela-

---

103. Fanta-Vagenshtein et al., "Technological Knowledge," 290.
104. Paradise and Rogoff, "Side by Side Learning," 132.
105. Mazamisa, "Reading from This Place," 72.
106. Diamond, "Epilogue," 301.
107. Ong, *Orality and Literacy*, 12.
108. Dehaene et al., "How Learning to Read Changes," 1359–64.
109. Dehaene et al., "How Learning to Read Changes,"; Knowland and Thomas, "Educating the Adult Brain."
110. Thigpen, *Connected Learning*, 111.
111. Papacharissi, "Unbearable Lightness of Information," 4.

tionship revolution," urging those involved in technology to "re-orient their worldview around relationships."[112]

Those who value books, especially sacred books but are not necessarily literate occupy the upper left quadrant. Arrington in researching the Lisu in China found they held to their Christian faith through a "liturgical literacy," prizing their Bibles and hymnals, songs of the faith.[113] "Scribal culture" occupies this quadrant as well,[114] with those who value such events as recitation from a Jewish rabbi, teaching from an Indian *guru*, or the chanting of Buddhist monks.

---

112. Schrage, "Relationship Revolution."
113. Arrington, "Hymns of the Everlasting Hills," 5.
114. Botha, "Mute Manuscripts."

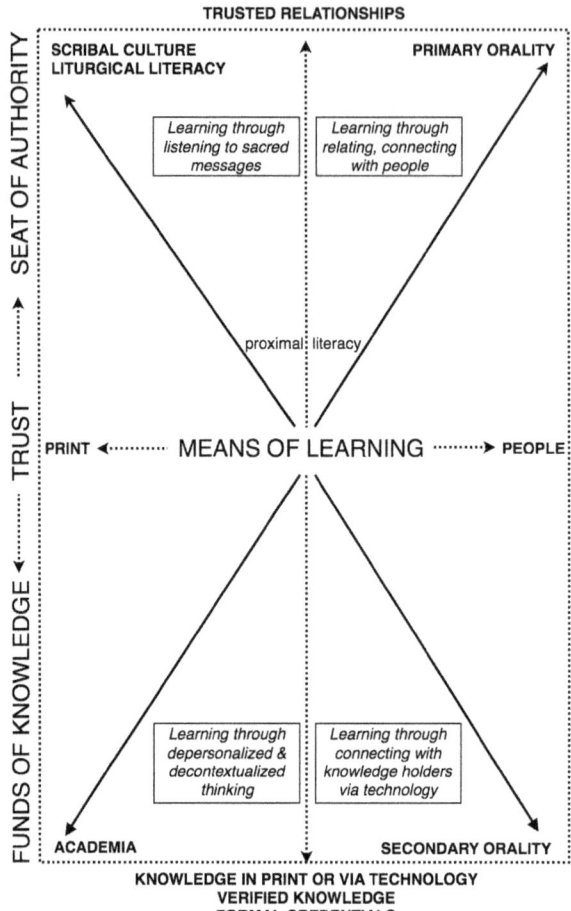

Figure 2.2. Learning Quadrants[115]

"People can learn from sacred texts in any quadrant and that is reflected in the complexity of this diagram."[116] Besides this quadrant majoring on liturgical literacy and scribal culture, learners in the top right quadrant would not read a sacred text. Instead, they might listen to recordings or live storytelling sessions. Those in the secondary orality quadrant might prefer a digital application on their phone or a YouTube video or a Facebook Live sermon. Others in the bottom left quadrant might delve into hermeneutics and ancient origins of texts, exploring source language meanings.

---

115. Thigpen, *Connected Learning*, 138.
116. Thigpen, "Connected Learning: A Grounded Theory," 143.

In the center of the diagram lies the intersection of so many worlds. In the space bridging between learning from people and learning from print lies literacy brokering and proximate or proximal literacy, learning from someone who can read.[117] In many of life's situations, this concept, this bridge between worlds, provides a lifeline for connected learners.

Each quadrant represents a way of learning worthy of respect and having specific needs. Connected learners eschewing print cannot move from quadrant to quadrant, but as an academic, I can choose. If I want to cook a favorite dish, I might not consult a book. I might operate as a connected learner and call my mother for instructions or watch her make the dish. I might choose digital orality and watch a YouTube video.

Sadly, in research and the literature, one quadrant takes precedence. Formal schooling seems to be preferred over informal and non-formal avenues.[118] However, "equating 'education' with 'formal schooling,' reflects epistemological ethnocentrism by suggesting that the educational traditions . . . which are informal, are tied to the social life of the community . . . are not 'legitimate' forms of education."[119] People desire to learn, but adult education efforts tend to offer literacy as a first course of action, forcing folks to learn in ways they eschew. In teaching Hmong immigrants, Hvitfeldt noticed they felt compelled to make a "paradigm shift from a familiar learning paradigm to the unfamiliar"—"two conflicting learning paradigms."[120]

I respect literacy and its benefits. Some of the participants in my study did learn to read. However, many do not. I believe we commit a grave error when we do not provide learning apart from literacy. When we only provide text-based resources, we alienate a large segment of the world's population. Since so many types of learners can be found along the axes of these quadrants, why do we impose the learning of those in one quadrant upon the culture of those in other quadrants? Why this hegemony? When education applauds learner-centered education, why do we not adapt to the learning needs of connected learners? This inequity must be remembered when reconstructing orality.

---

117. See Basu et al., *Isolated and Proximate Illiteracy*; Maddox, "Worlds Apart?" for more information on proximate literacy. Regarding literacy brokering, see Perry, "Genres."

118. Montandon, "Formes Sociales," 237.

119. Diouf et al., "Adult Learning in a Non-Western Context," 33.

120. Hvitfeldt, "Traditional Culture, Perceptual Style, and Learning," 4.

The Recommendations

In reconstructing oral learning and moving forward, I advise focusing on a number of issues:

- adapting terminology,
- promoting relational learning,
- implementing no-failure learning with the elimination of shame and a focus on dignity, and
- employing effective pedagogies/andragogy (see Figure 2.3).

I briefly discuss these elements in these concluding remarks.

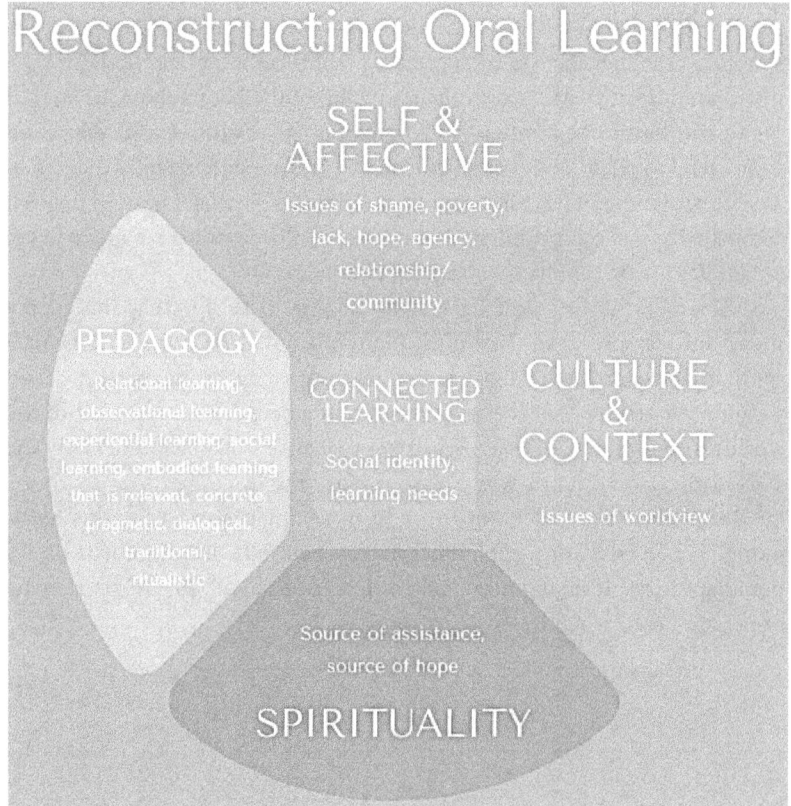

Figure 2.3. Reconstructing Oral Learning

I would definitely prefer to abandon the terms "oral preference learner" and "oral learner," as well as the term "orality," as these are all unfortunate misnomers, masking the "principal ways ALFE truly learn and the global and holistic ways incorporated in connected learning."[121] I teach a course on orality, and students are constantly mistaking it for auditory learning or mere verbal communication. We all communicate orally. Connected learning is more than that. This way of learning is not exclusively oral, but also foundational, natural, visual, social, concrete, pragmatic, and holistic. Implementing more correct terminology, we avoid the Great Divide and the dichotomies of the past because we all begin our learning journeys in the upper right quadrant of the Learning Quadrants diagram. Since humans learn from infancy by relational or connected means, this kind of learning persists throughout life, especially in those with limited education.[122]

Orality is more than a way of knowing. I found oral learning to be a social identity set in a worldview, that it was not a preference, but an identity and a situation imposed by society and circumstances, which then becomes the style of learning needed. The situation is a cultural ontology, a way of being, and an "under-recognized and under-served" one.[123] Arterianus-Owanga also found orality to be an identity.[124] More importantly, this type of learning culture is not a disease or a deficiency. It is natural and organic, much like the ways in which we are socialized from birth. West agreed, calling orality a sociocultural identity, one in which we are socialized into this way of being.[125]

On a foundational level, what we presently call *orality* is a social identity, an ontology, complete with a connected/relational way of knowing and learning. Only when we reconstruct the concepts in this way can we relate and teach in a manner that connected learners prefer, rescue them from shame, and provide meaningful learning opportunities that are not text-based. Coomaraswamy complained, "To impose our literacy (and our contemporary 'literature') upon a cultured but illiterate people is to destroy their culture in the name of our own."[126] The hegemony of literacy must cease and opportunities for oral learning increase.

Secondly, a proper reconstruction of connected learning focuses on the personal aspects of this learning need. In teaching the Christian faith, Saint Augustine reminded learners when the Ethiopian eunuch read the prophet Isaiah and did not understand (Acts 8:26–39), God sent a person–someone

---

121. Thigpen, *Connected Learning*, 153.
122. Thigpen, *Connected Learning*, 157–58.
123. West, "Re-eventing of Theological Education," 1.
124. Arterianus-Owanga, "Orality is My Reality."
125. West, "Re-eventing of Theological Education."
126. Coomaraswamy, *Bugbear of Literacy*, 54.

who "sat with him, and in human words and human language opened up to him what was hidden in that passage."[127] Augustine also told his non-reading followers: "We are your books."[128] God came to earth as a man to communicate with us. He personally connected with humanity. Indeed, "truth is not a statement at all, but is nothing less than a *person*."[129] Some time ago a learning group emphasized "people as informal, extended resources for learning" or PIER learning.[130] We must employ this PIER concept and embody truth for connected learners, as well as being books, reading for others, and giving them all the benefits of proximate literacy.

Johnson advised: "If shame can interfere with a student's feeling of community . . . community may also be the best remedy."[131] People can do more than become sources for learning; they can also become implements of healing. "What if medicine's first principle were also education's?"—"First, do no harm."[132] Boyden and Bourdillon related, "Emphasizing success at school as a criterion for success in life can be debilitating for those whose interest and aptitudes lie elsewhere, and who are stigmatized as failures on account of their school performance."[133] Lienhard felt, "Shame outweighs death,"[134] so learning opportunities that extinguish shame must be promoted.

Weiss et al. and Francis et al. found learning itself to be healing,[135] so we must provide learning options apart from literacy. Childs and Greenfield found that many cultures without formal education naturally promote "no failure learning,"[136] avoiding "school-induced shame" or "educational wounds."[137] "The drive to learn in humans is something so strong, so defining of human nature according to anthropologists, that it should still amaze us as truly remarkable that we have been able to design a social institution that can teach children to fail at learning."[138]

---

127. McCarthy, "'We are Your Books,'" 183.
128. McCarthy, "'We are Your Books,'" 183.
129. Soukup, "In Commemoration," 837.
130. Hill, "People as Informal, Extended Resources for Learning."
131. Johnson, "Considering Shame and Its Implications for Student Learning," 13.
132. Gray, "What If Medicine's First Principle were also Education's?"
133. Boyden and Bourdillon, "Reflections," 273.
134. Lienhard, "Restoring Relationships," 97.
135. Weiss et al., "Literacy Education as Treatment for Depression"; Francis et al., "Does Literacy Education Improve Symptoms of Depression?"
136. Childs and Greenfield, "Informal Modes of Learning and Teaching," 285.
137. Shelton, "Heart of Literacy," 3–4.
138. Paradise, "What's Different About Learning in Schools?," 276–77.

> No one failed in the rites of passage among the Arunta. But minorities fail in formal educational settings . . . The school experience early on defines them as potential failures or even learning disabled, and there is always the implication that even if they put up with such definitions and endure the school, they are not assured of a positive gain at the end. The long initiation ritual of the school is for many minorities a long drawn out degradation ritual.[139]

The final recommendation, then, deals with pedagogy or andragogy. Crabtree and Sapp wrote an article with a provocative and applicable title: "Your Culture, My Classroom, Whose Pedagogy?"[140] Of course, the answer is, "The learner's pedagogy!" As this research discovered, the process of connected learning is relational, social, connected, holistic, encompassing, and integrated into all areas of life; reflexive and closely related to self-efficacy and the avoidance of shame; redemptive, closely connected to spirituality and faith, which provided hope, purpose, and assistance; relevant, contextual, and highly linked to experience; and needs to be repackaged in appropriate and accessible technologies.[141] Ramirez-Esparza et al. likewise concurred, promoting an "apprentice-mentor or socialization model in which observation and learning through practice allows one to move from legitimate peripheral participation to fuller participation through contextualized practice."[142]

Li found the meeting of literacy and non-reading to be a "cultural mismatch"[143] and Cutz an "emic-etic conflict."[144] Therefore, we must cultivate effective and appropriate pedagogies for connected learners. The appropriate pedagogies would include observational learning with examples and mentoring, apprenticeships, etc. An example would be people like Rebekah Naylor, who created a village model for mothers who lacked the knowledge to prepare nutritious meals for their malnourished children.[145] According to Ardila et al., "it is not totally accurate to assume that people with low levels of education are somehow 'deprived.' It may be more accurate to assume they have developed different types of learning, more procedural, pragmatic, and

---

139. Spindler and Spindler, *Fifty Years of Anthropology and Education*, 187.
140. Crabtree and Sapp, "Your Culture, My Classroom, Whose Pedagogy?"
141. Thigpen, *Connected Learning*, 177.
142. Ramirez-Esparza et al., "Socio-Interactive Practices and Personality," 544.
143. Li, *Culturally Contested Pedagogy*, 196.
144. Cutz, "Emic-Etic Conflicts," 64.
145. Morris, "Fellow Servants Honor Dr. Rebekah Naylor," para. 8.

sensory oriented."[146] DeCapua and Marshall's MALP emphasized "immediate relevance, interconnectedness, shared responsibility, oral transmission, and pragmatic tasks."[147] Wilson advised using "context-oriented" learning styles and use of "apprenticeship—'learning by example through experience.'"[148] Highly literate Fasheh noted his illiterate mother learned by "observing, doing, reflecting, relating, and producing," and that "her knowledge sprang from life and was connected to life."[149]

In conclusion, what is orality/oral learning? After deconstructing, examining, and researching the construct, how do we move forward? How do we rescue the term and the field and reconstruct orality? The chart above is an attempt at such a reconstruction of oral learning, incorporating my latest research.

Given this research, we can distance ourselves from simple dichotomies as portrayed by Ong. We can embrace the complex construct and the Learning Quadrants, which helps us acknowledge the continuum and complexities of primary orality, of secondary orality, of scribal literacy and liturgical literacy versus academic learning. We can also recognize and affirm ALFE learn by entirely different means than print learners and call them by their rightful name, according to how they prefer to learn. We can affirm the assets they possess and call them "connected" or "relational learners," as we advocate for their right to learn through connection.

In an astute evaluation of orality versus literacy, Watson wrote:

> Each way of living has its own lineage, its own noesis with its own rules and a completely different set of skills needed to navigate it successfully. Both ways are deficient in a certain *sense* . . . but one deficiency—illiteracy—puts people at a disadvantage for accessing power and privilege, while the other—orality—puts people at a disadvantage for accessing relationship and belonging. On the other hand, regardless of where we end up in maturity, all humans spring from oral roots.[150]

She continued to remark, "The noesis of orality brings the possibility of a healing gift, in the sense that much of what we in hyperliterate academic cultures lack is precisely what oral cultures possess. It is appropriate therefore to speak not only of the challenges of orality, but of the *gift of*

---

146. Ardila et al., "Illiteracy," 697.
147. DeCapua and Marshall, "Students," 167.
148. Wilson, "Let the Earth Hear His Voice," 41.
149. Fasheh, "How to Eradicate Illiteracy without Eradicating Illiterates," 53.
150. Watson, "Interpreting Across the Abyss," 240–41.

orality."[151] In reconstructing oral learning, we reconstruct a gift, one shared by a majority of the world.

Bibliography

Aikman, Sheila. *Intercultural Education and Literacy: An Ethnographic Study of Indigenous Knowledge and Learning in the Peruvian Amazon.* EBSCO Reader version. 1999.

Ardila, Alfredo, et al. "Illiteracy: The Neuropsychology of Cognition without Reading." *Archives of Clinical Neuropsychology* 25 (2010) 689–712.

Arrington, Aminta. "Hymns as Theological Mediator: The Lisu of South-West China and Their Music." *Studies in World Christianity* 21 (2015) 140–60.

———. *Hymns of the Everlasting Hills: The Written Word in an Oral Culture in Southwest China.* PhD diss., Biola University, 2014.

Aterianus-Owanga, Alice. "Orality Is My Reality: The Identity Stakes of the Oral Creation in Libreville Hop-Hop Practices." *Journal of African Cultural Studies* 27 (2015) 146–58.

Avoseh, Majai B. "Proverbs as Theoretical Frameworks for Lifelong Learning in Indigenous African Education." *Adult Education Quarterly* 63 (2012) 236–50.

Basu, Kaushik, et al. *Isolated and Proximate Illiteracy and Why These Concepts Matter in Measuring Literacy and Designing Education Programs.* Working Paper No. 00-W02. Nashville: Vanderbilt University, 2000.

Bentley, R. Alexander, and Michael J. O'Brien. "Tipping Points among Social Learners: Tools from Varied Disciplines." *Current Zoology* 58 (2012) 298–306.

Bigelow, Martha H. "Orality and Literacy within the Somali Diaspora." *Language Learning: A Journal of Research in Language Studies* 60 (2010) 25–57.

Blankstein, Alan M. *Failure is Not an Option: 6 Principles that Advance Student Achievement.* Thousand Oaks, CA: Corwin, 2013.

Bogale, Gebeyehu W., et al. "Reaching the Hearts and Minds of Illiterate Women in the Amhara Highland of Ethiopia: Development and Pre-Testing of Oral HIV/AIDS Prevention Messages." *Journal of Social Aspects of HIV/AIDS* 7 (2010) 2–9.

Botha, Pieter J. J. "Letter Writing and Oral Communication in Antiquity: Suggested Implications for the Interpretation of Paul's Letter to the Galatians." *Scriptura* 42 (1992) 14–34.

———. "Mute Manuscripts: Analysing a Neglected Aspect of Ancient Communication." *Theologia Evangelica* 23 (1990) 35–47.

Boyden, Jo, and Michael Bourdillon. "Reflections: Inequality, School, and Social Change." In *Growing Up in Poverty: Findings from Young Lives,* edited by M. Bourdillon and J. Boyden, 269–80. New York: Palgrave Macmillan, 2014.

Bradt, Kevin M. *Story as a Way of Knowing.* Kansas City, KS: Sheed & Ward, 1997.

Brod, Shirley. *What Non-Readers and Beginning Readers Need to Know: Performance-Based ESL Adult Literacy.* Denver, CO: Spring Institute for International Learning, 1999.

Bruner, Jerome. *Actual Minds, Possible Worlds.* Cambridge, MA: Harvard University, 1986.

---

151. Watson, "Interpreting Across the Abyss," 242.

Cheng, I-Hsuan. "Case Studies of Integrated Pedagogy in Vocational Education: A Three-Tier Approach to Empowering Vulnerable Youth in Urban Cambodia." *International Journal of Educational Development* 30 (2010) 438–46.

Childs, Carla P., and Patricia M. Greenfield. "Informal Modes of Learning and Teaching: The Case of Zinacanteco Weaving." In *Studies in Cross-Cultural Psychology*, edited by N. Warren, 2:269–304. London: Academic, 1980.

Colter, Angela. "The Audience You Didn't Know You Had." *Contents Magazine* 2 (2012). http://contentsmagazine.com/articles/the-audience-you-didnt-know-you-had/.

Coomaraswamy, Ananda K. *The Bugbear of Literacy*. London: Dennis Dobson, 1947. http://www.worldwisdom.com/public/library/ default.aspx

Crabtree, Robbin D., and David Alan Sapp. "Your Culture, My Classroom, Whose Pedagogy? Negotiating Effective Teaching and Learning in Brazil." *Journal of Studies in International Education* 8 (2004) 105–32.

Cruikshank, Julie. "Orality and Literacy: Reflections across Disciplines": Review of the book *Orality and Literacy: Reflections across Disciplines*, edited by Keith Thor Carlson et al. *Canadian Journal of History* 47 (2012) 712–13.

Cutz, German R. "Emic-Etic Conflicts as Explanation of Nonparticipation in Adult Education among the Maya of Western Guatemala." *Adult Education Quarterly* 51 (2000) 64–75.

DeCapua, Andrea, and Helaine W. Marshall. "Serving ELLs with Limited or Interrupted Education: Intervention that Works." *TESOL Journal* 1 (2010) 49–70.

———. "Students with Limited or Interrupted Formal Education in US Classrooms." *The Urban Review* 42 (2010) 159–73.

Dehaene, Stanislas, et al. "How Learning to Read Changes the Cortical Networks for Vision and Language." *Science* 330 (2010) 1359–64.

de Vries, Lourens. "New Guinea Communities without Writing and Views of Primary Orality." *Anthropos* 98 (2003) 397–405.

Diamond, S. "Epilogue." In *Anthropological Perspectives on Education*, edited by M. Wax et al., 300–306. New York: Basic, 1971.

Diouf, Waly, et al. "Adult Learning in a Non-Western Context: The Influence of Culture in a Senegalese Farming Village." *Adult Education Quarterly* 51 (2000) 32–44.

Einstein, Albert, and Alice Calaprice. *The Ultimate Quotable Einstein*. Princeton: Princeton University Press, 2011.

Fanta-Vagenshtein, Yarden. "How Illiterate People Learn: Case study of Ethiopian Adults in Israel." *Journal of Literacy and Technology* 9 (2008) 26–55.

Fanta-Vagenshtein, Yarden, et al. "Technological Knowledge among Non-Literate Ethiopian Adults in Israel." *Knowledge, Technology, and Policy* 22 (2009) 287–302.

Fasheh, Munir. "How to Eradicate Illiteracy Without Eradicating Illiterates?" In *Literacy as Freedom*, edited by N. Aksornkool, 48–73. Paris: UNESCO Literacy and Non-Formal Education Section, 2003.

Fingeret, Arlene. *The Illiterate Underclass: Demythologizing and American Stigma*. PhD diss., Syracuse University, 1982.

Finkelstein, Sidney. *Sense and Nonsense of McLuhan*. New York: International, 1968.

Finnegan, Ruth. "Orality and Literacy: Epic Heroes of Human Destiny?" *International Journal of Learning* 10 (2003) 1551–60.

———. "Literacy versus Non-Literacy: The Great Divide? Some Comments on the Significance of "Literature" In Non-Literate Cultures." In *Modes of Thought: Essays on Thinking in Western and Non-Western Societies,* edited by R. Horton, 112–44. London: Faber, 1973.

Flanders, Christopher. *About Face: Rethinking Face for 21st Century Mission.* Eugene, OR: Pickwick, 2011.

Foley, John Miles. "Word in Tradition, Words in Text: A Response." *Semeia* 65 (1995) 169–79.

Foster, Stuart J. "Oral Theology in Lomwe Songs." *International Bulletin of Missionary Research* 32 (2008) 130–34.

Francis, Laurie, et al. "Does Literacy Education Improve Symptoms of Depression and Self-Efficacy in Individuals with Low Literacy and Depressive Symptoms? A Preliminary Investigation." *Journal of the American Board of Family Medicine* 20 (2007) 23–27.

Goodman, Madeline, et al. *Literacy, Numeracy, and Problem Solving in Technology-Rich Environments Among U.S. Adults: Results from the Program for the International Assessment of Adult Competencies 2012.* Washington, DC: National Center for Education Statistics Institute of Education Sciences U.S. Department of Education, 2013.

Gray, Peter. "What If Medicine's First Principle Were Also Education's?" *Psychology Today.* September 10, 2016. https://www.psychologytoday.com/blog/freedom-learn/201609/what-if-medicine-s-first-principle-were-also-education-s.

Hardman, Joel C. "A Community of Learners: Cambodians in an Adult ESL Classroom." *Language Teaching Research* 3 (1999) 145–66.

Hadisi, Mwana. "Exploring the Performance, Semantic, and Cognitive Dimensions of Orality. *Missiology: An International Review* 40 (2012) 443–53.

Hiebert, Paul G. *Transforming Worldviews: An Anthropological Understanding of How People Change.* Grand Rapids: Baker Academic, 2008.

Hill, Dianne. "People as Informal, Extended Resources for Learning." In *Proceedings of the Ninth International Symposium on Aviation Psychology,* edited by R. Jensen and L. Rakovan, 1219–22. Columbus, OH: The Ohio State University Aviation Psychology Laboratory, 1997.

Hvitfeldt, Christina. "Traditional Culture, Perceptual Style, and Learning: The Classroom Behavior of Hmong Adults." *Adult Education Quarterly* 36 (1986) 65–77.

International Orality Network and Lausanne Committee for World Evangelization. *Making Disciples of Oral Learners.* Lima, NY: Elim, 2005.

Ito, Mizuko, et al. *Connected Learning: An Agenda for Research and Design.* Irvine, CA: Digital Media and Learning Research Hub, 2013.

Johnson, Diane E. "Considering Shame and Its Implications for Student Learning." *College Student Journal* 46 (2012) 3–17.

Jousse, Marcel. *The Oral Style.* Translated by Edgard Sienaert and Richard Whitaker. New York: Routledge, 2015.

Keysser, Christian. *A People Reborn.* Pasadena, CA: William Carey, 1980.

Knowland, Victoria C., and Michael S. C. Thomas. "Educating the Adult Brain: How the Neuroscience of Learning Can Inform Educational Policy." *International Review of Education* 60 (2014) 99–122.

Lado, Ana. "Ways in Which Spanish-Speaking Illiterates Differ from Literates in ESL Classrooms." *ERIC Digest,* 1990. https://eric.ed.gov/?id=ED367195.

Li, Guofang. *Culturally Contested Pedagogy: Battles of Literacy and Schooling between Mainstream Teachers and Asian Immigrant Parents.* EBSCO Reader version, 2006.

Lienhard, Ruth. "Restoring Relationships: Theological Reflections on Shame and Honor among the Daba and Bana of Cameroon." PhD diss., Fuller Theological Seminary, 2010.

Lovejoy, Grant. "The Extent of Orality: 2012 Update." *Orality Journal* 1 (2012) 11–40.

Maddox, Brian. "Worlds Apart? Ethnographic Reflections on 'Effective Literacy' and Intrahousehold Externalities." *World Development* 35 (2007) 532–41.

Mazamisa, Welile. "Reading from This Place: From Orality to Literacy/Textuality and Back." *Scriptura* 9 (1991) 67–72.

Mayers, Marvin K. *Christianity Confronts Culture: A Strategy for Cross-Cultural Evangelism.* Grand Rapids: Zondervan, 1987.

McCarthy, Michael C. "'We are Your Books': Augustine, the Bible, and the Practice of Authority." *Journal of the American Academy of Religion* 75 (2007) 324–52.

McIntyre, Roy C. *Using Ceremonies to Disciple Oral Learners among the Tribal People in Bangladesh.* DMiss diss., Asbury Theological Seminary, 2005.

Merriam, Sharan B., and Gabo Ntseane. "Transformational Learning in Botswana: How Culture Shapes the Process." *Adult Education Quarterly* 58 (2008) 183–97.

Merriam, Sharan B., and Mazanah Mohamad. "How Cultural Values Shape Learning in Older Adulthood: The Case of Malaysia." *Adult Education Quarterly* 51 (2000) 45–63.

Merrifield, Juliet, and Mary Beth Bingman. "Living and Learning: Strategies for Survival in a Literate World." In *34th Annual Adult Education Research Conference (AERC) Proceedings.* University Park, PA: Pennsylvania State University, 1993.

Moll, Luis C., et al. "Funds of Knowledge for Teaching: Using a Qualitative Approach to Connect Homes and Classrooms." *Theory into Practice* 31 (1992) 132–41.

Montandon, Cleopatre. "Forme Sociales, Formes D'education Et Figures Theoriques" ["Social Forms, Forms of Education, and Theoretical Figures"]. In *Formel? Informel? Les formes de l'éducation* [*Formal? Informal? The Forms of Education*], edited by C. Montandon and O. Maulini, 223–43. Brussels, Belgium: De Boeck University, 2005.

Moon, W. Jay. "Discipling through the Eyes of Oral Learners." *Missiology: An International Review* 38 (2010) 127–40.

———. "Rituals and Symbols in Community Development." *Missiology: An International Review* 40 (2012) 141–52.

———. "Understanding Oral Learners." *Teaching Theology and Religion* 15 (2012) 29–39.

———. *Using Proverbs to Contextualize Christianity in the Bulisa Culture of Ghana, West Africa.* PhD diss., Asbury Theological Seminary, 2005.

———. "Using Rituals to Disciple Oral Learners: Part 1." *Orality Journal* 2 (2009) 43–64.

Morris, Mark. "Fellow Servants Honor Dr. Rebekah Naylor." February 13, 2009. http://www.missionleader.com/?p=338

Motty, Bauta D. "Contextualizing Theological Education in Africa: A Case of ECWA Theological Seminary, Jos, Nigeria." In *Beyond Literate Western Models: Contextualizing Theological Education in Oral Contexts,* edited by Samuel Chiang and Grant Lovejoy, 153–62. Hong Kong: International Orality Network, 2013.

Ong, Walter J. *Orality and Literacy: The Technologizing of the Word.* New York: Routledge, 1982.

———. *Rhetoric, Romance, and Technology: Studies in the Interaction of Expression and Culture.* Ithaca, NY: Cornell University, 1971.

Orenstein, Myrna. "Picking Up the Clues: Understanding Undiagnosed Learning Disabilities, Shame, and Imprisoned Intelligence." *Journal of College Student Psychotherapy* 15 (2000) 35–46.

Oughton, Helen. "Funds of Knowledge: A Conceptual Critique." *Studies in the Education of Adults* 42 (2010) 63–78.

Papacharissi, Zizi. "The Unbearable Lightness of Information and the Impossible Gravitas of Knowledge: Big Data and the Makings of a Digital Orality." *Media, Culture, and Society* 37 (2015) 1–6.

Paradise, Ruth M. "What's Different about Learning in Schools as Compared to Family and Community Settings?" *Human Development* 41 (1998) 270–78.

Paradise, Ruth, and Barbara Rogoff. "Side by Side Learning: Learning by Observing and Pitching In." *Ethos* 37 (2009) 102–38.

Parker, Veronica A. *Adults' Perspectives on the Impact of Low-Level Literacy/ Functional/ Illiteracy on Their Lives: A Case Study of Literacy Program Participants.* EdD diss., University of Houston, 1999.

Perry, Kristen H. "Genres, Context, and Literacy Practices: Literacy Brokering among Sudanese Refugee Families," *Reading Research Quarterly* 44 (2009) 256–76.

Ramirez-Esparza, Nairan, et al. "Socio-Interactive Practices and Personality in Adult Learners of English with Little Formal Education." *Language Learning* 62 (2012) 541–70.

Rhoads, David. "Biblical Performance Criticism: Performance as Research." *Oral Tradition* 25 (2010) 157–98.

Rodriguez, Gloria M. "Power and Agency in Education: Exploring the Pedagogical Dimensions of Funds of Knowledge." *Review of Research in Education* 37 (2013) 87–120.

Ryan, Annette, et al. "Wise Women: Mentoring as Relational Learning in Perinatal Nursing Practice." *Journal of Clinical Nursing* 19 (2010) 183–91.

Schrage, Michael. "The Relationship Revolution." *Technology and Society: The Merrill Lynch Forum,* 2001. http://web.archive.org/web/20030602035010/http://www.ml.com/woml/forum/relation3.htm.

Shelton, Leslie H. *The Heart of Literacy: Transforming School-Induced Shame and Recovering the Competent Self.* PhD diss., The Union Institute, 2001.

Shuter, Robert. "The Hmong of Laos: Orality, Communication, and Acculturation." In *Intercultural Communication: A Reader,* edited by L. A. Samovar and R. E. Porter, 102–8. Belmont, CA: Wadsworth, 1985.

Simmel, Georg. "The Sociological Significance of the 'Stranger." In *Introduction to the Science of Sociology,* edited by R. Park and E. Burgess, 322–27. Chicago: University of Chicago, 1921.

Smith, John D. "Worlds Apart: Orality, Literacy, and the Rajasthani Folk *Mahabharata*." *Oral Tradition* 5 (1990) 3–19.

Smith-Hefner, Nancy J. "Education, Gender, and Generational Conflict among Khmer Refugees." *Anthropology and Education Quarterly* 24 (1993) 135–58.

Soukup, Paul A. "In Commemoration: Walter Ong and the State of Theology." *Theological Studies* 73 (2012) 824–40.

Spindler, George, and Louise Spindler. *Fifty Years of Anthropology and Education: 1950–2000: A Spindler Anthology*. Mahway, NJ: Taylor & Francis, 2009.

Sterne, Jonathan. "The Theology of Sound: A Critique of Orality." *Canadian Journal of Communication* 36 (2011) 207–26.

Stock, Brian. *Listening for the Text: On the Uses of the Past*. Philadelphia: University of Pennsylvania, 1996.

Street, Brian V. *Autonomous and Ideological Models of Literacy: Approaches from New Literacy Studies*, 1995. http://www.philbu.net/media- anthropology/street_newliteracy.pdf.

———. *Social Literacies: Critical Approaches to Literacy in Development, Ethnography and Education*. New York: Routledge, 1995.

Swearingen, C. Jan. "Oral Hermeneutics during the Transition to Literacy: The Contemporary Debate." *Cultural Anthropology* 1 (1986) 138–56.

Tanner, Kathleen. "Adult Dyslexia and the 'Conundrum of Failure.'" *Disability and Society* 24 (2009) 785–97.

Taylor, Stephen C. R. *A Study of the Relationship between Christian Education and the Belief System of Thai Christians*. DMin thesis, International Theological Seminary, Los Angeles, 1999.

Thigpen, Lynn. *Connected Learning: A Grounded Theory Study of How Cambodian Adults with Limited Formal Education Learn*. PhD diss.., Biola University, 2016.

———. *Connected Learning: How Adults with Limited formal Education Learn*. Eugene, OR: Pickwick, 2020.

———. "The Dark Side of Orality." In *Honor, Shame, and the Gospel*, edited by Christopher Flanders and Werner Mischke. Littleton, CO: William Carey, 2020.

———. "The Oral Bible School." 2005. http://theoralbibleschool.com.

Thompson, LaNette W. "The Nonliterate and the Transfer of Knowledge in West Africa." MA thesis, The University of Texas at Arlington, 1998.

———. *Perceptions of Teaching Nonliterate Adults in Oral Cultures: A Modified Delphi Study*. PhD diss., Baylor University, 2015.

United Nations Development Program (UNDP). "About Cambodia." 2013. https://web.archive.org/web/20130821021354/http://www.kh.undp.org/content/cambodia/en/home/countryinfo.

United Nations Development Program (UNDP). "About Cambodia." 2016. http://www.kh.undp.org/content/Cambodia/en/home/countryinfo.

van de Craats, et al. "Research on Low-Educated Second Language and Literacy Acquisition." In *Low-Educated Adult Second Language and Literacy Acquisition: Proceedings of the Inaugural Symposium, Tilburg University, August 2005*, edited by I. van de Craats et al., 7–24. Utrecht, The Netherlands: LOT, 2005.

Vautrot, Leona. *"Why Don't They Come?" Perceptions of Illiterate Adults in an Appalachian Mountain Region Regarding Nonparticipation in an Adult Literacy Program*. PhD diss., University of New Orleans, New Orleans, LA, 2004.

Velez-Ibanez, Carlos G., and James B. Greenberg. "Formation and Transformation of Funds of Knowledge among U.S.-Mexican Households." *Anthropology and Education Quarterly* 23 (1992) 313–35.

Watkins, Chris, and Peter Mortimore. "Pedagogy: What Do We Know?" In *Understanding Pedagogy and Its Impact on Learning*, edited by P. Mortimore, 1–19. Thousand Oaks, CA: SAGE, 1999.

Watson, Jill A. *Interpreting across the Abyss: A Hermeneutic Exploration of Initial Literacy Development by High School English Language Learners with Limited Formal Schooling.* PhD diss., University of Minnesota, 2010.

Weiss, Barry D., et al. "Literacy Education as Treatment for Depression in Patients with Limited Literacy and Depression: A Randomized Controlled Trial." *Journal of General Internal Medicine* 21 (2006) 823–28.

West, Russell W. "The Re-Eventing of Theological Education: Toward a Pedagogy of Leadership Formation in the Verbomoteur Mode." Paper presented at the International Orality Network Forum, Asbury Theological Seminary, Wilmore, KY, April 2014.

Wilson, John D. "Let the Earth Hear His Voice." *International Journal of Frontier Missions* 14 (1997) 177–82.

Wydick, Bruce, and Travis J. Lybbert. "Poverty, Aspirations, and the Economics of Hope." Paper presented at the Economics of Global Poverty Conference, Gordon College, Wenham, MA, 2015.

3

The Metanarrative of Scripture
A Critical Factor in Cross-Cultural Ministry

Wiley Scot Keen

The thesis of this chapter is quite simple. I maintain that story is essential to human communication and is the primary means by which worldviews are shaped and expressed. For that reason, it is in the best interest of cross-cultural ministries to be well versed in the metanarrative of the host audience as well as the metanarrative of Scripture. In fact, it is *critical*. This word was chosen carefully. Merriam-Webster defines "critical" as *indispensable* or *essential*.[1] By learning the metanarrative of the host audience, missionaries grasp worldview and that which shapes it. This in turn creates the platform from which to bring the rival narratives of the host audience into tension with God's narrative. This approach also enables the missionary to utilize the power of God's story to bring transformation among the host audience. Metanarrative is a critical factor in cross-cultural ministry.

The Universality of Narrative

Story is so characteristic of humanity that our species has been called *Homo Narrans*.[2] Roland Barthes commented on this universality of narrative by saying, "[N]arrative is present in every age, in every place, in every society; it begins with the very history of mankind and there nowhere is nor has been a people without narrative . . . narrative is international, trans-historical, transcultural: it is simply there, like life itself."[3]

---

1. "Critical." https://www.merriam-webster.com/dictionary/critical.

2. Niles, *Homo Narrans*, 3. See also Fisher, *Human Communication as Narration*, xiii.

3. Barthes, *Image, Music, Text*, 79.

Because of the universality of narrative, Hayden White says we must identify what kind of insight narrative provides into the nature of real events.[4] For one, the very existence of narrative—whether oral or written—is an attempt to rank the significance of events in sequence and interpret their significance. "It is this need or impulse to rank events with respect to their significance for the culture or group that is writing its own history that makes a narrative representation of real events possible."[5] To illustrate this human impulse to rank events and find correlation between those events, White appealed to *The Annals of Saint Gall*, a list of historical events in Gaul from 700 to 900 C.E. At first glance, the list of natural and social events appears incomprehensible with no story, conclusion or central subject.[6] However, White says this first glance is insufficient, because "there must be a story since there is surely a plot—if by 'plot' we mean a structure of relationships by which the events contained in the account are endowed with a meaning by being identified as parts of an integrated whole."[7]

The human "impulse to rank events" is an attempt to make sense of experiences by way of story.[8] Events are understood by the way in which they correlate to other events. A narrative is an arrangement of events in relation to one another, with the underlying belief that the meaning of the events must be seen in light of their correlations. Stories, therefore, are the foundational way in which humans configure ideas; we live by seeing ourselves within a story.[9]

Narrative is a mode of communication rooted in the human need to make sense of life.[10] Not only is human rationality structured narratively, narrative is also the vehicle through which behaviors and beliefs are communicated to others.[11] Narrative both informs and expresses worldview. The stories that we have been taught and embraced form the paradigmatic lens through which we view the world.

---

4. White, "Value of Narrativity," 10.
5. White, "Value of Narrativity," 14.
6. White, "Value of Narrativity," 12–13.
7. White, "Value of Narrativity," 13.
8. Turner, *Literary Mind*, v.
9. Lubeck, "Talking Story," 1–2.
10. Lubeck, "Talking Story," 1.
11. Lubeck, "Talking Story," 6.

Metanarrative and Worldview

Metanarrative Defined

Jean-Francois Lyotard is credited with coining the term "metanarrative (maître-récit)." Lyotard contrasted meta/master narratives with local narratives.[12] Metanarratives distinguish themselves from local narratives because they are institutionalized and, consequently, they legitimize.[13] A metanarrative is, "any overarching universal account of reality and human life that purports to explain everything."[14]

Metanarrative and Enculturation

The intersection of local narratives and metanarratives is germane to the topic at hand. Local narratives (as well as the various events and experiences of life) are understood in light of the metanarrative one holds. As Michael Matthews contends, "One's cultural/perceived metanarrative is the foundation any person (illiterate or literate) has for determining meaning."[15] Allow me to illustrate with a . . . *story*.

> Years ago, my son purchased an Australian Shepherd pup. The owners were ready to say goodbye to the entire litter, and somehow by the time we left their house, we left with two puppies instead of one. The alpha dog quickly established her dominance and maintained this dominance by frequently pinning her litter mate to the ground. Over the years, these contests became quite intense. One day my daughter ran into the house and yelled, "Dad, Freckles is killing Floss." I ran outside and found that the alpha dog was biting her litter mate's neck, which was stained with blood. When I tried to pull her off, I realized that her tooth was hung in her litter mate's collar. The blood was not from the jugular vein; it was from her own mouth! Because there was a history of violent attacks through which the alpha dog maintained her dominance, we interpreted an isolated event accordingly. Our understanding (or *misunderstanding*) was based on the narratives that had formed our perspective concerning our dogs.

---

12. Klein, "History and Theory," 281.
13. Klein, "History and Theory," 282.
14. Wolter, "Metanarrative," 506.
15. Matthews, *Is There a Reader of This Text*, 85.

Bringing this back to the topic at hand, the events and experiences of life are filtered through and (mis)understood by the metanarrative we have been taught. David Naugle argues this from a *philosophical* vantagepoint: "A weltanschauung [worldview]—as the primary system of narrative signs that articulate a vision of reality and lie at the base of individual and collective life—is the most significant set of presuppositions on the basis of which interpretation operates."[16] Michael Matthews defends this same concept from a *missiological* perspective and contends that every person operates from a worldview that is based on a metanarrative.[17] Matthews witnessed this first-hand as a missionary in Siberia when one of his teammates shared John 3:16 with a Yukatian hitch-hiker. Matthews observed, "You have only one hermeneutical option. You can only interpret these (very few) foreign and 'holy words' in light of what you already know."[18] Again, "Nothing is interpreted in life by anybody, anywhere, at any time without being filtered through and influenced by a comprehensive metanarrative."[19]

Not even Lyotard could escape the concept of metanarrative, which he disdained. Ray Lubeck explains that, in making a judgment call concerning various metanarratives, postmodernism is self-defeating because it sees itself as an irreducible metanarrative.[20] "The postmodernist is thus caught in a performative contradiction, arguing against the necessity of metanarratives precisely by (surreptitious) appeal to a metanarrative."[21] Thus, disciplines which are sometimes presented as objectively evaluating facts with no presuppositions are themselves built upon philosophical commitments.[22] These predetermined commitments are based on narratives.[23] The pervasive influence of a metanarrative within a culture is rooted in the fact that these metanarratives are communally shared and perpetuated by recognized authorities.[24]

---

16. Naugle, *Worldview*, 313.
17. Matthews, *Is There a Reader*, 1.
18. Matthews, *Novel Approach*, xxvi.
19. Matthews, *Is There a Reader*, 201.
20. Lubeck, "Talking Story," 11.
21. Middleton and Walsh, *Truth Is Stranger*, 77.
22. Moreland, *Scientism and Secularism*, 23.
23. Lubeck, "Talking Story," 4.
24. Matthews, *Novel Approach*, 124.

Metanarratives and Authority

All worldviews contain various cultural universals, regardless of the worldview or the culture in which they are found.[25] One of those elements is *authority*. "Various levels of authority develop within a grand story over time. They become accepted by and firmly embedded in any society . . . This perceived ultimate authority is . . . primarily responsible for telling and governing of the overarching story of reality within that culture."[26] The Bible presents itself as *the* Metanarrative, the overarching account of reality that explains all other things. This means that a faithful and comprehensive presentation of the Metanarrative of Scripture will necessarily confront the controlling narratives of a given culture, and the ultimate epistemological authorities recognized by those cultures. Missiologists must draw cultural narratives into tension with God's narrative. This would confront an animistic culture by claiming that the shaman is not the ultimate authority; God's Word is. It would confront a humanistic society by stating that human reason is not the ultimate authority; God's Word is. Again, the Bible claims to be *the* meta-story. When the message of the Bible is absorbed and distorted by cultural metanarratives, the recognition of its ultimate authority has been sacrificed.

Metanarratives and Host Audience: Summary

Narrative is universal. A study of man necessarily includes story. When a missionary immerses themself in culture study, they do so by soliciting stories from their host people. When they organize and interpret the recorded data, they do so in narrative constructs. Given enough time, they will inevitably find an overarching metanarrative that shapes the worldview of the host people. The concept of metanarrative is critical for cross-cultural ministry because all cultures interpret life through a worldview grid that has been shaped and expressed through story. By learning the metanarrative of a given culture, we not only gain relevancy, we also reduce the risk of syncretism by positioning ourselves to present God's Word for what it truly is–the ultimate Metanarrative.

---

25. Matthews, *Novel Approach*, 109.
26. Matthews, *Novel Approach*, 124.

The Transformational Power of God's Story

While articulations of the storyline differ, evangelicals largely agree that the Bible presents one overarching story.[27] This section of the chapter highlights the transformational power of that story.

Metanarrative of Scripture and Authority

Michael Goheen connects the metanarrative of Scripture to the authority of Scripture. He reasons that, when we read the Bible in a fragmentary way, it is easily subsumed into the larger cultural story surrounding it, which allows the humanistic cultural story to shape our lives more than the biblical story.[28] Thus he concludes, "We can understand its authority only if we receive it as an all-embracing story."[29] Of course, narrative is only one of many genre found in Scripture. Nevertheless, the non-narrative portions of Scripture are located within a larger meta-story that claims to be *the* meta-story that defines reality. To divorce propositional statements from the meta-story is to undermine the authority of the meta-story.

Embrace a Biblical Worldview

Jeanine K. Brown asserts that, "Stories help us configure a coherent view of ourselves and our life experiences; they are integrally related to our worldview."[30] Narrative and worldview are inseparable. As Mark Turner stated, "*Story* is a basic principle of mind. Most of our experience, our knowledge, and our thinking is organized as stories."[31] In fact, story is the essential shape of a worldview.[32] Duvall and Hays claim that every person has a metanarrative

---

27. E.g., Johnson, *Dispensational Biblical Theology*, 32. Johnson (obviously) holds to dispensational theology. Leland Ryken, *Words of Delight*, 31. Ryken is a literary expert who maintains that the Bible has the structure of a metanarrative. Wright, *How God Became King*, 66. Wright comes from yet another theological vantage point but still maintains the overall narrative structure of the Bible.

28. Goheen, "Urgency," 473–74.

29. Goheen, "Urgency," 473.

30. Brown. *Scripture as Communication,* 43.

31. Turner, *Literary Mind*, v.

32. Turner, *Literary Mind*, 147.

and that they use their metanarrative to make sense of life.[33] "Everyone believes in or buys into a big story, whether they realize it or not."[34]

This intersection of worldview and narrative was articulated by J. R. Middleton and B. J. Walsh. In their book *The Transforming Vision,* they noted four questions that all cultures ask:

1. "Where are we?
2. Who are we?
3. What's wrong? and
4. What's the remedy?"[35]

Upon later reflection they realized that these questions are fundamental to narrative which compelled them to write a second work, *Truth is Stranger Than It Used to Be.* In this book they connected components of narrative to each of their original four questions:

1. "Where are we? *Setting,*
2. Who are we? *Characters,*
3. What's wrong? *Conflict,* and
4. What's the remedy? *Resolution.*"[36]

These observations have major implications for ministry. Narrative is the paradigm through which all peoples view the world. Narrative is also the medium by which a worldview is communicated to others. Therefore, effective evangelism and discipleship must be accomplished by challenging rival narratives with God's metanarrative. This is conducted towards the ultimate goal of believers embracing God's story and their place within it. On this foundation, Sharon Short argues that evangelism is ultimately a call to switch stories and sanctification is a call to live in light of the story of God.[37] We see this played out on the pages of Scripture. Ruth abandoned the stories/worldview of Moab for the Story of God (Ruth 1:16–17 cf. 2:12). Moses abandoned the treasures of Egypt and identified himself with the God of the Hebrews because of the stories he had embraced (Heb

---

33. Duvall and Hays, *Living God's Word,* 14.
34. Duvall and Hays, *Living God's Word,* 14.
35. Walsh and Middleton, *Transforming Vision,* 35.
36. Middleton and Walsh, *Truth Is Stranger,* 64. This concept is made explicit in Lubeck, "Talking Story," 8.
37. Short, "Formed By Story," 116–17.

11:23–28). These men and women of God embraced a biblical worldview via the influential narratives they were taught.

If believers are going to embrace a biblical worldview, they must see that the multiplicity of ideas being proclaimed in a given culture are ultimately alternative stories (coming from the father of lies), and must therefore be held in contradistinction to God's story.[38] As Duvall and Hays contend, "When you give no thought to your guiding story, then you are simply being swept along by the most powerful currents of your culture."[39] Bartholomew and Goheen share the same conviction:

> The dominant story of modern culture is rooted in idolatry: an ultimate confidence in humanity to achieve its own salvation. Thus, instead of allowing the Bible to shape us, we may in fact be allowing our culture to shape the Bible for us. Our view of the world and even our faith will be molded by one or the other: either the biblical story is our foundation, or the Bible itself becomes subsumed with the modern story . . . If our lives are to be shaped and formed by Scripture, we need to know the biblical story well, to feel it in our bones.[40]

Believers are delivered from syncretism when they learn to see beyond the ideas and values of their culture to the very stories (and philosophical assumptions) behind them. In turn, they must embrace the biblical story as *the* story of reality. "[The Biblical story] is to function as the controlling story . . . an authoritative worldview."[41]

Impact of Narrative for Discipleship

Narrative Invites Reflection

Stories are powerful because they invite reflection. Bruce Baloian said, "Perhaps one of the reasons we humans do not forget stories is because the primary human engagement with reality is story. Therefore, the stories heard or seen can be pondered again and again and new insights can emerge in the various situations people find themselves in until their story matches the biblical stories."[42] According to N. T. Wright, one of the

---

38. Matthews, "Is There a Reader," 86.
39. Duvall and Hays, *Living God's Word*, 20.
40. Bartholomew and Goheen, *Drama of Scripture*, 197.
41. Bartholomew and Goheen, "Story and Biblical Theology," 155.
42. Baloian, "Teaching the Ineffable," 70.

reasons Jesus used story (parable) is that it invited his hearers to reflect upon the part they played in God's story, whether good or bad.[43] As believers reflect upon the spiritual values communicated via story, they are challenged to embrace the values communicated from that story—including the desire to fit into God's story.

Narrative is Disarming

Stories impact spiritual formation because of the manner in which they communicate and challenge believers. "Stories disarm us, allowing the truth to penetrate where propositional truths may simply be deflected or ignored."[44] N. T. Wright contends:

> Stories are, actually, peculiarly good at modifying or subverting other stories and their worldviews. Where head-on attack would certainly fail, the parable hides the wisdom of the serpent behind the innocence of the dove, gaining entrance and favour which can then be used to change assumptions which the hearer would otherwise keep hidden away for safety.[45]

The classic example of this concept is Nathan's confrontation of David for his sin with Bathsheba (2 Sam 12). Nathan's parable enabled David to be drawn into and identify with the story before realizing that he was himself the antagonist! As noted earlier, Jesus often used parables (a type of story) to challenge worldview.

Narrative is an Exercise in Ethics

Stories also impact spiritual formation by drawing the reader into the narrative and engaging them in the decision-making process. Daniel Carroll comments:

> Narrative works in ethics in several ways. One is, it actually pictures the problem . . . and you can identify with the situation . . . What novels do is engage you in the decision-making process . . . engaging your ethical sensibilities and train[ing] you . . . A good literary piece will draw you into the narrative and not only picture for you the scene, but also engage you ethically so that

---

43. Wright, *New Testament*, 77.
44. Tripplett, "God's Transforming Story," 308.
45. Wright, *New Testament*, 40.

you're thinking through what options you would take if you were in that same place, and you also see the good and the bad consequences of the choices that the characters are making . . . Literary theory sees this and we need to bring it into the biblical discussion more and more.[46]

As believers become increasingly familiar with the narratives and metanarrative of Scripture, they will undoubtedly see the consistency of God's character, faithfulness to His promises, and the reward of living by faith. As readers see the hopes of antagonist's disappointed and expectations of believers fulfilled, they will be shaped by this characterization, and persuaded to align themselves with God and His purposes.[47]

Narrative Influences Values

Walter Fisher proposes that narrative is inherently ethical and is the supreme instrument for building values and goals which then motivate human conduct.[48] This is because of the correlation between metanarrative and worldview.[49] Metanarrative and worldview lie inseparably at the core of every culture and stand as the basis for all values held within that culture. As Walsh and Middleton contend, "A world view is never merely a vision *of* life. It is always a vision *for* life as well . . . Our worldview determines our values . . . It sorts out what is important from what is not, what is of highest value from what is least."[50]

Desire to fit into God's Story: Reason for Being

Metanarrative and Orientation

Alasdair MacIntyre said, "I can only answer the question 'What am I to do?' if I can answer the prior question 'Of what story or stories do I find myself a part?'"[51] One's concept of reality is based on the stories that they embrace (e.g., Creation, the Big Bang, etc.). This philosophy of reality is pragmatic

---

46. Bock, "Table Podcast."
47. Ryken, *Words of Delight*, 83.
48. Fisher, *Human Communication*, 65.
49. Turner, *Literary Mind*, v.
50. Walsh and Middleton, *Transforming Vision*, 32.
51. MacIntyre, *After Virtue*, 216. Double space??

because, "Our perception of reality dictates how we live in it."[52] Craig Bartholomew and Michael Goheen are very pointed concerning the practical importance of metanarrative in a believer's life: "If our lives are to be shaped by the story of Scripture, we need to understand two things well: the biblical story is a compelling unity on which we may depend, and each of us has a place within that story."[53] By recognizing one's place in the biblical story one is thereby motivated to fit into that story.

In contrast, if believers view the Bible as a giant book of principles and commands without seeing the overarching story, they may be collecting and applying truth piecemeal. Duvall and Hays assert, "A person will never truly experience the Great Story if they remain content with adding bits and pieces of it to their life, especially if they are really living according to a different grand story."[54] Again, "Participating in God's mission in this world brings ultimate meaning and purpose in life because it centers our life in God himself and his purposes rather than in ourselves."[55]

The literature articulates three primary means by which believers would be compelled to fit into God's story as a result of the metanarrative:

1. by recognizing the trajectory of God's activity in history,
2. through gaining an awareness of their identity as God's people, and
3. by understanding one's ultimate destiny.

Metanarrative and Trajectory

Regarding the emphasis of the trajectory in the metanarrative, N. T. Wright articulates the biblical story in the framework of a five-act play and concludes that the present period of history (Act 5) is a time in which believers are called to continue God's work as set by the trajectory of His actions in history up to this present time (Acts 1–4).[56] This concept of trajectory is recognized by others as well. Duvall and Hays take their cue from the book of Acts and conclude, "This section of the Story also challenges us to regard evangelism as a priority for the church."[57] Bartholomew and Goheen also recognize the evangelistic thrust of the metanarrative:

---

52. Matthews, *Novel Approach*, 26.
53. Bartholomew and Goheen, *Drama of Scripture*, 12.
54. Duvall and Hays, *Living God's Word*, 303.
55. Duvall and Hays, *Living God's Word*, 301.
56. Wright, *New Testament*, 140–41.
57. Duvall and Hays, *Living God's Word*, 270.

The goal of God's redemptive work is to restore his creation from the effects of sin upon it. In his death Jesus has conquered sin, and in his resurrection, he has inaugurated a new era of salvation and recovery. The kingdom banquet is ready to be enjoyed, but it does not begin just yet. More peoples must first be gathered to the banquet table so that they too may taste of the renewing power of the coming age. This in-between time, after Jesus' first coming and before he comes again, is a time of mission for the exalted Christ, the Spirit, and the church.[58]

As noted above, one's perception of where history is going impacts the way(s) in which they seek to fit in to God's story. This is a double-edged sword in that, if one is mistaken as to what God is seeking to accomplish in the world at a given point in time, then they may find their life being lived in futility of purpose. For example, some believers expect to see the increasing betterment of society through the progress of the gospel.[59] This would lead proponents of this view to seek to bring in the kingdom through their social and evangelistic efforts. Others claim to enter the trajectory of God's story by seeking to renew the earth *now* in light of the fact that it will ultimately be renewed in the eschaton.[60] Those who see this present age as a time of invitation—a time in which guests are being gathered for the final banquet—will adjust accordingly, seeking to prepare guests via evangelism and discipleship. Again, one's understanding of where history is going will be impacted by the trajectory (whether it be real or perceived) they understand from the Metanarrative.

Metanarrative and Identity

Christopher Wright adds to the element of *trajectory* the aspect of *identity*. Wright contends that the imperatives of Scripture are typically based on indicatives.[61] He illustrates this with Israel, whose imperatives (Exod 20) were based on her identity (Exod 19).[62] Wright also notes that Israel's election was not the rejection of other nations but for the sake of those nations.[63] Wright then extends this identity and mission to the church because of her position *in Christ*. "This story is also our story, for if we are in Christ then, according

58. Bartholomew and Goheen, *Drama of Scripture*, 171.
59. Walvoord, *Millennial Kingdom*, 30.
60. Srokosz, "God's Story," 166.
61. Wright, "Mission as a Matrix," 129.
62. Wright, "Mission as a Matrix," 129.
63. Wright, "Mission as a Matrix," 135.

to Paul, we are also in Abraham and heirs according to the promise."[64] Thus for Wright, identity gives greater depth to the mission of the church, grounding its activity in its identity. While considerable debate occurs regarding the similarities and distinctions between the role of Israel and the Church in redemptive history, both Covenant and Dispensational theologians would agree that identity informs activity. Thus Wright states:

> So then, our mission certainly flows from the authority of the Bible. But that is far richer and deeper than simply obeying a biblical command. Rather, obedience to the Great Commission, and even the Great Commission itself, are set within the context of these realities. The Great Commission is not something extra or exotic. Rather, the authority of the Great Commission is embedded in the reality of the God whose universal authority Jesus has been given, in the reality of the *story* it presupposes and envisages, and in the reality of the *people* who are now to become a self-replicating community of disciples among all nations. This is the God we worship, this is the story we are part of, this is the people to whom we belong. How should we then live? What then is our mission?[65]

Eugene Merrill sees *identity* as one of the major reasons for which the Pentateuch was written. He contends that:

> The original purpose of the Torah was not to provide modern readers insight into creation or the flood or other great turning points . . . but to address questions raised by Israel itself concerning its (then) present situation, what lay ahead, and, most important, its historical roots. Who are we? Why are we here? What purpose does God have in mind for us? . . . In order for Israel to have a fuller understanding of its role as a kingdom of priests and a holy nation, Moses had to transport them back to the beginning—the absolute beginning—to creation itself.[66]

Israel's ability to carry out her purpose as a nation was thus tied to her sense of identity as gained from the metanarrative. This concept was so critical for Israel that she was instructed through the Law to pass on this sense of identity to successive generations (e.g., Exod 13:14–16; Deut 26:1–11; Ps 78:1–8). As Graeme Goldsworthy commented, "The only explanation for the laws and regulations that can be given to a curious child

---

64. Wright, "Mission as a Matrix," 128.
65. Wright, "Mission as a Matrix," 129.
66. Merrill, *Everlasting Dominion*, 38.

is the historical act of redemption by which they were freed from slavery in Egypt (Deut 6:20–25)."[67]

The value for God's people gaining their sense of identity based on how they relate to the biblical story is far reaching as it gives people a sense of purpose and direction in life. In contrast, when people are not taught about their identity from the word of God, culture will define that role for them.

> We are defined by so many stories. There are so many stories that, in our culture, make a claim to us; claim to define us. The biblical story is the story that speaks *the* truth about who we are, why we are here, what the purpose is for our life, and yet we're so often drawn to these other stories and let them make their claims on us.[68]

Christians take their sense of identity from story: one of the cultural stories that surround them or the biblical story. As believers find identity in the metanarrative of Scripture, the literature supports the concept that they will be motivated to embrace their place within that story.

Metanarrative and Telos[69]

Akin to the concepts of trajectory (where God is moving history) and identity (who we are as defined by Scripture) is the concept of telos (our ultimate destiny). Michael Matthews argues, "The purpose underneath an action . . . is driven to a great extent by a sense of destiny. The reason for much human behavior and action is tied to the perception of how the perceived story of life in this world ends."[70] Every culture holds some notion of eschatology. It is natural to then align oneself with their final expectation. In his critique of Enlightenment thought, Lesslie Newbigin claims, "Eschatology went from being the return of Christ to human reason increasing in understanding until finally all evils that enslave humanity would be conquered."[71] In our day, it might be argued that technology is the answer. In fact, technological and scientific advancements in health care do indeed impact the way we view life.

---

67. Goldsworthy, *According to Plan*, 153.
68. Hawk, "Biblical Metanarrative."
69. MacIntyre, *After Virtue*, 217.
70. Matthews, *Novel Approach*, 138.
71. Newbigin, *Foolishness to the Greeks,* 28.

Our ultimate destiny, the post-humanists contend, is to transcend our weak biological bodies and be born again into eternal machines. Obviously, these two stories are at odds. In one story, God is the source of our resurrection and eternal life; in the other, technology becomes our god who enables our ascension into eternal life.[72]

Thus, one's concept of *telos* (whatever that concept might be) impacts one's expectations, which, in turn, impacts the way they live. Metanarrative impacts discipleship.

Concluding Reflections

The concept of *metanarrative* is a critical (and often neglected) factor in cross-cultural ministry. Narrative is universal among humanity, thus relating to anthropology. Narrative is essential to human communication and is the primary means of enculturation used to establish identity, meaning, purpose, and values. Thus, metanarrative is necessarily related to cross-cultural ministry. All cultures interpret life through a worldview grid that has been shaped and expressed through story.

The metanarrative of Scripture is critical for cross-cultural church planting. The Gospel of Christ takes on its greatest significance when placed against the backdrop of the Metanarrative of Scripture. In fact, the Great Commission is the extension of God's plan that is sourced in Genesis and developed throughout the plotline of the entire Bible. Narrative is effective for discipleship because of the *way* it communicates (disarming, inviting reflection, etc.). The Metanarrative of Scripture is crucial for discipleship because of *what* it communicates (setting a trajectory, providing a sense of identity, and articulating telos).

Effective cross-cultural ministry demands a grasp of metanarrative-one's own, that of the host audience, and the Metanarrative of Scripture as a whole. Missionaries proficient with metanarrative are able to utilize this universal medium to bring competing worldviews into tension with Scripture and influence peoples to embrace a biblical worldview.

---

72. Dyer, *From the Garden to the City*, 41.

Bibliography

Baloian, Bruce Edward. "Teaching the Ineffable Through Narrative." *Evangelical Quarterly* 88 (2016) 56–70.

Barthes, Roland. *Image, Music, Text.* Translated by Stephen Heath. New York: Hill and Wang, 1978.

Bartholomew, Craig G. "Biblical Theology and Biblical Interpretation." In *Out of Egypt: Biblical Theology and Biblical Interpretation,* edited by Craig Bartholomew et al., 1–22. Grand Rapids: Zondervan, 2004.

Bartholomew, Craig et al., eds. *Out of Egypt: Biblical Theology and Biblical Interpretation.* Grand Rapids: Zondervan, 2004.

Bartholomew, Craig G., and Michael W. Goheen. *The Drama of Scripture.* Grand Rapids: Baker Academic, 2004.

———. "Story and Biblical Theology." In *Out of Egypt: Biblical Theology and Biblical Interpretation,* edited by Craig Bartholomew et al., 144–71. Grand Rapids: Zondervan, 2004.

Bock, Darrell. "The Table Podcast: How Does Narrative Teach Theology and Ethics?" Interview with M. Daniel Carroll. https://www.dts.edu/thetable/play/old-testament-ethics-1#759.

Brown, Jeanine K. *Scripture as Communication: Introducing Biblical Hermeneutics.* Grand Rapids: Baker Academic, 2007.

Duvall, J. Scott and J. Daniel Hays. *Living God's Word: Discovering Our Place in the Great Story of Scripture.* Grand Rapids: Zondervan, 2012.

Dyer, John. *From the Garden to the City: The Redeeming and Corrupting Power of Technology.* Grand Rapids: Kregel, 2011.

Fisher, Walter. *Human Communication as Narration: Toward a Philosophy of Reason, Value, and Action.* Columbia: University of South Carolina, 1989.

Goheen, Michael W. "The Urgency of Reading the Bible as One Story." *Theology Today* 64 (2008) 469–83.

Goldsworthy, Graeme. *According to Plan.* Downers Grove, IL: InterVarsity, 1991.

———. "Evangelicalism and Biblical Theology." In *The Futures of Evangelicalism,* edited by Craig Bartholomew et al., 124–48. Grand Rapids: Kregel, 2003.

Hawk, Daniel. "The Biblical Metanarrative." Logos Mobil Ed Conversations. https://itunes.apple.com/us/podcast/mobil-ed-conversations/id860915911?mt=2.

Johnson, Elliot. *A Dispensational Biblical Theology.* Allen, TX: Bold Grace Ministries, 2016.

Klein, Kerwin K. "History and Theory." *History and Theory* 34 (1995) 275–98.

Lubeck, Ray. "Talking Story: Narrative Thought, Worldviews, and Postmodernism." Paper Presented at ETS Meeting, Orlando, FL, November 20, 1998.

MacIntyre, Alasdair. *After Virtue.* 3rd ed. Notre Dame, IN: University of Notre Dame Press, 2007.

Matthews, Michael. *A Novel Approach: The Significance of Story and Interpreting and Communicating Reality.* Victoria, BC: Tellwell, 2017.

———. *Is There a Reader of this Text?* PhD diss., Trinity Theological Seminary, 2016.

Merrill, Eugene. *Everlasting Dominion: A Theology of the Old Testament.* Nashville: B & H, 2006.

Middleton, J. Richard and Brian J. Walsh. *Truth Is Stranger Than It Used to Be: A Biblical Faith in a Postmodern Age.* Downers Grove, IL: InterVarsity, 1995.

Moreland, J. P. *Scientism and Secularism*. Wheaton: Crossway, 2018.
Naugle, David. *Worldview: The History of a Concept*. Grand Rapids: Eerdmans, 2002.
Newbigin, Lesslie. *Foolishness to the Greeks: The Gospel and Western Culture*. Grand Rapids: Eerdmans, 1986.
Niles, John D. *Homo Narrans: The Poetics and Anthropology of Oral Literature*. Philadelphia: University of Pennsylvania, 1999.
Ryken, Leland. *Words of Delight*. 2nd ed. Grand Rapids: Baker, 1992.
Short, Sharon Warkentin. "Formed by Story: The Metanarrative of the Bible as Doctrine." *Christian Education Journal* 9 (2012) 110–23.
Srokosz, Meric. "God's Story and the Earth's Story: Grounding our Concern for the Environment in the Biblical Metanarrative." *Science and Christian Belief* 20 (2008) 163–74.
Triplett, Suzy. "God's Transforming Story: How the Metanarrative of Scripture can Change Lives." *Evangelical Quarterly* 52 (2016) 308–16. https://www-emqonline-com.dts.idm.oclc.org/print/3529.
Turner, Mark. *The Literary Mind*. New York: Oxford, 1996.
Walsh, Brian J., and J. Richard Middleton. *The Transforming Vision: Shaping a Christian Worldview*. Downers Grove, IL: InterVarsity, 1984.
Walvoord, John F. *The Millennial Kingdom*. Grand Rapids: Zondervan, 1959.
White, Hayden. "The Value of Narrativity in the Representation of Reality." *Critical Inquiry* 7 (1980) 5–27.
Wolter, Albert. "Metanarrative." In *Dictionary for Theological Interpretation of the Bible*, edited by Kevin J. Vanhoozer, 506–7. Grand Rapids: Baker, 2005.
Wright, Christopher J. H. "Mission as a Matrix for Hermeneutics and Biblical Theology." In *Out of Egypt: Biblical Theology and Biblical Interpretation*, edited by Craig Bartholomew et al., 102–43. Grand Rapids: Zondervan, 2004.
Wright, N. T. *How God Became King*. New York: Harper One, 2016.
———. *The New Testament and the People of God*. Vol. 1. *Christian Origins and the Question of God*. Minneapolis: Fortress, 1992.

Part 2
Horizon: The Classroom

4

Theological Institutions and Orality

Paying Attention to the Theological Intelligence (TQ) of Oral Learners

Larry W. Caldwell

A FEW DISCLAIMERS ARE in order before I proceed. First, I am not an expert in orality. My entire academic career has predominately been with native readers and reading preference learners,[1] as well as with those who were required to choose a preference for reading somewhere along their academic journey. That being said, however, I have also learned over the years that theological education, as it currently stands in all its reading dominance, will never meet the theological training needs of the vast majority of pastors and lay leaders who are oral learners. I have come to see that the vast majority of Bible schools and seminaries worldwide turn a blind eye to the oral realities of their learners, learners who either come from (and will return to) oral contexts, or learners (both Western and non-Western) who may know how to read but who prefer not to.

In light of these realities, what changes must theological institutions make? This chapter will explore some changes that I believe are necessary in three parts: first, examining the hegemony of the reading culture that dominates theological education worldwide and its effects on the relevancy of current training programs; second, examining how Bible schools and

---

1. I prefer the designation "learner" instead of "student" and will use it throughout the chapter. A "student" is typically thought of in relationship to a hierarchy of teacher-student roles and expectations, often implying the student as the passive receiver of the content as given by the all-knowing teacher. In contrast, a "learner" is co-equal with the teacher who, though admittedly further along in their learning journey on a particular topic, is also ideally still a learner; in fact, they are both learning together through the guidance of the teacher.

seminaries might better incorporate orally-based pedagogical models into both the teaching and learning that occurs in their training programs by paying attention to the Theological Intelligence (TQ) of all their learners; and third, examining one theological seminary—Sioux Falls Seminary—and how we are attempting to incorporate orality into the mainstream of our programs at all levels, from BA to doctoral. The chapter will conclude with several recommendations for Bible schools and seminaries.

But first I would like to begin with a story . . .

> Jing-boy became a follower of Jesus as a young boy in a remote rural tribal area of a non-Western country. Though he had some "formal" schooling, the local reader-dominant educational system was rudimentary. But Jing-boy was steeped in the more "informal" local oral cultural ways and, as a teenager, distinguished himself in his ability to communicate the Bible in ways that made sense with both his fellow teenagers as well as with his elders in the community. He often preached in the small bamboo and thatched-roof local church, and all spoke well of him. A Western missionary to Jing-boy's people group observed Jing-boy's leadership gifting and convinced Jing-boy's family to send him several hundred miles away to the nearest city to attend Bible college and receive formal Bible training. Since no one in their family, and few in the area, had ever gone away to college, everyone was excited about Jing-boy's opportunity.
>
> Jing-boy, however, struggled at the Bible college. Though intellectually gifted, he had never studied so hard in his life: reading books, writing assignments, taking written quizzes and tests. In his mind it was like having to learn an entirely new way of thinking. Somehow, though, Jing-boy made it through Bible college; in fact, he excelled. When he went back home during the summers, however, his local friends and family started to find it more and more difficult to understand what Jing-boy was talking about when he was invited to preach. For now, when he preached, he often spoke of context, original languages, and what so-and-so Western person said about the Bible; and every time he preached, he had three points that he wanted to get across. To his friends and family, it was almost as if Jing-boy was speaking a foreign language.
>
> Jing-boy himself grew increasingly frustrated every time he journeyed home. However, he did so well in Bible college that, upon graduation, he was given a big scholarship by the Western missionaries to travel to an even larger city for a seminary

education. Here Jing-boy again excelled, but he didn't go home as often, and when he did, he really didn't have much in common with his own people. Eventually Jing-boy ended up teaching at the seminary in the big city. He seldom returned home, and when he did, he was rarely invited to speak in church.

Jing-boy's story is a composite of several individuals I have known over the years. At least five salient points emerge from his story:

1. He was extracted from his own culture and cognitive environment;[2]
2. His local orality-based cognitive environment, and oral system of learning, were not considered adequate for church leadership by the local Western missionary;
3. The Western missionaries thought that he needed to learn another educational system—a reading preference system—in order for him to excel in his spiritual giftings;
4. He struggled in learning the new reading culture but soon viewed it as superior to his own oral culture's learning style; and
5. As his new reading-culture knowledge and ability grew, he increasingly could not communicate with his own people.

So, what is wrong with these five points in regard to Jing-boy's story?

The Hegemony of the Reading Culture of the Academy

Well, obviously, many of these points are wrong. Though the motivations of the Western missionaries were not necessarily malevolent,[3] the fact is they were rooted in a colonial mentality of "West is best," including the Western educational system. Elsewhere I have written on colonization and its effects on theological and missiological education, especially in the dismissing of

---

2. Kevin Higgins's understanding of a person's cognitive environment is helpful when talking about both formal and informal systems of learning. Higgins examined relevance theory and its understanding of cognitive environment, especially its implications for communication. Higgins, following the work of Dan Sperber and Deirdre Wilson, describes cognitive environment as "a set of assumptions which the individual is capable of mentally representing and accepting as true" which "includes a person's current and potential matrix of ideas, memories, experiences and perceptions." Kevin Higgins, "Diverse Voices," 190.

3. In fact, some argue that the motivations of such missionaries are mostly benevolent; who wants to remain in the cognitive environment of orality when one can learn how to read? See, for example, the comments of Wes Seng in "Symposium," 160–71.

local ways of teaching and learning.⁴ As a result, I will limit my comments on colonization to the following:

> colonization—and the resulting paternalism that has oftentimes remained—has affected theological and missiological education in many ways, but primarily with regards to curriculum relevance and to dismissing local ways of teaching and learning. Recent ethnographic research has come to label the influence of colonization as "authoritative knowledge." A result of colonization is that those who are colonized eventually take on as authoritative a certain way of thinking or knowing that was at first foreign to that particular culture.⁵

It is the concept of authoritative knowledge that is especially pertinent to any discussion of the place of orality in theological institutions both past and present. Anthropologist Brigitte Jordan expands on the oftentimes insidious role of authoritative knowledge:

> frequently one kind of knowledge gains ascendance and legitimacy. A consequence of the legitimation of one kind of knowing as authoritative is the devaluation, often the dismissal, of all other kinds of knowing ... The constitution of authoritative knowledge is an ongoing social process that both builds and reflects power relationships within a community of practice. It does this in such a way that all participants come to see the current social order as a natural order, that is, the way things (obviously) are.⁶

Such was the case with Jing-boy. The American colonizers, including the Western missionaries, brought a foreign understanding of what formal Bible college should be. The colonized, Jing-boy and his tribal people, saw such formal schooling, and the required print-based learning, as the way things should be done. So, of course, Jing-boy was forced (even if it was voluntary) to adapt to an entirely new way of thinking and learning that he saw as authoritative and therefore did not question. He eventually viewed

---

4. Caldwell, "Interpreting the Bible *with* the Poor"; Caldwell, "How Asian is Asian Theological Education?"; Caldwell, "Ethnohermeneutics."

5. Caldwell, "Interpreting the Bible *with* the Poor," 5.

6. Jordan, "Authoritative Knowledge," 56. Further, Linda Tuhiwai Smith refers to authoritative knowledge as "civilized knowledge," whereby "[t]he globalization of knowledge and Western culture constantly reaffirms the West's view of itself as the centre of legitimate knowledge, the arbiter of what counts as knowledge and the source of 'civilized' knowledge." Smith, *Decolonizing Methodologies*, 66.

it as superior to his own culture's way of doing things and subsequently lost relevancy with his own people.

Unfortunately, Jing-boy's experience continues to occur worldwide in theological institutions today. We must acknowledge, at the very least, that much of the curricula—as well as the educational models and techniques that are used—have been unquestionably set up the way the print-dominant colonizers did it. All parties have unquestionably assumed that print learning is superior to other learning approaches. However, it does not have to be this way. We must look for other alternatives, including using both curriculum and educational techniques, that are culturally appropriate for all learners, both readers and non-readers alike. As educational anthropologist George D. Spindler says:

> a transcultural perspective on education is essential, for education is a cultural process and occurs in a social context. Without attention to cultural difference and the way education serves those differences, we have no way of achieving perspective on our own culture and the way our educational system serves it or of building a comprehensive picture of education as affected by culture.[7]

A transcultural perspective on education is imperative today given the fact that, according to orality expert L. Lynn Thigpen, only two percent of the world's population is able to read at the high level required for success in most theological institutions.[8]

Furthermore, this transcultural perspective on education is not just for those working with oral learners in the non-Western world. Increasingly, the seemingly more literate Western world is not as literate as is commonly thought, with an increasing number of oral preference learners in the West.[9] As a result, it is important for theological institutions to look at the individual learners whom these institutions serve—both in the West and non-West—more holistically than they may have done so in the past.

---

7. Spindler, *Education and Cultural Process*, 272.

8. Thigpen, *Connected Learning*, 3. The two percent figure is taken from the 2012 study done by the Program for the International Assessment of Adult Competencies (PIAAC); cf. Thigpen, *Connected Learning*, 3 for further PIAAC survey results.

9. See especially Moon, "'I Love to Learn"; Moon, "Discipling"; Moon, "Understanding Oral Learners"; Thigpen, *Connected Learning*, 3.

How Bible Schools and Seminaries Might Better Incorporate Oral-based Pedagogical Models

I believe one way that Bible schools and seminaries today might better accommodate oral learners is by viewing the individual learners in terms of what I call their "theological intelligence," or TQ. We are all familiar with IQ (the measurement of a person's reasoning ability, or rational intelligence), and EQ (the measurement of a person's emotional intelligence).[10] We generally assume that all individuals have both an IQ and an EQ, though we are increasingly seeing how these two measurements can be culturally determined and biased. However, despite the limitations, both IQ and EQ can be helpful measures of how an individual will succeed/perform in certain situations.

Like IQ and EQ, I would argue that every person has a TQ. I define theological intelligence as follows:

> Theological Intelligence (TQ) is the innate ability that every individual has to think theologically within the confines of their own cultural context and cognitive environment. They are able to do this through having mastered the techniques of their culturally appropriate educational systems (both informal and/or formal). As a result, each individual is able to successfully comprehend their culture's theology—and communicate that theology—to their own people in ways that are both culturally appropriate and understandable.[11]

As social ethicist Patricia A. Lamoureux points out, (in evaluating the research of EQ pioneer Daniel Goleman), both IQ and EQ "are not

---

10. Mention should also be made here about CQ, or cultural intelligence: the measure of a person's cultural intelligence, especially in relationship to engaging individuals who are culturally different from oneself. Since CQ is generally seen as a subset of EQ, I will not deal with it here. See Livermore, *Cultural Intelligence* for more information concerning CQ.

11. Such culturally appropriate understanding and communication will involve the use of culturally appropriate hermeneutical approaches to cultures, whether oral-dominant or print-dominant. Paying attention to the hermeneutical approaches of a specific culture is what the discipline of ethnohermeneutics is all about. Because of space limitations I will not go into greater detail on ethnohermeneutics here, nor its implications for oral learning. For further study of ethnohermeneutics see Caldwell ("Towards the New Discipline of Ethnohermeneutics," "Towards an Ethnohermeneutical Model," and "Reconsidering Our Biblical Roots" pts. 1 and 2) for the theoretical background to the discipline, and Caldwell, *Doing Bible Interpretation!* for the more practical application of ethnohermeneutics for all cultures, oral or reading. See also the groundbreaking work of Steffen and Bjoraker, *Return of Oral Hermeneutics*; see also Barber, *Anthropology of Texts*; and Moon, *African Proverbs*.

inherently opposing competencies, but rather separate yet interconnected ones... which operate, for the most part, in tight harmony."[12] In the same way, I would argue that an individual's TQ builds on, and is connected with, both their IQ and EQ.

Here is another way of saying all of this: TQ is the innate ability that every person utilizes to understand and express religious concepts and philosophies in terms of their own culture and cognitive environment. TQ is a fully orbed understanding of theology appropriately learned in one's cultural context. Whether Muslim, Buddhist, Christian, animist, or whatever, each individual has the TQ to both think theologically, and to communicate those theological thoughts, in ways that have been shaped by their unique cultures and cognitive environments. As a result, there are several sub-points in relation to TQ:

1. Every individual has a TQ; individual TQs are developed over the lifetime of the individual, with foundational TQs typically in place by the individual's teenage years;

2. All TQ's are equal. There should be no privileging of one TQ over another; in other words, all learning styles that undergird one's TQ—whether orally-based or reading-based—are culturally conditioned, hence all learning styles are valid and equal;

3. Cultures default to the TQ that works best for them in light of their own cognitive environment; and, similarity,

4. Both informal and formal educational systems within the culture will default to the culture's dominant TQ.

What all of this means for Bible schools and seminaries worldwide is that we must both understand and value the individual TQs of our learners and take them seriously as we develop specific training programs. Unfortunately, most theological institutions worldwide tend to disregard the TQ of their learners. Instead, they typically default to the authoritative knowledge of reading cultures to the neglect of the TQ of oral cultures and, increasingly, to the TQ of their learners who are readers but who have a preference for oral learning. In the past, the "academy" (which in a real sense is the "gate keeper" of authoritative knowledge) determined that academic theological knowledge is best achieved through:

- book learning;
- credit hours and seat-time;

12 Lamoureux, "Integrated Approach," 143.

- a top-down process where the teacher pours content into the learner;
- independent research done silently in a library;
- results presented logically and systematically;
- assessment linked to quizzes, tests and academic paper writing; and
- little concern for formation and practical application.

As a result, the academy determined that what is to be considered "academic" needs to fall within the above categories; the academy defaulted to an understanding of "academic" in terms of a typically privileged Western understanding of what TQ is.[13] Any alternative TQ was categorized as inferior and "non-academic."

But here we must raise the question, "Who says?" Is defaulting to the hegemony of a print-based reading TQ the only, or primary, way to go in terms of theological education? I think not. An understanding and valuing of all TQs causes us to redefine what is, and what is not, "academic." As a result, cannot the learning styles and educational methods worked out in the cognitive environments of oral learners be considered just as "academic"? I think so. An oral-based academic TQ, therefore, will consider the following elements:

- group learning that is connected and relational learning;[14]
- learning achieved through both formal and informal gatherings of the community;
- learning that values "hands on" learning experiences more than lectures;
- peer learning where the "elder[15]/teacher" guides the group in communal scholarship, coming to proper conclusions through extended and lively conversations;
- results—both individual and group—presented appropriately according to the cognitive environment of the specific group;

---

13. Moore and Sherwood speak of the invention of the biblical scholar in *The Invention of the Biblical Scholar*; cross reference Van Wolde, *Reframing Biblical Studies*, esp. chapter 1 and her discussion of the frameworks of thinking in biblical studies. In like manner, I think that it is appropriate to speak of the invention of the theological institution, as well as the invention of what is considered academic.

14. Cf. Thigpen, *Connected Learning*.

15. Note that in oral learning wisdom and age are often more highly valued than academic expertise.

- assessment linked to the individual and group's ability to actually communicate theology to others in the same cultural context; and
- much concern for formation and practical application.[16]

Increasingly there is a growing interest in theological educational models that are a hybrid: flexible enough to meet the educational needs of both reading-based and oral-based learners.[17] My own experience at Sioux Falls Seminary demonstrates how such a hybrid might work.

What Sioux Falls Seminary Is Doing[18]

Historically, for 160 years—like most seminaries—Sioux Falls Seminary (SFS) was exclusively a reading-dominant seminary. Then, in 2014, SFS developed and launched what we call the Kairos Project.[19] The Kairos Project is a whole new philosophy of how to do theological education, emphasizing theological education that is affordable, accessible, relevant and faithful. It is the "accessible" and "relevant" pieces that are particularly germane to the topic of this chapter.

Accessibility and relevancy can be seen in a variety of ways. First, Kairos is a competency-based theological education (CBTE) model that emphasizes mentor teams (made up of a faculty mentor, a vocational mentor, a personal mentor, and the learner) who help learners achieve competency in outcomes specifically designed for their specific degree.[20] Second, because it is competency-based, Kairos emphasizes learning experiences that are accessible to those learners that God places in our midst, no matter where God has called them to serve nor what learning style they prefer. Our primary goal is to meet learners *where they are*, both literally and figuratively. We take seriously the learner's TQ. Third, Kairos emphasizes the importance of

16. The elements listed here are but a select few. For additional elements see Steffen and Bjoraker, *Return of Oral Hermeneutics,* esp. 65–72; cf. Steffen, "Pedagogical Conversions," 141–59.

17. See, for example, some of the responses to the views of Seng, "Symposium"; see also the chapters in this book by Cameron D. Armstrong and A. Steven Evans.

18. Note that Sioux Falls Seminary never purposefully intended to address the educational needs of oral or oral-preference learners. Rather, an increased sensitivity to the oral realities of our learners was a natural occurrence that flowed out of our development of the Kairos Project, described below.

19. Space constraints do not allow me to go into detail concerning Kairos. For more information, see the following link: https://sfseminary.edu/prospective-students/programs/kairos/.

20. SFS offers degrees from the BA to the DMin, with 15 outcomes for the BA, 6 outcomes for the MA, 9 outcomes for the MDiv and 5 outcomes for the DMin.

the learner's vocational context and allows the mentor team to determine what kind of learning is most necessary, and appropriate, for the learner, and how such learning should occur and be assessed. Fourth, Kairos seeks to fully integrate each learner's life, vocation and calling into their educational journey of discipleship.

Accessibility and relevancy involve a key shift in thinking for all in the Kairos Project: learners and mentors alike. This key shift views knowledge as more than just content. I believe one of the past impediments to seeing the validity of oral learning was (and still is) the academy's limited understanding of knowledge as primarily content. If academic knowledge is limited to content, and content is primarily gained through reading and writing, then to be "academic," a theological institution must have an educational pedagogy that defaults to the reading of written documents (printed texts and articles), as well as to the production of written documents (papers and written answers on tests and quizzes) that, taken together, somehow demonstrate the overall competency of their learners. Instead, for the Kairos Project, knowledge is defined as involving three essential pieces: content, character, and craft. As Kairos Project Executive Partner David Williams says:

> Without all three of these aspects of knowing, something essential is missing. By speaking of knowledge as content, character, and craft, we constantly are forced to integrate and thus to remember that content isn't the goal no matter how good, credible, or important that content may be . . .
>
> This linguistic change isn't merely semantic. It dramatically changes the educational journey. If knowledge is a three-fold mutuality between content, character, and craft, then the pathway students take toward an educational outcome, the assessment as to how well they have achieved that outcome, as well as whom needs to be working with the student on the journey toward embodiment of that outcome must reflect this integrated nature of knowledge. This is why in Kairos the mentor team includes a faculty mentor, a vocational mentor, and a personal mentor. It is only when we look through all three lenses that we can adequately assess a student's knowledge.
>
> An institutional shift toward a more robust, integrated understanding of knowledge does imply a shift away from the previous role content has played. This is inevitable. When knowledge was identified with content then delivering content was at the center of the institution. That is no longer the case. This "decentering" of content and content delivery in the educational process in order to include attention to character and

craft is a far reaching and sometimes painful process. It may be painful, but it is good.[21]

I have quoted much from Williams because this emphasis of SFS on the "three-fold" understanding of knowledge as a "mutuality between content, character, and craft" is the key to designing educational pedagogy—from start to finish—that can privilege *both* the reading learner *and* the oral learner, as well as the emerging oral preference learner. Of course, there has to be some content, but the more holistic three-fold view of character and craft, allows us more pedagogical options.

So how does accessibility and relevancy work out, practically speaking, at SFS? Let me briefly touch on three ways. First, for SFS, this means that though we still default to reading-related methodologies—since the majority of our learners still come from reading-dominant TQ cognitive environments—we at the same time recognize and value those learners whose TQs are more orally-based. We ask this simple question: How does the specific learner prefer to learn? As a result, some of us are trying to incorporate more stories into our lectures rather than just content monologues.[22] We are also allowing ample time for group discussions on content presentations. For specific assignments learners are usually given the option to either write a paper or prepare an oral video response. Though textbooks are still used, we allow learners to find print or oral parallels in their own language or trade language for greater clarity. Likewise, by seeing knowledge as content, character and craft, we use the vocational mentor to help us, in William's words, "better understand how writing functions in a specific vocation. Writing can be significantly different if one is a pastor, a chaplain, a social worker, a businessperson, or an academic."[23] Here the vocational context in which ministry for the learner happens helps to determine what is considered "academic" for that specific vocational context. Likewise, if the vocational context is primarily oral, then presentations that demonstrate competency will be more orally based, especially if this is the TQ of the learner as well.

One example that especially demonstrates how the learner's vocational context is taken seriously here at SFS involves our DMin program; more specifically the required DMin final project. Many seminaries view the DMin final project as a mini-PhD dissertation, and have subsequently

21. David Williams, "Knowing is Integrative—Part 1."

22. I, personally, have been challenged to use more stories in my teaching through the influence of theologian C. S. Song. Song, in his prescient book, *In the Beginning Were Stories, Not Texts*, 6, argues: "Who says theology has to be ideas and concepts? Who has decided that theology has to be doctrines, axioms, propositions?" See also Steffen, *Reconnecting God's Story to Ministry* and Steffen, "Pedagogical Conversations."

23. Williams, "Knowing is Integrative—Part 3."

chosen to model their DMin final project along the lines of the PhD dissertation. As a result, their DMin emphasis is upon research seminars, high-level academic research, dissertation proposal defenses, doctoral committees, a formal dissertation defense, extensive dissertation rewrites, proper formatting and style as with a dissertation, and so on. While there is nothing inherently wrong with this approach, it tends to lengthen out both the number of units necessary for the DMin degree, as well as the time and energy needed to complete it. This understanding of the DMin final project also tends to eventually end with a written academic document that sits on an obscure shelf somewhere in the bowels of the seminary library, never to be seen (or read) again.

Not so for the SFS DMin final project. For us the final project is a *ministry/vocational* project. It is a doctoral-level summative project that reflects academic rigor addressing both the nature and the practice of ministry/vocation. The project *is for the church or ministry/vocation* that the learner actively participates in; it *is not primarily for the academy*, though there are certain academic components to it. The project especially addresses appropriate biblical, theological, sociological and cultural issues that are pertinent to the learner's ministry/vocational context. As a result, the project results not in a written dissertation (unless that is the learner's ministry/vocational context). Instead, it results in a media form (visual, auditory, print, electronic, and/or web-based, and so on) created to address a specific ministry/vocational context/situation. The DMin final project is devised—from start to finish—to be useful to the Church. As such, the project is easily adapted to the needs of oral learners and oral contexts if such is the cultural, ministry, or vocational context of the DMin learner.

Secondly, since most oral TQ learners typically come from, and will return to, ministry in oral-based vocational contexts, we at SFS seminary are seeing that learning and assessment should be adapted to methodologies that are more typically oral. We give both reading-dominant and oral-dominant learners the opportunity to write up a response to an assignment or to present their results orally, oftentimes through some kind of a video report. Unfortunately, oftentimes reader-dominant academics view such video reporting as less than academic. The truth of the matter, however, is that oral summations or presentations are not necessarily easy. They can entail much thought and preparation, oftentimes involving the same amount of time as the preparation of a written document. In fact, at SFS we have determined in our Coursework Rubric that one minute of oral presentation is equivalent to approximately one hour of preparation, and our oral assignments are geared accordingly.[24]

Thirdly, we here at SFS are finding that increased sensitivity to oral learners also includes peer-learning in groups, working on and presenting assignments as a group, and even group assessment. This latter item—group assessment—is one of the hardest for the academy to grasp. Assessments have become so individualized that we seldom think that there might be another way. The fact is, all types of learning can be evaluated in terms of knowledge acquisition, ability to function within the explicit TQ category, and whether or not the resulting applications are relevant to particular TQ contexts. At SFS all learners have the same targets for the various outcomes, but they are allowed to demonstrate competence according to their own unique learning styles and cultural backgrounds. I often use peer group assessment in my masters-level and doctoral seminars, to good success. I have found that peer group assessment can be brutally honest while at the same time be very affirming for the learner, leading the learner to an increased ability to carry out ministry in their vocational context.

Recommendations

There are many recommendations of this study for Bible schools and seminaries, as well as for those who both teach and learn in such theological institutions. I will address a few of the most pertinent. Ironically, the main subjects of this study—oral learners—will never read this; nevertheless, these recommendations will hopefully help those of us who are readers to better relate to those who are not.

Recommendations for Theological Institutions:

1. Pay attention to theological intelligence (TQ)

   We of the academy must admit that our place of privilege and power has caused us to default to the TQ of readers (where we are most comfortable), embracing a print culture and the print technology that goes along with it. This default has been to the detriment of oral learners. Such privilege and power have no place in Bible colleges and

---

24. For example, if an assignment requires an eight- to ten-page written paper, we allow for the substitution of an eight to ten-minute oral video presentation, at the learner's discretion, expecting both assignments to take approximately eight to ten hours of preparation.

seminaries today, especially as we seek to help meet the training needs of the whole Church. We must acknowledge the mistakes of our past and agree to move forward to better understanding the TQ of *all* of our learners, including oral learners and oral-preference learners.

2. Develop appropriate curricula

We need to develop courses, and other academic learning experiences, with the TQ needs of oral learners in mind. This is especially crucial in academic settings (particularly in the non-Western world) where the majority of learners come from oral cultures and cognitive environments. Increasingly, the preponderance of oral-preference learners, especially in the West, requires us to rethink our curricula.

3. Adjust assignments and assessments appropriately

Like curricula, both assignments and assessments must be re-thought in light of the needs of oral learners. This will involve less attention to individualized learning and evaluation and more attention to the involvement of the group in both processes. Developing both learning outcomes and assessment tools that more holistically deal with learners, regardless of specific reading or oral learning preferences, will aid both groups.

Recommendations for Educators

1. Embrace the TQ challenge

Value the TQs of your individual learners, and be willing to adjust your teaching, assignments and assessments accordingly. For most educators this will be a huge challenge. But, given the realities of the trained leadership needs of the worldwide Church today, we have no other choice.

2. Exercise humility

We educators have oftentimes enjoyed the privilege and power of academia and we oftentimes expect others to go through the same challenges in their educational journeys that we were forced to go through. But what we must all come to see is that learning *The Chicago Manual of Style*—and being able to correctly cite sources, footnote, and compile bibliographies, and the like—really has nothing whatsoever to do with whether or not something is to be considered "academic." Yes, the minority of our learners whose vocational context is, or will be, an academic one will indeed need to learn the rules of *Chicago*. However, for the vast majority (99 percent?) of our learners such intimacy with *Chicago* is not necessary.

The reality is that those in academic power have invented such supposedly "academic standards" which result in—paraphrasing here the apostle Peter—"putting on the necks of the disciples a yoke that neither we nor our fathers have been able to bear" (Acts 15:10 NIV). We educators must move beyond our privilege and power (and I daresay, our pride) and thereby truly meet our learners where they are at; all of our learners, including oral learners.

3. Recognize that it will not be quick and easy

Do not expect quick solutions to the reality of oral learners. Be in it for the long haul. Changing curricula, courses, teaching styles, assignments, and assessments is a marathon not a sprint. We here at SFS are still trying to figure out how to best meet the educational needs of our oral and oral-preference learners. Even after seven years we still have a long way to go.

Recommendations for Learners:

1. Fully embrace your TQ

   Whether you are reading-dominant, or oral-dominant, or somewhere in-between, fully embrace the TQ that God has allowed you to grow up in. Recognize that there are real strengths (and weaknesses) to each approach. Realize that as much as you value your TQ so, too, does the one whose TQ is different from yours.

2. Value the TQs of others

   This is especially for reading-dominant learners since the TQ of reading still dominates our Bible colleges and seminaries. You have had the privilege of growing up in a culture and cognitive environment that values reading. Oral-dominant learners have grown up in cultures and cognitive environments that value oral learning. There is no better or worse to either way; they are just different. As you encounter oral and oral-preference learners in your schools and programs try to better understand why they think the way they do. Advocate on their behalf. Value and learn from them. They will help you understand the many oral-preference learners in your own culture and, especially, your own ministry context.

Furthermore, be aware that oral learners often feel shame, or are ashamed of their oral learning background. As a reader you have the opportunity to help them see that they are not "second class" in God's eyes, nor should they be considered as such in the eyes of reading cultures and reading-dominant theological institutions.[25]

Concluding Reflections

While theological institutions have a long journey ahead in meeting the TQ realties of oral learners, a growing awareness of oral learners, and their unique educational needs, is beginning to happen.[26] My dream is that the Jing-boys of our world will soon be able to receive a theological education that is indeed both accessible and relevant. Furthermore, I dream that oral learners will no longer be regarded as "second class citizens" in the world of the academy but instead their educational backgrounds and learning preferences will be respected and utilized just like those of the dominant reading cultures. When this happens, Bible colleges and seminaries worldwide will be closer to truly meeting the training needs of the Christian constituencies that they serve.

Bibliography

Barber, Karin. *The Anthropology of Texts, Persons and Publics. Oral and Written Culture in Africa and Beyond*. Cambridge: Cambridge University, 2007.

Caldwell, Larry W. *Doing Bible Interpretation! Making the Bible Come Alive for Yourself and Your People*. Sioux Falls, SD: Lazy Oaks, 2016.

———. "Ethnohermeneutics and Advanced Theological Studies: Towards Culturally Appropriate Methodologies for Doctoral Programs." In *Challenging Tradition. Innovation in Advanced Theological Education*, edited by Perry Shaw and Havilah Dharamraj, 287–308. Carlisle, UK: Langham Partnership, 2018.

———. "How Asian Is Asian Theological Education?" In *Tending the Seedbeds: Educational Perspectives on Theological Education in Asia*, edited by Allan Harness, 23–45. Quezon City: Asia Theological Association, 2010.

———. "Interpreting the Bible *With* the Poor." In *Social Engagement: The Challenge of the Social in Missiological Education*, 165–190. The 2013 Proceedings of the

---

25. See Thigpen, *Connected Learning*, for the feelings of shame that non-readers oftentimes feel in relationship to those from reading-dominant cultures.

26. See, for example, Biola University's course—ISCL 744—Narrative in Scripture and Teaching—which is "[a]n investigation and demonstration of the narrative/story genre in teaching and curricula design"; cf. https://catalog.biola.edu/courses/iscl/.

Association of Professors of Mission. Wilmore, KY: First Fruits, 2013. http://place.asburyseminary.edu/firstfruitspapers/20.

———. "Reconsidering Our Biblical Roots: Bible Interpretation, the Apostle Paul and Mission Today. Part 1." *International Journal of Frontier Missiology* 29 (2012) 91–100. http://www.ijfm.org/PDFs_IJFM/29_2_PDFs/IJFM_29_2-Caldwell.pdf.

———. "Reconsidering Our Biblical Roots: Bible Interpretation, the Apostle Paul and Mission Today. Part 2." *International Journal of Frontier Missiology* 29 (2012) 113–21. http://www.ijfm.org/PDFs_IJFM/29_3_PDFs/IJFM_29_3-Caldwell-Pt2.pdf.

———. "Towards an Ethnohermeneutical Model for a Lowland Filipino Context." *Journal of Asian Mission* 7 (2005) 169–93.

———. "Towards the New Discipline of Ethnohermeneutics: Questioning the Relevancy of Western Hermeneutical Methods in the Asian Context." *Journal of Asian Mission* 1 (1999) 21–43.

Higgins, Kevin. "Diverse Voices: Hearing Scripture Speak in a Multicultural Movement." *International Journal of Frontier Missiology* 27 (2010) 189–96.

Jordan, Brigitte. "Authoritative Knowledge and Its Construction." In *Childbirth and Authoritative Knowledge*, edited by Robbie E. Davis-Floyd and Carolyn F. Sargent, 55–79. Berkeley, CA: University of California, 1997.

Lamoureux, Patricia A. "An Integrated Approach to Theological Education." *Theological Education* 36 (1999) 141–56.

Livermore, David A. *Cultural Intelligence. Improving Your CQ To Engage Our Multicultural World*. Grand Rapids: Baker, 2009.

Moon, W. Jay. *African Proverbs Reveal Christianity in Culture*. American Society of Missiology Monograph Series 5. Eugene, OR: Pickwick, 2009.

———. "Discipling Through the Eyes of Oral Learners." *Missiology* 38 (2010) 127–40.

———. "I Love to Learn but I Don't Like to Read: The Rise of Secondary Oral Learning." *Orality Journal* 2 (2013) 55–65.

———. "Understanding Oral Learners." *Teaching Theology and Religion* 14 (2012) 29–39.

Moore, Stephen D., and Yvonne Sherwood. *The Invention of the Biblical Scholar. A Critical Manifesto*. Minneapolis: Fortress, 2011.

Seng, Wes. "Symposium: Has the Use of Orality Been Taken Too Far?" *Evangelical Missions Quarterly* 52 (2016) 160–71.

Smith, Linda Tuhiwai. *Decolonizing Methodologies. Research and Indigenous Peoples*. 2nd ed. Dunedin, NZ: Otago University, 2012.

Song, C. S. *In the Beginning Were Stories, Not Texts. Story Theology*. Eugene, OR: Cascade, 2011.

Spindler, George D. *Education and Cultural Process. Anthropological Approaches*. 3rd ed. Long Grove, IL: Waveland, 1997.

Steffen, Tom. *Reconnecting God's Story to Ministry. Cross-cultural Storytelling at Home and Abroad*. Rev. ed. Waynesboro, GA: Authentic, 2005.

———. "Pedagogical Conversions: From Propositions to Story and Symbol." *Missiology: An International Review* 38 (2010) 141–59.

Steffen, Tom, and William Bjoraker. *The Return of Oral Hermeneutics. As Good Today as It Was for the Hebrew Bible and First-Century Christianity*. Eugene, OR: Wipf & Stock, 2020.

Thigpen, L. Lynn. *Connected Learning. How Adults with Limited Formal Education Learn*, American Society of Missiology Monograph Series 44. Eugene, OR: Pickwick, 2020.

Van Wolde, Ellen. *Reframing Biblical Studies: When Language and Text Meet Culture, Cognition and Context*. Winona Lake, IN: Eisenbrauns, 2009.

Williams, David. "Knowing Is Integrative-Part 1." 2020. https://sfseminary.edu/story-center/knowing-is-integrative-pt.-1.

———. "Knowing Is Integrative-Part 3." 2020. https://sfseminary.edu/story-center/knowing-is-integrative-pt.-3.

5

Storying in Seminary
Romanian Theology Students Using Oral-Based Teaching Methods[1]

CAMERON D. ARMSTRONG

"THIS WAY OF STUDYING motivates me to be more involved in evangelism!" My Romanian student, Maria, excitedly wrote this comment in her evaluation of my Introduction to Evangelism course. It is a comment I will forever treasure. As a missionary professor at the Bucharest Baptist Theological Institute in Romania, such affirming words served to validate my efforts. Until that point, I was unsure how my highly educated Romanian group would respond to a seminary class using narrative tools originally designed for low literate cultures. After that experience, however, I resolved to press on further to understand if more educated Romanians could experience breakthroughs like Maria's.

Oral ministry strategies similar to the format I used during the seminary class with Maria developed over several decades into what is now called storying.[2] Using theoretical premises put forth by literacy scholar Walter Ong,[3] missionaries to non-literate and low literate cultures began to orally teach biblical stories in chronological form. By adapting their methods, missionaries found storying touched their host culture's learning preferences closer than text-based models, especially if the people did not esteem literacy as significant to daily life.

Text-based learning, however, is greatly esteemed in Romania. According to the UNESCO Institute for Statistics (2013), Romania officially reports

---

1. This chapter is taken from various sections within my recently completed dissertation. Armstrong, "Finding Yourself in Stories."

2. International Orality Network [ION] and Lausanne Committee for World Evangelization [LCWE], *Making disciples of oral learners*; Steffen, *Worldview-Based Storying*.

3. Ong, *Interfaces of the Word*; Ong, *Orality and Literacy*.

a 9 percent literacy rate.[4] As such, highly literate ministry models are the norm among pastors, missionaries, and churches. These Christian leaders use printed materials that emphasize abstract thinking common in churches and theological institutions in the global West. Yet Romanians also exhibit signs of learning preferences beyond traditionally literate models of reading and writing, including a strong tendency toward oral learning.[5]

Studies in recent years have focused largely on oral ministry among often rural cultures exhibit low literacy levels.[6] In Ong's terms, such groups are called *primary* oral cultures.[7] In theological education, a growing body of research has been conducted on ministry among oral preference cultures, which Ong called *secondary* oral cultures.[8] Such discussions are helpful, as theorists now view the oral and literate categories as simplistic, choosing instead to understand a culture's tendency toward orality and literacy as more of a graded continuum than a "great divide."[9]

While several scholars are beginning to ask how this experiential distinction might be bridged,[10] theoretical and ministerial studies still tend toward theological education in primary oral contexts.[11] Nevertheless, secondary oral ministry is experiencing a burgeoning focus. In an article entitled "Teaching Ducks to Swim," Jay Moon encouraged theological educators to utilize both oral and print-based models to allow students to learn using both learning preference styles.[12] And though Moon's work is a welcomed call to practitioners, theological education studies among the secondary oral peoples of Eastern Europe are scarce and not readily apparent.

All of these factors led me to ask, what would be Romanian theology students' perceptions toward an oral preference teaching model? Due to this lack of focus in the literature, the following study seeks to fill this gap by examining secondary oral teaching methodology in the theological education classroom in Romania.

---

4. UNESCO Institute for Statistics, *Adult and Youth Literacy*.

5. Dumitrescu et al., "Comparison," 3571–77; Ong, *Orality and Literacy*.

6. De Neui, *Communicating Christ*; ION and LCWE, *Making Disciples of Oral Learners*.

7. Ong, *Orality and Literacy*, 11.

8. Ong, *Orality and Literacy*, 11.

9. Biakolo, "On the Theoretical Foundations of Orality and Literacy," 42; Finnegan, *Oral and Beyond*; Steffen and Bjoraker, *Return of Oral Hermeneutics*.

10. Steffen, *Reconnecting God's Story to Ministry*; Moon, "Encouraging Ducks to Swim."

11. Chiang and Lovejoy, *Beyond Literate Western Models*.

12. Moon, "Encouraging Ducks to Swim."

Literature Review

In this section, I first explain several relevant educational theories that intersect with my study. I then trace the development of theological education, particularly as it relates to global contexts. Third, I explore the "maturation process" of orality literature and its touchpoints with theological education.[13] Since orality is the overall focus of this book, I spend considerably less time developing orality theory. Finally, the section concludes by further narrowing the focus to theological education in Romania, ultimately depicting the conspicuous absence of theological education using orality-based teaching concepts. The Venn diagram in Figure 5.1 depicts these intersections.

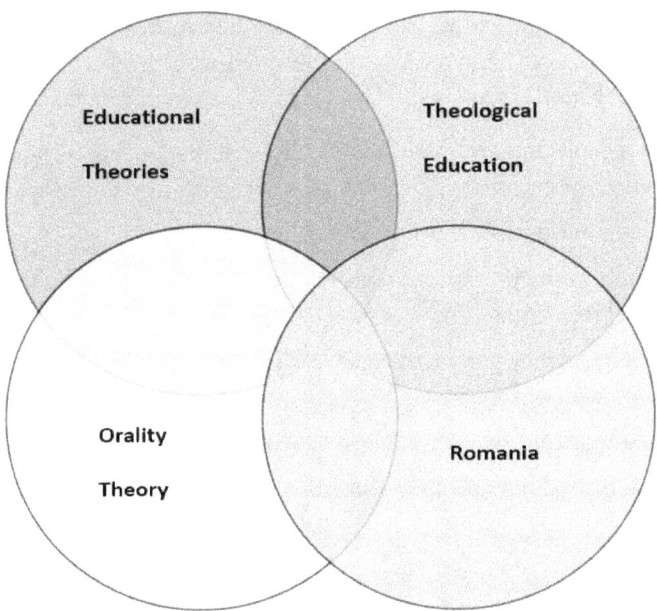

Figure 5.1. Literature Review Intersections

Education Theories

The particular theories I highlight in this section include andragogy, transformative learning, and learning style theories. For a study centered on

---

13. Steffen, *Worldview-Based Storying*.

theological education among adults, these theories appear especially pertinent. Each theory is introduced below.

Andragogy

Adult learning theory, or andragogy, is the study of how adults learn. Since the present study concerns the education of adults, andragogy merits prime placement in this study's theoretical presentation. Merriam and Bierema defined adults as people whose "age, social roles, or self-perception, define them as adults."[14]

Adult learners approach the learning process with a wealth of life experience that should be built upon and not ignored. This fact clearly distinguishes andragogy from pedagogy. According to Merriam, the field of adult education began to coalesce in the 1960s with the work of Malcolm Knowles.[15] Knowles proposed six principal characteristics of adult learners:

1. As people mature, their self-concept moves from dependence to independence.
2. Adults accumulate a growing reservoir of experience.
3. Adults' desire to learn is closely related to developmental tasks in their social role.
4. Change in time perspective comes with maturity, from future-oriented to immediate application.
5. Adults are mostly internally motivated.
6. Adults need to know the reason for learning.[16]

Transformative Learning Theory

Transformative learning theory was developed in the decades following the advent of adult education theory. After studying the effects of women returning to either postsecondary education or the workplace after an extended amount of time, Mezirow proposed that the learning process ignites a "disorienting dilemma" that leads to examination, reflection, and

---

14. Merriam and Bierema, *Adult Learning*, 12
15. Merriam, "Adult Learning Theory."
16. Knowles, *Modern Practice of Adult Education*.

change of the status quo.[17] The process of transformative learning takes learners through ten steps:

1. Disorienting dilemma
2. Self-examination
3. Sense of alienation
4. Relating discontent to others
5. Explaining options of new behavior
6. Building confidence in new ways
7. Planning a course of action
8. Knowledge to implement plans
9. Experimenting with new roles
10. Reintegration[18]

Learning Style Theory

First developed by Kolb, learning style theory has proven effective in multiple educational arenas.[19] For each of the four learning styles, which Kolb termed divergers, assimilators, convergers, and accommodators, learners better understand how they prefer to receive and comprehend new information. Divergers prefer less information at one time, perceive it concretely, and seek meaning along the way. Assimilators perceive information abstractly, are logical, but are not as concerned with practical application. Convergers perceive information abstractly but process it through concrete, active application and experimentation. Accommodators both learn and process information concretely and seek to apply their knowledge in the real world.[20] Allowing students to self-evaluate how they receive and process new information assists educators in developing lesson plans that cater to each of the four learning styles.

In their review of the scholarly literature on learning styles theory, Pashler and his colleagues contended the proposed learning style evaluation

---

17. Mezirow, "Perspective Transformation."
18. Christie et al., "Putting Transformative Learning Theory into Practice," 11–12.
19. Kolb, *Individual Learning Styles and the Learning Process*.
20. Kolb, *Individual Learning Styles and the Learning Process*.

tools are inconclusive.[21] Yet this does not mean that learning style theory should be disregarded:

> [I]t is undoubtedly the case that a particular student will sometimes benefit from having a particular kind of course content presented in one way versus another. One suspects that educators' attraction to the idea of learning styles partly reflects their (correctly) noticing how often one student may achieve enlightenment from an approach that seems useless for another student.[22]

Theological Education

Narrowing to theological education (TE) specifically, I first present TE historically. The section then outlines advancements in TE in global contexts. It also should be noted that Christian TE within an evangelical Protestant perspective will receive special attention, because that is the context within the overall study.

History

Taken from the widest lens as learning about God and God's world, theological education is chronologically as old as humanity itself. For in the beginning, God created humans to know him and fill the earth with people that know him (Gen. 1:26–28). One seminal work on the history of theological education was written by Banks, who placed the genesis of theological education in Old Testament times and called attention to how Jewish families taught future generations the stories of the patriarchs.[23] Even formal teaching from a rabbi emphasized character development as the "heart of wisdom," and Banks posited that such emphasis carried through the Reformation.[24] Only after the Reformation was theological education considered a formal science; one that may be honed by scholars in schools of higher learning.

In the transition to a select group of people deemed fit for clerical service, communities that took seriously the task of pastoral formation began

---

21. Pashler et al., "Learning Styles."
22. Pashler et al., "Learning Styles," 116.
23. Banks, *Reenvisioning Theological Education*.
24. Banks, *Reenvisioning Theological Education*, Part 1, chapter 1, The Significance of Personal Formation section, para. 7.

to solidify. Monastic and convent schools, alongside their urban counterpart, "cathedral schools," became centers of learning for all matters of study, but especially philosophy and theology.[25]

In the Enlightenment period (18th century), scholars generally agree that theological education became more formalized with Berlin University professor Friedrich Schleiermacher's attempt to "professionalize" the study of theology and "justify [its] presence in the academic world."[26] Such justification further distanced academic theology from that taught in the churches; an issue that persists to this day.

Global Contributions

In *The Next Christendom,* Jenkins shocked the theological world by demonstrating that the epicenter of Christianity has shifted to the Southern Hemisphere, particularly Africa.[27] Walls also came to similar conclusions, yet his work is often not as well-known in North America as Jenkins.[28] Based on such writings, the Western church has slowly begun the process of bringing non-Western voices to the "theological roundtable."

To provide a broad-brush picture of how theological education is being done around the world, the World Council of Churches, the Institute for Cross-Cultural Theological Education, and the Centre for the Study of Global partnered to survey 1,650 church leaders and theological educators from around the world Christianity.[29] Ranging from formal seminaries to informal Bible institutes, the survey spanned over 7,000 worldwide institutions. The data yielded 15 conclusions concerning the state of theological education, including the value of newer, innovative techniques. Focusing on theological education is considered the "most important" issue facing global Christianity.[30] Therefore, in both highly literate and non-literate contexts, churches are calling for more developed models of theological education.

To conclude this section on TE, suffice it to say that the research depicted that TE is a vital endeavor for the future health of the church. Because Christians are called to both "reach out" through evangelistic and

---

25. Gonzalez, *History of Theological Education.*
26. Gonzalez, *History of Theological Education,* chapter 14, para. 7.
27. Jenkins, *Next Christendom.*
28. Walls, *Missionary Movement in Christian History.*
29. Esterline et al., "Global Survey."
30. Esterline et al., "Global Survey," 1–8.

church planting efforts *and* "teach" mature, sound doctrine, TE remains an ongoing and necessary push.[31]

Orality Theory

As mentioned above, I have chosen to spend less time on orality theory because it is the overall focus of this book. Nevertheless, some preliminary comments are worthwhile, especially as concerns the present study. In particular, the section offers specific touchpoints between orality, mission studies, and theological education.

Orality as a discipline can be traced back by many to the work of Walter Ong, who provided much of the academic definitions and launching points for orality theory. Ong's *Orality and Literacy* proposed essential cognitive distinctions between "literate" and "oral" groups.[32] In separating objects from their visualized symbols, or words, literacy leads to levels of abstraction unrecognized by non-literate groups. It is in Ong that the original categories of "primary" and "secondary" orality are offered:

> I style the orality of a culture totally untouched by any knowledge of writing or print, 'primary orality.' It is "primary" by contrast with the 'secondary orality' of present-day high-technology culture, in which a new orality is sustained by telephone, radio, television, and other electronic devices that depend for their existence and functioning on writing and print.[33]

Building on Ong's work, Fisher demonstrated that humans are essentially storytellers, finding and passing on their deepest values through narrative.[34] Cognitively, humans appear wired for telling and responding to stories. Fisher called this the ancient form of "narrative logic," which he defined as follows:

> Narrative rationality is its logic. The essential components of this logic are the following. Human communication is tested against the principles of probability (coherence) and fidelity (truthfulness and reliability). Probability, whether a story 'hangs together,' is assessed in three ways: by its argumentative or structural coherence; by its material coherence, that is, by comparing and contrasting stories told in other discourses (a story may be

---

31. Sills, *Reaching and Teaching*.
32. Ong, *Orality and Literacy*.
33. Ong, *Orality and Literacy*, 10–11.
34. Fisher, *Human Communication*.

internally consistent, but important facts may be omitted, counterarguments ignored, and relevant issues overlooked); and by characterological coherence.[35]

Orality in Missions and TE

Steffen demonstrated that using oral strategies for theological teaching is not a new development.[36] McIlwain recognized the necessity of using narrative for biblical teaching with his work in the Philippines in the 1970s, which he called Chronological Bible Teaching (CBT).[37] Over the next several years, Southern Baptist missionaries refined CBT in order to focus simply on the biblical stories themselves, instead of inserting personal exposition.[38] Since this time, oral learning through the use of telling and retelling biblical stories has become a major emphasis for the modern mission movement and is making headway in both rural and urban settings.[39]

Recently, the International Orality Network hosted four conferences on the topic of using orality strategies in TE.[40] Both formal and informal contexts were represented, discussing how orality strategies are being used in the Majority World. Although work is being done in formal and informal institutions, one weakness of these conferences is the lack of representation from post-Communist countries like Romania.

Romania

Modern Romanian culture appears to be marked by several significant elements. I briefly note only three

a. the prominent value distinctions of individualism-collectivism and power distance,

b. honor and shame, and

c. Eastern Orthodoxy.

---

35. Fisher, *Human Communication*, 47.
36. Steffen, *Worldview-Based Storying*.
37. McIwain, *Building on Firm Foundations*.
38. Steffen and Terry, "Sweeping Story."
39. Steffen, "Chronological Practices."
40. Chiang and Lovejoy, *Beyond Literate Western Models*; Chiang and Lovejoy, *Beyond Literate Western Practices*.

First, data gathered by Hofstede and the subsequent site known as Hofstede Insights depicted a fairly low (30 percent) value of individualism among Romanians.[41] This value means that the majority of Romanians choose not to make decisions individually but prefer to involve members of their group (family, friends, etc.). For power distance, meaning how clear power differentials are perceived, Romanians score 90 percent. Group-based decision-making often comes through participatory interaction that weigh the reactions of other members. As such, this dynamic is closely tied to the second cultural element outlined below.

Second, honor and shame tendencies can be found throughout Romanian cultural interactions. Vertical hierarchy based on communal status and role is the norm. Gallagher also made this connection to Romanian history:

> Romanians have been viewed as subjects rather than citizens by successive regimes of contrasting political hues. There is no doubt that the legacy of vertical dependence and exploitation inherited from foreign rule, particularly in the provinces of Wallachia and Moldavia, cast a long shadow over the independent Romanian state.[42]

Romanians are keenly aware of how their actions will be perceived among the collective. This perception is especially prevalent in the smaller cities and rural areas, where families and neighbors interact on a daily basis.[43]

Third, the Eastern Orthodox religion is the faith of the vast majority of Romanians (87 percent). Even with the secularizing trends in North American and Western European countries, Romania cannot be labeled a "secularizing" nation.[44] Eastern Orthodox leaders believe that there is an unbroken link between the Early Church and the modern, Eastern Orthodox Church.[45] Liturgy, celebration of saints, and tradition, therefore, is precious to the Orthodox believer and must be held closely. Emphasis is placed on the sovereignty and mystery of God, especially when God the Son took on flesh and dwelt among sinners. It has been said that, whereas Protestant and Catholic Christianity are largely concerned with the personal and knowable aspects of God, Orthodoxy looms large in its concern with the majesty and supremacy of God over humanity. Based more on creating a mystical

---

41. Hofstede, *Culture's Consequences*; Hofstede Insights, "Compare Countries [digital tool]."

42. Gallagher, *Modern Romania*, 1.

43. Armstrong, "Honor and Shame"; Raiser, "Future of Theological Education."

44. Stahl, "Has Romania Become a Secular Society?"

45. Clendenen, *Eastern Orthodox Christianity*.

experience with God than calling believers to interact with the written biblical text, Eastern Orthodox cathedrals are designed in such a way that all five senses are caught up in learning and imbibing church tradition.[46] Much of the Orthodox tradition utilizes oral-based learning methods. While true that the priests read the liturgy during services, the entire experience is targeted at all five senses: smelling the incense, hearing the melodic voice of the priest, touching the ground and icons, seeing the beautifully-painted pictures, and tasting with the brush of the lips the icons set along the margins of the church. Orthodox believers are thus taught that their services are holistic, which is far more oral than literate as a concept.

Research Method and Design

Using qualitative data gathered through the use of interviews with 16 students from two seminary classes, I designed a research project in order to understand how Romanians might perceive classes taught using oral-based teaching methods. Qualitative research leans heavily on verbal data based on interviews and field observation.[47] Qualitative research seeks to capture individual stories, meanings, and thoughts.

Initial interviews were conducted by a Romania research assistant. This choice was made to lessen potential power distance issues, such as students simply telling their professor what they think I'd want to hear, and possible language barriers that might disrupt the conversation flow. Each interview lasted approximately 30 minutes, was recorded by the research assistant and immediately emailed to me, and then I transcribed the interviews from Romanian to English. Themes were generated based on the qualitative data.

Findings

The central understanding to emerge from this study's collected data is that oral-based teaching methods, such as storying, create a transformative impact through a process of disorienting first impressions, novel learning experiences, reorienting realizations, and finding oneself in the stories. These concepts are encountered in a semi-linear fashion as learners engage biblical narratives through oral-based methods (see Figure 5.2).

46. Clendenen, *Eastern Orthodox Christianity*; Letham, *Through Western* Eyes; Spann, *Witnessing to People of Eastern Orthodox Background*; St. Athanasius Orthodox Academy, *Orthodox Study Bible*.

47. Charmaz, *Constructing Grounded* Theory; Merriam and Tisdell, *Qualitative Research*.

94 PART 2: HORIZON: THE CLASSROOM

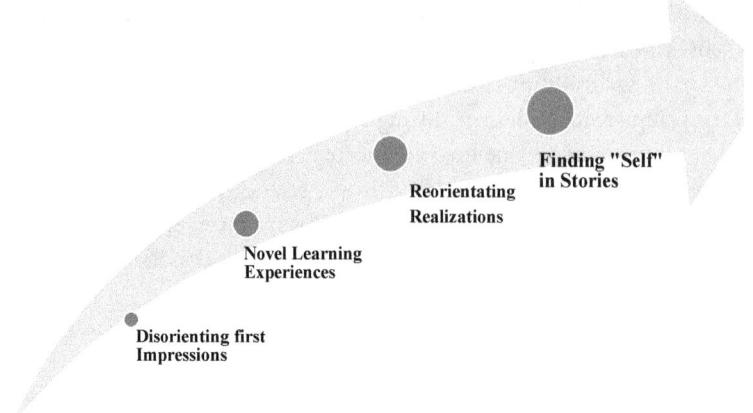

Figure 5.2 Central Understanding 5.2.

Disorienting First Impressions

Shuffling into the classroom on the first day of the semester, students expected a theology class like the others: interesting material delivered primarily through lecture and perhaps some discussion. After explaining the course as playing a role in my dissertation study, students were surprised to hear the Parable of the Sower (Mark 4:1–9) delivered as a story.

Răzvan recalled that first day well. Commenting on his first thoughts, he said, "At first it seemed boring and banal. I had the impression that we were being treated like children in the college student environment." Indeed, many students had the same thoughts. No matter how well the story appeared to hold their attention, the idea that storytelling is something childish is difficult to renounce.

Some students felt, at the outset, that they had entered a church Sunday School class. Gina noted that this was how she felt her colleagues reacted, although she liked that it was something new and interesting. "It gave me a good feeling," Gina declared. "I also heard remarks [like], 'We are in Sunday School.'"

Several students also commented on their first impressions being the high level of involvement among students. Instead of merely sitting and listening to a lecture, discussion and the voicing of opinions played an integral role in the lesson. Further, the fact that students understood each lesson's structure of telling, retelling, and discussing proved a source of interest.

Laura, a self-described "quieter student," noted, "Everyone interacted very much. I don't think there was anyone who did not speak."

Still, the highly interactive method of storying is quite different from traditional theological education models. Due to this fact, some students were bound to be a bit more skeptical. Călin was one of the more skeptical students, yet he admitted this could be because he is older than the typical university student. When asked how he felt his colleagues reacted to the storying method, Călin predicted, "[My colleagues] liked it, too. The only minus was the fact that it was just a style presented. Most liked it. Probably 50–60 percent. And probably the other 40 percent liked it okay."

Novel Learning Experiences

One of the most significant themes discovered in the interviews is the students' perceptions of how the learning experiences impacted them, especially concerning their understanding the material easily. All participants declared, in their own way, an ability to comprehend the material and how it made a great impact on their learning.

"I think it is a style that is easier to understand because we are used to watching movies. In general, from when you are a kid, they tell us stories that you can remember. And I think this helps, to say something in the form of a story." Raluca's connection between stories and films supports the idea that narratives are memorable.

When abstract ideas are framed in a story, students felt they understood the purposes better. Daniel likened it to *The Screwtape Letters* by C. S. Lewis, one of his favorite books. Through the medium of letters written from a powerful demon to his less powerful demon nephew, readers capture the narrative of a Christian being tempted to renounce his faith in various ways. "The fact that he tells it like a story helps me very much to understand everything that he wants to say," Daniel said.

Reorienting Realizations

As students moved through the learning process, they reflected on new realizations. The students began to connect their experiences with previous courses and professors that motivated them.

Students claimed their attention was captured in classes where they were challenged to explore and research for themselves. In the theology classroom, this may mean digging into the Bible or supplemental texts to find further explanations. Gianina, a social work student, posited that the most helpful theological teaching "challenges students to read and understand more for themselves." In such a way, students develop their own belief system. Assumptions are challenged and subsequently revised. In her interview, Florica reported that, although she had grown up in church and thought everything would be familiar, she observed new details in every lesson: "I realized the fact that I had learned some aspects that before I had not learned or understood or processed very much intellectually. And it helped me." For Florica, different forms of teaching captivated her and moved beyond an intellectual experience only.

Interestingly, oral-based teaching methods appeared to connect these motivating factors. As noted above, Daniel claimed that learning through stories generates faster recall. Daniel viewed the method as "more practical, more efficient, and more beneficial" than traditional models. When asked if he will remember these lessons years from now, Daniel answered positively. "You know," he added, "it was like a soul searching, so to speak, from God." Daniel not only found himself learning new things about the stories but learning new things about himself. Daniel found that he thrives when learning in this fashion. "Yes, I will use it [in the future]," Daniel concluded.

Finding "Self" in the Stories

Perhaps the most intimate experiences shared during the interview process occurred as the participants described how hearing and retelling the biblical stories affected them personally. Besides thinking only outwardly concerning how they might utilize oral methods in speaking with others, the students declared that the stories also touched them emotionally and spiritually.

When asked how teaching and learning through the use of oral methods like storying and drama made him feel, Daniel reacted quite emotionally. "So, believe me," Daniel answered, "in many of the stories the professor taught us, I found myself in them." Pausing a moment, Daniel then asked my research assistant, "Can I give an example?" My research assistant's response: "Of course."

Daniel gave the example of the parable of the Prodigal Son from Luke 15:

> Like the parable of the prodigal son, that Brother Cameron taught us. How he left his home and he goes far away from his father. I found myself again in this parable. Because I was far from God. If I were to apply this to my life, [then] this story mirrors some of the situations of my life. And it had a great impact.

Răzvan maintained, "[People] will find themselves immediately in stories." Florica became exceptionally open when asked how she might apply the course material to her life. Florica's response is so rich that it merits quotation at length:

> Especially in this last period I was going through a period of sort of confusion, which I really didn't know what to do with my life after university. A period that matured me. And I am beginning to be more serious in my relationship with God and with people around me, more so than before I began university. No, I already feel a transformation. And even I remembered many things I recalled from this course and when I felt sad or did not feel God close, I think about the parable of the lost sheep and that God leaves everything and comes after me. It makes me feel important when I wasn't feeling this way. Or, I don't know, we also had the parable of the Pharisee and Tax Collector. And I sat and thought that many times in church you have the tendency to judge others and somehow you think you are better than them or like them but in fact it is not true. And I had a moment when I thought myself better than someone and, immediately, I remembered this parable.

Discussion

In this section, I discuss how my findings relate to existing literature, specifically as it relates to adult education theory, transformative learning theory, and learning style theory. Finally, I briefly situate my study within similar inquiries into the use of orality methods in pedagogy.

Adult Education Theory

To reiterate, adult learning theory is the study of how adults learn. The field of adult education builds upon the foundational work of Malcolm Knowles. Knowles proposed six distinguishing characteristics of adult learners, as mentioned above.[48]

Due to these factors, adult education theory fits well with the findings of this study for several reasons. The student participants are all adults who have *independently* chosen to study theology at Bucharest Baptist Theological Institute (Characteristic 1) based on their *prior experiences* and eagerness

---

48. Knowles, *Modern Practice of Adult Education*.

for further theological education (Characteristic 2). They can, if they wish, choose to discontinue their studies, thus their motivation is mostly *internal* (Characteristic 5). Yet the students have found *personal reasons* for studying theology at this institution, largely due to a desire for spiritual and ministerial equipping (Characteristic 3). The students' desire teaching that is *immediately applicable* to everyday life (Characteristic 4) and that provides the *rationale for learning* and curriculum development (Characteristic 6).

In the findings, students time and again noted how they chose theological studies in order to develop themselves personally. They were aware of how the material and the teaching methodologies used built upon their previous life experiences. In *The Adult Learner*, Knowles, Holton, and Swanson discussed how this awareness in adult learners intrinsically concerns changes that are "expected to occur."[49] Facilitating such change, then, becomes the role of the educator. As students claimed in their interviews, engaging with the biblical stories enhanced their theological understanding. Interestingly, learning the material using oral-based methods also caused them to consider how their personal life stories mimicked or paralleled those from the Bible.

According to adult education theory, adult learners ultimately desire teaching that is applicable to their everyday life. Such teaching must not be only applicable at a hypothetical, later time, but applicable in the moment. Students believed that much of the teaching methods used at the Bucharest Baptist Theological Institute are less effective because they fail to do this. In contrast, oral-based teaching methods are seated in relationships. Thus, oral-based methods are by nature designed to be applied. It was for this reason that the parables and other biblical stories learned were told and retold in the classroom.

Transformative Learning Theory

As mentioned above, transformative learning theory was first developed by Jack Mezirow, who proposed that the learning process ignites a "disorienting dilemma" that leads to examination, reflection, and change of the status quo.[50] The process of transformative learning details ten steps.

Transformative learning theory is appropriate for this discussion of oral-based teaching models because the findings display learners who critically reflected on their prior learning experiences and reevaluated their understandings based on new perceptions. The process described as the

---

49. Knowles and Swanson, *Adult Learner*, 10.
50. Mezirow, "Perspective Transformation."

central understanding of this study's findings illustrate the transformative learning process described by Mezirow and his colleagues. The "disorienting dilemma" (Step 1) is evident in multiple students' reflections on their experiences using oral-based methods. Students then examined their prior experiences with more traditional education models (Step 2), especially those that are teacher-oriented and lecture-based, students noted a significant distinction in the student-focused oral methods. At first, the oral-based methods seemed out-of-place (Step 3), with students evening "relating their discontent to others" by asking if they were in Sunday School instead of a theology class (Step 4).

Further, some students used the interviews to voice the cognitive and affective transformation they experienced. Specifically, in the area of evangelism, students declared they now approach the task differently (Step 5). Instead of taking the posture of argument and defense, for example, students noted the use of storying is more conversational and gives both conversation parties pause and consideration. To use transformative learning theory terms, students found that oral-based teaching methods assist in constructing new personal and theological meanings and implications (Step 6). For many of the student participants, this was a liberating revelation. The students then began to use their newfound perspectives to construct ideas for how oral-based methods might be integrated into their ministries, coursework, and even in other content areas (Steps 7–10).

Learning Styles Theory

As mentioned above, learning style theory was developed by Kolb and his colleagues in the 1970s.[51] Kolb believed that learning is a four-step process involving concrete experience, reflective observation, abstract conceptualization, and active experimentation. Students display a desire for greater or lesser abstraction and concrete experimentation.

The research on learning styles is significant for this study because oral-based teaching models are meant to

1. engage multiple learning methods, besides simply the traditional lecture, and
2. incorporate multiple student perspectives by "hearing" voices other than the professor and course texts.

---

51. Kolb, *Individual Learning Styles*.

Indeed, courses based on text-driven models do not tend to diversify instruction. The findings show a strong desire for diversified pedagogical models, since students consider that creative methods enhance the learning process and result in real world application.

In this study on oral-based teaching methods, attention was especially given to audio-verbal instruction and repetition. Students recalled in their interviews that such an approach was unique among the content of other courses. Students remarked that such verbal repetition of the biblical stories had a great impact on their learning the material and applying it to their own lives.

Further, the findings of this study displayed a frustration with lecture-based teaching as the *only* form of instruction used in the classroom. In such courses, students relayed that information was successfully transmitted but quickly forgotten. Just as in the seminal work *What's the Use of Lectures?* Bligh does not suggest scrapping lectures entirely; instead, the research shows that additional instructional methods are necessary.[52] Comparatively, the findings of this study agree and go further by demonstrating how oral-based methods capture attention. Oral-based methods are active learning methods which both transmit information and promote memory and thought.

Related Orality Studies

The final major section of this discussion section concerns similar orality studies. Citing examples from the cross-cultural mission field and changing mindsets based on the rise of technology, Jagerson claimed that Christian educators would do well to incorporate insights from orality theorists into their curriculums: "With the rise of globalization worldwide and pluralism at home, teaching methods that are able to communicate to a broad spectrum of cultures are increasingly imperative."[53] Jagerson cited a personal example of sharing a biblical story on an airplane with a Czech woman, in which the using the form of story caused the woman to become fascinated and wanted to learn more about Jesus.[54]

In multiple works, Steffen has called for theological education to reconsider the prominent place of narrative in Scripture.[55] Narrative appears

---

52. Bligh, *What's the Use of Lectures?*
53. Jagerson, "Harnessing the Power of Narrative," 273.
54. Jagerson, "Harnessing the Power of Narrative," 272.
55. Steffen, "Chronological Practices; Steffen, "Discoveries Made"; Steffen, "Saving the Locals from Our Theologies."

more than any other literary genre. In a recent article, Steffen recalled coming to this realization:

> One day out of the blue, I asked myself, while there are multiple genres in Scripture, what if there were just three—propositions, narrative, and poetry? What percentage would I assign each?
>
> After conducting some investigation, I eventually came to some surprising findings. My favorite genre, propositions, came in dead last at around 10 percent. Poetry followed with 25–35 percent. Narrative won the contest at 55–65 percent . . . [I]t can categorically be stated that narrative is the predominant genre of Scripture.[56]

In another article, Steffen goes further by declaring that a failure to take into account the oral aspects of Scripture will result in an eclipsed theology that remains peculiarly Western. Calling the 80 percent of the world's population the "Oral Majority," he wrote,

> Theologians and Bible teachers must learn to enter the Oral Majority world to be better able to appreciate the great emphasis oral tradition has played in completing and communicating the canon . . . We must learn to appreciate the oral nature of Scripture if we are to gain a more complete picture of her Author, and be able to communicate more clearly with the Oral Majority . . . This will require paradigm shifts. Only then will thick theology result that helps produce spiritual-social flourishment and fruitfulness; only then will we be able to save locals from our theologies.[57]

Concluding Reflections

The central understanding to emerge from this study's collected data is that oral-based teaching methods, such as storying, create a transformative impact through a process of disorienting first impressions, novel learning experiences, reorienting realizations, and finding oneself in the stories. Study participants perceived oral preference teaching methods as effective for several reasons. First, participants referred to the memorable nature of the use of oral-based methods. In contrast with the traditional delivery model of lecture and students as passive learners, oral-based methods

---

56. Steffen, "Discoveries Made," 172.
57. Steffen, "Saving the Locals from Our Theologies," 57–58.

accent interaction. Students are given the opportunity to share their own perspectives and applications.

Second, students noted that the oral-based methods stirred within them a passion for further learning of the biblical and theological material. Instead of learning course content by rote and later forgetting it, the participants noted how learning the material through oral-based methods caused a greater appreciation for the biblical text and its context.

Third, students considered oral-based methods to be effective in other educational contexts. Whether in institutional (formal), ecclesial (informal), or personal (non-formal) contexts, students offered potentially transferrable educational contexts where the use of oral-based methods could assist in the learning process.

As such, I list below six implications and applications to emerge from this study:

Implication 1: Students Find Non-Lecture-Based Teaching Methods Stimulating

Application 1: Diversify Instruction

Implication 2: Students Value the Professor Hearing Their Perspective

Application 2: Select Instructional Activities that Encourage Students to Speak

Implication 3: Creative Teaching Enhances Understanding

Application 3: Teach for Understanding as the End Goal

Implication 4: Students Want to Learn How to Apply Course Material

Application 4: Demonstrate How Course Material Applies to the Real World

Implication 5: Oral-Based Teaching Methods Capture Students' Attention

Application 5: Experiment with Oral-Based Methods

Implication 6: Oral-Based Teaching Methods Make a Memorable Impact

Application 6: Evaluate and Apply the Types of Oral-Based Teaching Methods That Make a Memorable Impact

To return to the anecdote given at the beginning of the introduction, I mentioned the vivid memory of Maria, a social work student, declaring her newfound love for practicing evangelism through the telling of Bible stories. Maria's comment, given roughly a year before this study was conducted, is the heartbeat of every teacher of evangelism. To see students not only excited about content material but actually using it in real life for the glory of God is the purpose of theological education, as I view it. This study has shown that students also desire that, too, yet some students may find traditional teaching methods a hindrance to practical application. Incorporating oral-based teaching methods may help remedy the situation.

Bibliography

Armstrong, Cameron D. *Finding Yourself in Stories: Romanian Theology Students' Experience Using Oral-Based Teaching Methods*. PhD diss., Biola University, 2020.
———. "Honor and Shame: Cross-Currents in Romanian Culture." *Jurnal Teologic* 14 (2015) 95–123.
Banks, Robert J. *Reenvisioning Theological Education: Exploring a Missional Alternative to Current Models*. Grand Rapids: Eerdmans 1999. Kindle.
Biakolo, Emevwo. "On the Theoretical Foundations of Orality and Literacy." *Research in African Literatures* 30 (1999) 42.
Bligh, Donald A. *What's the Use of Lectures?* New York: John Wiley & Sons, 2000.
Charmaz, Kathy. *Constructing Grounded Theory, 2nd edition*. Thousand Oaks, CA: Sage, 2014.
Chiang, Samuel E., and Lovejoy, Grant, eds. *Beyond Literate Western Models: Contextualizing Theological Education in Oral Contexts*. Wheaton, IL: Condeo, 2013.
Chiang, Samuel E., and Lovejoy, Grant, eds. *Beyond Literate Western Practices: Continuing Conversations in Orality and Theological Education*. Hong Kong: International Orality Network, 2014.
Christie, Michael, et al. "Putting Transformative Learning Theory into Practice." *Australian Journal of Adult Education* 55 (2015) 9–30.
Clendenen, Daniel B. *Eastern Orthodox Christianity: A Western Perspective*. Grand Rapids: Baker, 2012.
De Neui, Paul, ed. *Communicating Christ Through Story and Song: Orality in Buddhist Contexts*. Pasadena, CA: William Carey Library, 2008.
Dumitrescu, A. L, et al. "A Comparison between Learning Style Preferences of Undergraduate Students from Three Different Romanian Faculties—Using VARK." In L. Gómez Chova, A. López Martínez, I., and Candel Torres, eds., *ICERI2013 Proceedings*, 3571–77. Seville, Spain: IATED, 2013.
Esterline, David, et al. "Global Survey on Theological Education, 2011–2013: Summary of Main Findings: For WCC 10th Assembly." Busan, 30 Oct—8 Nov 2013. http://www.globethics.net/web/gtl/research/global-survey.
Finnegan, Ruth. *The Oral and Beyond: Doing Things with Words in Africa*. Chicago: University of Chicago, 2007.
Fisher, Walter R. *Human Communication as Narration: Toward a Philosophy of Reason, Value, and Action*. Columbia: University of South Carolina, 1987.
Gallagher, Tom. *Modern Romania: The End of Communism, the Failure of Democratic Reform, and the Theft of a Nation*. Washington Square: New York University, 2005.

Gonzalez, Justo L. *The History of Theological Education* Nashville: Abingdon, 2015. Kindle.

Hofstede, Geert. *Culture's Consequences: International Differences in Work-Related Values.* Beverly Hills, CA: Sage, 1980.

Hofstede Insights. "Compare Countries [Digital tool]." https://www.hofstede-insights.com/product/compare-countries/.

International Orality Network & Lausanne Committee for World Evangelization. *Making Disciples of Oral Learners.* Lima, NY: Elim, 2005.

Jagerson, Jennifer. "Harnessing the Power of Narrative: Literacy and Orality in Christian Education." *Christian Education Journal* 11 (2014) 259–75.

Jenkins, Philip. *The Next Christendom: The Coming of Global Christianity.* 3rd ed. London: Oxford University, 2011.

Knowles, Malcolm S. *The Modern Practice of Adult Education: From Pedagogy to Andragogy.* Englewood Cliffs, NJ: Cambridge Adult Education, 1980.

Knowles, Malcolm S., et al. *The Adult Learner: The Definitive Classic in Adult Education and Human Resource Development.* 6th ed. Burlington, MA: Elsevier, 2005.

Kolb, David A. *Individual Learning Styles and the Learning Process* (Working paper no. 535–71). Cambridge, MA: Sloan School of Management, MIT, 1971.

Letham, Robert. *Through Western Eyes: Eastern Orthodoxy, a Reformed Perspective.* Geanies House, UK: Christian Focus, 2007.

McIlwain, Trevor. *Building on Firm Foundations, Vol. 1: Guidelines for Evangelism and Teaching Believers.* Orlando, FL: New Tribes Mission, 2005.

Merriam, Sharan B. "Adult Learning Theory: Evolution and Future Directions." *PAACE Journal of Lifelong Learning* 26 (2017) 21–37.

Merriam, Sharan B., and Elizabeth J. Tisdell. *Qualitative Research: A Guide to Design and Implementation.* 4th ed. San Francisco: Jossey-Bass, 2016.

Merriam, Sharan B., and Laura L. Bierema, *Adult Learning: Linking Theory and Practice.* San Francisco: Jossey-Bass, 2014.

Mezirow, Jack. "Perspective Transformation." *Adult Education Quarterly* 28 (1978) 100–10.

Moon, W. Jay. "Encouraging Ducks to Swim: Suggestions for Seminary Professors Teaching Oral Learners." *William Carey International Development Journal* 2 (2013) 3–10.

Ong, Walter J. *Interfaces of the Word: Studies in the Evolution of Consciousness and Cultur.* 1st ed. Ithaca, NY: Cornell University, 1977.

———. *Orality and Literacy.* New ed. London: Routledge, 1982.

Pashler, Harold, et al. "Learning Styles: Concepts and Evidence." *Psychological Science in the Public Interest* 9 (2009) 105–19.

Raiser, Konrad. "The Future of Theological Education in Central and Eastern Europe: Challenges for Ecumenical Learning in the 21st century." *International Review of Mission* 98 (2009) 49–63.

Stahl, Irina. "Has Romania Become a Secular Society?" *Revista română de sociologie* 27 (2016) 135–49.

Sills, M. David. *Reaching and Teaching: A Call to Great Commission Obedience.* Chicago: Moody, 2010.

Spann, Matthew. *Witnessing to People of Eastern Orthodox Background: Turning Barriers of Belief into Bridges to Personal Faith.* PhD diss., Southwestern Baptist Theological Seminary, 2001.

St. Athanasius Orthodox Academy. *The Orthodox Study Bible*. Nashville: Thomas Nelson, 1993.

Steffen, Tom. "Chronological Practices and Possibilities in the Urban World." *Global Missiology* 4 (2013). ttp://ojs.globalmissiology.org/index.php/english/ article/view/1215.

———. "Discoveries Made While Reconnecting God's Story to Ministry." *Christian Education Journal* 14 (2017) 160–83.

———. *Reconnecting God's Story to Ministry: Cross-Cultural Storytelling at Home and Abroad*. Rev. ed. Waynesboro, GA: Authentic Media, 2005.

———. "Saving the Locals from our Theologies: Part Two." *Journal of Asian Mission* 19 (2018) 37–61.

———. *Worldview-Based Storying: The Integration of Symbol, Story, and Ritual in the Orality Movement*. Richmond, VA: Orality Resources International, 2018. Kindle.

Steffen, Tom, and Bjoraker, William. *The Return of Oral Hermeneutics: As Good Today as It Was for the Hebrew Bible and First-Century Christianity*. Richmond, VA: Orality Resources International, 2020.

Steffen, Tom, and Terry, J. O. "The Sweeping Story of Scripture Taught through Time." *Missiology: An International Review* 35 (2007) 315–35.

UNESCO Institute for Statistics. *Adult and Youth Literacy: National, Regional and Global Trends, 1985–2015* (UIS Information Paper). http://www.uis.unesco.org/Education/Documents/literacy-statistics-trends-1985-2015.pdf.

Walls, Andrew F. *The Missionary Movement in Christian History: Studies in the Transmission of Faith*. Maryknoll, NY: Orbis, 1996.

6

For a Time Such as This

Oral Bible Schools Take Root in Sub-Saharan Africa

A. Steven Evans

ORAL BIBLE SCHOOLS. WHILE not a new concept in Sub-Saharan Africa, it is certainly an evolving one. Over the past two decades, the idea of such Bible and theological schools has moved from a novelty to a necessity. "The concept of Oral Bible Schools is innovative and strategic for the new world of missions we are living in," said a Bible translator and consultant in South Africa, who served as a top official for southern Africa with a major global Bible translation agency. "The reach of an Oral Bible School can be as wide as the reach of their storytellers who share the stories they've learned."[1]

This chapter looks at seven such schools in six countries of Sub-Saharan Africa, widely spread across a spectrum from a basic Oral Bible Storying approach to a more advanced approach that combines Oral Bible Storying with the methodology of a traditional Bible school or theological institute (see Figure 6.1). This author oversees two of the seven schools and consulted on two others. Emerging out of the oral schools is the recognition of an element of missiology called *self-theologizing*, as well as the rise of a hermeneutics based on the discovery of biblical truth embedded in narrative presentations and explorations of Scripture, rather than being instructed on what the Bible says and means. "Hermeneutics is taught along the way rather than in a class of its own," said an International Mission Board (IMB) strategy leader of their Congo Basin region. "Each story discussion reinforces the importance of understanding the passage in its context, the dangers and limitations of allegory, and the difference between interpretation and application."[2] He said that an understanding of theology in the scope of the biblical narrative

---

1. Sebastian Floor, email message to author, April 8, 2019.
2. Jay Shafto, email message to author, February 28, 2020.

begins to emerge. After a survey of the seven Oral Bible Schools in Sub-Saharan Africa, this chapter ends with a discussion on self-theologizing emerging out of Bible Storying, then challenges the reader to establish Oral Bible Schools within his or her own contexts.

Looking Back Twenty Years

One special day, twenty years ago, in the bush of East Africa, seventeen young men–many of whom could barely read or write and some not at all–received certificates from the world's largest evangelical seminary. They were surrounded by starvation, drought, and decades of civil war, and though each might find it difficult to read the certificate he held in his hands, they all received above average marks on their final exam, qualifying them to graduate. A legacy had been born, the first fruits of an associate professor of preaching who lived and taught half a world away. Grant Lovejoy, who is now Director of Orality Strategies at the IMB, had dreamed of this day and had worked hard for it. An ardent advocate of biblical and theological education for oral communicators, he worked to address the situation that an estimated 90 percent of the world's Christian missionaries are literates who teach using literate methods among a global population of four billion or more who are oral communicators. In response, Lovejoy and the academic institution he represented, Southwestern Baptist Theological Seminary (SWBTS), in Ft. Worth, Texas, developed a plan based on the concept of Chronological Bible Storying (CBS). His partners were to be missionaries of the IMB and their national colleagues.

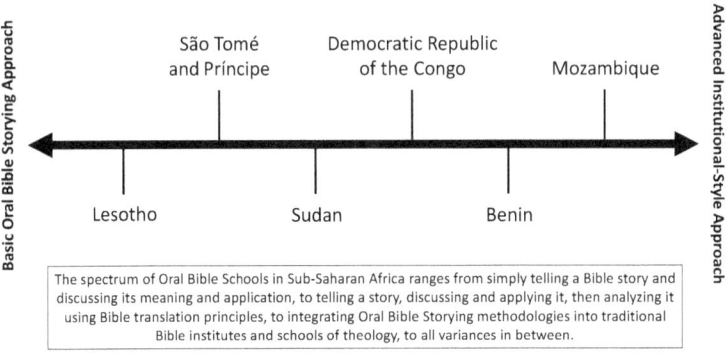

Figure 6.1. Oral Bible Schools Spectrum in Sub-Saharan Africa

"There are many ways to prepare people for leading in Christian ministry," Lovejoy said. "Probably the oldest way is to live with, learn from, and work alongside an accomplished leader. Jesus used this approach with the Twelve. Like apprentices to a master craftsman, they learned by close observation of his life and work and by his evaluation of their lives and work. This apprentice model of training and learning is ancient and used worldwide."[3]

It was this method of instruction that Lovejoy wanted to try, coupled with the concepts of CBS. He and SWBTS developed a program called *Tell the Generations*, agreeing to issue certificates to those who qualified, according to criteria set up by Lovejoy and approved by the seminary. He said, "Chronological Bible Storying, which was developed to address the needs of oral communicators, has a demonstrated effectiveness in teaching oral communicators Scripture in ways that enhance their understanding of the Bible, theology, and its relevance to their lives. It also gives oral communicators new confidence to share their faith, because they can do it in a culturally appropriate form, through storytelling."[4]

Back in the bush of a then-united Sudan, a local center to train evangelists in the south of the country had been established four years earlier by a partnering organization, but something was not working, and leadership was frustrated. Baptist missionaries in the area agreed to help by providing curriculum and teachers. Through his IMB contacts, Lovejoy became involved. They agreed to implement a curriculum that used an approach modeled on CBS. An IMB missionary, a pastor from a neighboring country, and Lovejoy initiated the teaching. The best-educated students had about ten years of schooling, but the area's schools often met sporadically and without the benefit of books or qualified teachers. Several students had little or no schooling. Lovejoy and the Baptist missionary developed a new program and left it in the hands of the pastor and another IMB missionary who joined him.

By the end of their training, students admitted that they had entered with little Bible knowledge. "For example, various students acknowledged that they entered knowing little of the Old Testament," Lovejoy said. "They did not understand the relationship between God and Jesus, did not know the characteristics of God, did not know that God created the angelic beings, had not heard of being born again, and did not know that Christians should not seek help from local deities."[5] Lovejoy added that these students were unable to communicate the Christian faith to other people. "By the time the

---

3. Lovejoy, "Report on Tell the Generations," 10.
4. Lovejoy, "Report on Tell the Generations," 12.
5. Lovejoy, "Report on Tell the Generations," 1.

training was over they had dramatically improved their understanding of all of these matters and many more," he said.[6]

Over the next two years, the training took place under adverse circumstances related to an ongoing, raging, civil war, drought-related hunger, and the absence of medical care. After an initial rocky six months trying to establish an appropriate teaching pattern, it became apparent that the approach being used was too literate, both in aim and in methodology. The first missionary returned for a visit and changes were initiated changes designed to restore a more oral, functional approach. In an informal discussion, the missionary heard reports that villagers had recently killed a hyena, a cause of great celebration. At the celebration, the villagers sung a song they composed to celebrate the event. They also created a dance that communicated what had happened. They did the same with respect to a conflict over water that had recently been resolved in their favor. With these two cultural events as examples, the leaders of the training were able to guide students to create a song and drama to reinforce the learning and communication of each biblical story they learned–three stories per week. The fact that it was familiar culturally made it easier for students to do it and also made it easier for the teachers to demand it as part of the learning process.

Within a matter of weeks, the introduction of song brought a new zeal to the daily classroom sessions. "Students were finding learning fun," Lovejoy said. "Moreover, the songs made the learning easier as well. People in the area were glad to hear the songs, so this made it much easier for students to initiate opportunities to share what they were learning."[7] Students learned to tell each story, create at least one song to go with each story, and create dramas of the stories. They discussed the meaning of the stories and interpreted them in light of God's unfolding redemptive plan.

The students spontaneously shared Bible stories and story-songs in their communities, with rapid, massive spread of the biblical message a common consequence. During one month-long break, villagers were so eager to learn the songs and stories from the visiting students that they sat up far into the night–even all night–to hear the songs and stories. Many wanted to hear the stories and songs over and over again so that they could learn them well.

"Students reported seeing evidence that the biblical stories were producing changed lives," Lovejoy said, "such as people praying to God for healing instead of visiting a local magician. Students reported using biblical stories at funerals to correct the common practice of using magic

6. Lovejoy, "Report on Tell the Generations," 1.
7. Lovejoy, "Report on Tell the Generations," 2.

to determine whom to hold responsible for the death of the one being buried."[8] The students learned to organize and tell the stories in chronological clusters: creation, judgment, the exodus, etc. Teachers taught students the stories orally, dialogued at length with students about the stories, and then evaluated each student carefully as the students told and sang the stories and performed the dramas. Each week the teachers evaluated how the students handled the new stories introduced that week. The weekly schedule also included extensive periods of reviewing earlier stories and occasionally involved weekend trips to use what they were learning. This pattern continued until the end of training.

Finally, after two years of hard work, the students were ready to be put to the test. SWBTS and Baptist missionaries sent a team to evaluate the success of the program and the accomplishments of the students. Lovejoy was part of that team. Over a period of four days, the visiting team interviewed at length the teachers, members of the training center's board of governors, the students, and the local chief. Then the students underwent a six-hour oral exam. "Students achieved knowledge of approximately 135 biblical stories in their correct chronological sequence, spanning from Genesis to Revelation," Lovejoy said. "They were able to tell the stories, sing songs that told the stories, and enact dramas about each of the stories. Students could tell the stories singly or in clusters—such as the 'creation cluster'–dealing with the creation of the spirit world, creation of heavens and earth, and the creation of man and woman."[9]

Lovejoy continued,

> They demonstrated the ability to answer questions about both the facts and theology of the stories. They showed an excellent grasp of the gospel message, the nature of God, and their new life in Christ. Students drew quickly and skillfully on the stories to answer a variety of theological questions. Given a theological theme, they could quickly and accurately name multiple biblical stories in which that theme occurs. If asked, they could tell each story and elaborate on how it addresses the theme.[10]

Lovejoy concluded, "In six hours of oral examination and interviews, the seventeen graduating students answered 70 questions dealing with factual matters, plus another 50 open-ended questions such as, 'How will you use what you have learned?' Students answered the 70 factual questions correctly

---

8. Lovejoy, "Report on Tell the Generations," 3.
9. Lovejoy, "Report on Tell the Generations," 2.
10. Lovejoy, "Report on Tell the Generations," 3.

more than 85% of the time."[11] In addition, members of the center's board of governors reported that the graduates had far better biblical knowledge than the members of the board did, including the ordained members of the board. "The board chairman said that he wished members of the board of governors could take the training," noted Lovejoy.[12] He continued:

> The training process has successfully achieved its goals of enabling students to tell a large number of biblical stories accurately, to have a good understanding of those stories and the theology that they convey, and to have an eagerness to share the Christian message. The community received the stories and story-songs enthusiastically and have made them part of the culture and church life alike. Despite some deficiencies in the training process, students told of using their training effectively during vacation periods and seeing lives changed in their communities. They also expressed confidence in using biblical stories in ministry and articulated plans for using their training in the various ministry situations to which they will go after graduation. The pattern modeled in the classroom was very appropriate for the culture. Local members of the board praised the students' biblical knowledge.[13]

Lovejoy concluded, "It seems readily apparent that students have grown dramatically in their biblical and theological knowledge, their capacity to share their faith, and their grasp of the Christian life. As members of the board pointed out, everything that they have seen thus far is positive, but the final evaluation depends on seeing what happens when students go to their churches and serve."[14]

Two Sub-Saharan African Leaders State the Case for Oral Bible Schools

"The concept of Oral Bible Schools is innovative and strategic for the new world of missions we are living in," said South African Sebastian Floor, a Bible translation consultant and former Vice President of The Seed Company, Southern Africa Region.[15] "The reach of an Oral Bible School can be as wide as the reach of their storytellers who share the stories they've

   11. Lovejoy, "Report on Tell the Generations," 3.
   12. Lovejoy, "Report on Tell the Generations," 4.
   13. Lovejoy, "Report on Tell the Generations," 1.
   14. Lovejoy, "Report on Tell the Generations," 5.
   15. Sebastian Floor, email message to author, April 8, 2019.

learned," he said. "Thus, a large group of non-readers gain access to Bible knowledge and Bible literacy without first having to learn how to read. An additional advantage is that a bulk of Bible content can be taught in oral format, much more than what one can do during a two or three day traditional-style workshop."[16]

Floor was first introduced to the concept of Oral Bible Schools in 2009, when he learned of Africa Inland Mission's (AIM) efforts in the country of Lesotho. AIM started a school for shepherds in the mountains of eastern Lesotho. "Basically an unreached people group, these shepherds were completely illiterate, not welcome in established churches, and were not given the time to attend serious Bible training or discipleship at a church, let alone expanding their knowledge of the Scriptures at a normal resident Bible school," Floor said.[17] He explained that living conditions were harsh, as the shepherds looked after their patron's herds high in the mountains where temperatures dropped to below freezing in winter. The shepherds moved around in groups of three and slept in small stone shelters big enough for only two. One shepherd always needed to be awake, day or night.

"Through the Oral Bible School, one of each group of three shepherds was able to attend a few days of Bible storytelling during which time they were taken through the Scriptures and the main themes of the Bible," said Floor. "The impact for church planting, discipleship and evangelism was significant."[18]

What appeals to Floor about this approach is that "regular oral Bible storytelling" as a discipleship tool and a leadership training tool becomes "institutionalized."[19] By that he means the Bible school is now not something that occurs when somebody schedules and conducts a workshop for teaching or training, but is "regular, ongoing, and word spreads that such and such a course is available."[20]

Albeit now considered regular, there still seems to be a spontaneity about it, not only with when and where courses are held, but also with who would attend. Word of mouth among the shepherds creates not only a curiosity about the school and its courses, but also a desire to attend. Because of the rotating nature of a shepherd-trio, one can never know which one of the three might show up at a course, and any one of the three has the chance to attend if the schedule works out just right. Also, as stories are told and retold

---

16. Sebastian Floor, email message to author, April 8, 2019.
17. Sebastian Floor, email message to author, April 8, 2019.
18. Sebastian Floor, email message to author, April 8, 2019.
19. Sebastian Floor, email message to author, April 8, 2019.
20. Sebastian Floor, email message to author, April 8, 2019.

by shepherds among the broader target audience, Oral Bible School attendance increases. According to Floor, the Oral Bible School for the mountain shepherds of Lesotho is still going on.

Floor is advocating for similar Oral Bible Schools in Angola. "An Oral Bible School where techniques for Oral Bible Storying can be taught will fulfill an enormous need in Angola to get the Word of God out to small minority groups," he said. "Potential oral storytellers can be trained at the school, full-time for a few months, or at workshops during the year. The storying training can be accompanied by theological training, especially exegesis and biblical theology or history of revelation."[21] He listed 19 languages in six provinces of Angola that are needing such schools now. "The list is not exhaustive," Floor said. "There are more minority languages in other provinces that could get onto this list."[22]

Recently this author met with Baptist pastor Frederico Supaleta in Angola's Cunene province, a province not included on Floor's list. The province is located in the extreme south of Angola and borders the country of Namibia. Supaleta expressed a critical need for low-to-mid-level theological education in his province. There are no existing Bible or theological institutions nearby, and attending ones that do exist is a costly endeavor. It was agreed that an Oral Bible School like the ones being conducted in the Portuguese-speaking island-nation of São Tomé and Príncipe–discussed later in this chapter–would be ideal for Cunene. Such a school is being developed.

Monseigneur Idore Nyamuke is a Baptist pastor and 1st Vice President of Église *du Christ au Congo* (ECC). The ECC is a parastatal union of 95 Protestant denominations in the Democratic Republic of the Congo (DRC). Translated, the organization is Church of Christ in Congo, or, probably more appropriately, Christ's Church in Congo. Nyamuke is responsible for the organization's evangelism, discipleship, missions and church planting programs. He is a firm believer in the need for appropriate level theological or biblical education for the country's oral communicators.

"*L'accès à la Parole de Dieu* étant *bloqué, les gens sont privés du message transformateur de la Bible à cause du taux d'analphabétisme trop* élevée *car la majorité de la population est constituée des personnes qui communiquent oralement*," he said. "*Devant les réalités de cette situation, l'implantation* des écoles *bibliques sur l'oralité est une réponse de Dieu pour servir ces populations dispersées dans les villages.*"[23] What Nyamuke is saying is that access to the Word of God is limited due to the nation's high illiteracy rate. Because

---

21. Sebastian Floor, email message to author, May 14, 2020.
22. Sebastian Floor, email message to author, May 14, 2020.
23. Idore Nyamuke, email message to author, March 29, 2019.

of this, people are denied the transformative message of the Bible. The establishment of Oral Bible Schools is God's response to serve those oral communicators who are dispersed throughout the villages of DRC.

Furthermore, he said that Congolese tradition has been oral since the time of their ancestors, and that culture and tradition were transmitted orally from one generation to another. "*Dieu a donné aux analphabètes une mémoire forte capable de réciter en mémoire l'histoire de la famille, du clan ou du village, nous pouvons utiliser cette opportunité pour* évangéliser, *former des disciples avec cette stratégie de l' oralité*," he said.[24] That is, God gave illiterates a high capacity for memory, enabling them to convey from memory the history of the family, clan or village. "*Nous pouvons utiliser cette opportunité pour* évangéliser, *former des disciples avec cette stratégie de l' oralité*," Nyamuke said.[25] We can use this opportunity to evangelize and train disciples with this strategy of orality, he said.

Nyamuke said that the poverty level of many make it impossible for them to attend a classic or traditional Bible or theological education school. This is why Oral Bible Schools are necessary to reach the people. Thus, the schools become an essential missionary strategy to quickly and comprehensively carry the message of the Good News of Jesus to the people.

"*Donc la RDC a un besoin des stratégies orales de façon concrète* dans *nos propres sphères d'influence pour accomplir le mandat du Christ, celle de faire de toutes les nations des disciples ce Christ*," Nyamuke said. "*L'Église du Christ qui est au Congo veut utiliser les écoles bibliques sur l'oralité pour* équiper *les membres de nos* églises *dans l'avance du Royaume de Dieu*."[26] In conclusion, he said that DRC needs oral strategies in concrete ways to fulfill the mandate of Christ, that is, of making disciples of all nations. The ECC (*Église* du Christ au Congo) wants to use Oral Bible Schools to equip members of its churches to advance of the Kingdom of God.

Oral Bible Schools in Benin, West Africa

In 2002, the Benin Baptist Convention began a traditional French-language Bible school. Shortly after, they started an Oral Bible School in one of Benin's vernacular languages, and later, they started two additional oral schools in two more languages. In the schools, students gather for one-week each month to learn ten Bible stories and discuss doctrine and theology contained within them. They learn 150 stories over a three-year period.

24. Idore Nyamuke, email message to author, March 29, 2019.
25. Idore Nyamuke, email message to author, March 29, 2019.
26. Idore Nyamuke, email message to author, March 29, 2019.

Jeff Singerman, a leader of the IMB's Sub-Saharan Africa affinity, earned his PhD studying Benin's Oral Bible Schools. He set out to compare and contrast traditional theological education with oral theological education and offer models for use throughout Africa. "We must explore creative options with existing Bible schools and seminaries to give 'accreditation' and proper recognition to those who have completed an oral theological training," Singerman said.[27]

Singerman further noted that oral methodologies introduced to national believers is an important step in the bridging of a "theological cultural gap." "Benin Baptists wanted to see proper contextualization, but also to communicate God's word in a culturally appropriate way," Singerman said.[28] The intent is to grant a diploma for oral preference learners without offering them courses that are deemed too similar to the French classic theological training. Having them appear to be too much alike would create tension between the two graduating classes, he said.

According to Singerman, teachers at the schools understand that courses for the Oral Bible Schools need to be presented concretely, rather than in an abstract manner, due to the oral students' preferred learning style. "Students taught in a concrete or situational manner more readily adapt what they learn to practical pastoral situations," he said.[29] However, a committee of the Benin Baptist Bible Institute professors met to discuss theological and doctrinal issues found in the stories in order to prepare theological lessons that coincided with the stories. They would, if necessary, translate certain theological concepts into the Fon language to prepare lessons to coincide with the stories. Students were to receive recordings of the stories, along with theological explanations, to enhance their learning and understanding of theological concepts. These aids were to enable students to correctly interpret biblical stories without fear of promoting heresy. (It is interesting to note that over decades this author has experienced similar reactions to Oral Bible strategies–a fear that oral strategies lead to heresy.) The professors surmised that stories alone would not be sufficient to provide adequate pastoral training. Therefore, they adapted certain classes from the traditional program, while remembering teaching and learning styles preferred by oral learners.

Singerman's study concluded that oral theological education has paid off. "The orally trained pastors and their congregants believe that training has resulted in better communication, better understanding of scripture,

27. Singerman, "Orality Observations," 126.
28. Singerman, *Grounded Theory Study,* 135.
29. Singerman, *Grounded Theory Study.* 138.

greater faith, greater wisdom, church growth, and a better command of God's Word," he said. "Effective pastors share biblical stories."[30]

One of the Oral Bible School students said, "A Fon proverb states, 'A child that does not know his father's story is worthless and insults his father.' How can one know the Word of God without knowing the Father's story?"[31] The student's equating the proverb with knowing God the Father's story indicates that he believes a person who does not know God's stories is worthless and insults the Eternal Father. This student, along with others, believes that one factor that contributes to a competent and qualified pastor is his communication of biblical stories and his use of oral methodologies.

Congregations of those who attended the Oral Bible Schools said their pastors teach effectively, because the pastors utilize oral, biblical story methods in the vernacular. "Congregants consider pastors who employ oral methodologies in communicating biblical stories, as effective," Singerman said. "Oral methodologies facilitate the congregations' ability to remember the stories and extrapolate truths." He added that 96 respondents in his study stressed that effective pastors share biblical stories, and that these stories help church members grow in their faith.[32]

One church member summed up the value of biblical stories by saying that they that helped her live out her faith. "Stories retain our attention more than messages," she said. "Stories are more effective. We are more educated by the stories. I did not go to school, but I know the stories. It is easier for us to remember the stories than the reading of texts."[33]

Two Small Islands and One Big Opportunity for Oral Bible Schools

"All we hear is noise, noise, noise," said the elderly public school teacher. "Noise from the pulpit, and noise in our Sunday School rooms. We don't understand any of it. If we could just hear a story told once or twice, we could remember it and understand it. We could use it and teach it and apply it to our lives." She was a student of one of the modular Oral Bible School courses on the small Portuguese-speaking island of Príncipe, located off the west coast of Africa. The school was initiated at the invitation of a WEC International missionary couple who run a Bible Institute on Príncipe's sister island of São Tomé. The institute offers a two-year

30. Singerman, *Grounded Theory Study*, 191.
31. Singerman, *Grounded Theory Study*, 146.
32. Singerman, *Grounded Theory Study*, 155.
33. Singerman, *Grounded Theory Study*, 188.

academic program, comprising of systematic theology, hermeneutics, apologetics, Old Testament, New Testament, etc. However, the missionaries were not only ready to try something new and innovative but felt that a different approach was necessary. Many of their students were losing interest, failing courses, and even dropping out of the school. They had heard of Oral Bible Storying from participants of a Summer Institute of Linguistics (SIL) OneStory project on the island and were impressed with what they heard and observed. SIL is affiliated with Wycliffe Bible Translators and was doing a OneStory project with two of the island's Bible-less people groups/languages. The Storying trainers and consultants used the WEC guest house, run by the missionary couple, while they were on the island. After hearing of Oral Bible Storying, the missionary couple wondered if this methodology could be used in their Institute.

In 2017, this author was in São Tomé to visit pastors of the newly organized Baptist Convention of São Tomé and Príncipe and stayed at the WEC guest house. While there, he met the StoryTogether personnel and heard about the dilemma of the WEC missionaries, German nationals Joachim and Kerstin Schultze. While conveying their need for a new school program and curriculum, they indicated that they wanted it to be both oral and modular. This new program would not replace their traditional one, they said, but run parallel to it. In partnership with this author, two Oral Bible Schools were established—one on each island—and a total of eight core modules were developed. Additional elective modules were also considered.

The Oral Bible Schools consist of eight standalone Bible Storying modules that are configured in various ways. Four of the modules are each two-weeks in length and four are each one week in length. The overall program takes up to four years, depending on how the schedule is set up each year. Currently, each island has two courses per year. São Tomé is completing the four one-week courses, while Príncipe is finishing the two-week courses. Soon, the courses will flip, with São Tomé doing the two-week courses and Príncipe doing the one-week courses. Between the two schools, there are anywhere from 80–150 students participating in the courses each time.

Foundational to the program are the four ST4T Bible survey story sets: 1. Bible Foundations (panoramic survey of the Bible), 2. Church Formation (Acts 1–15), 3. Church on Mission (Acts 16–28), and 4. Life Transformation (the Epistles). These four modules consist of 72 stories from the Bible, with each module requiring two weeks. The ST4T foundational sets of stories are supplemented by four additional one-week modules:

1. Tell His Story (evangelism),
2. Understanding Your Salvation (basic discipleship),

3. Life of David Leadership Stories (leadership development), and

4. Four Fields Perspective Through Paul's Missionary Journeys (church planting).

The total number of Bible stories used in these four modules is 28. ST4T is an Orality and Bible Storying approach for evangelism and church formation developed by a team of specialists (including this author) in South Asia as an oral response to the popular T4T strategy for evangelism, discipleship and church formation. T4T stands for Training for Trainers, while ST4T stands for Storying Training for Trainers.[34] Four Fields is a strategy framework that involves entry, evangelism, discipleship, and church planting strategies.

As previously mentioned, each of the eight modules can stand alone, with participants picking and choosing which ones to attend or not attend. Certificates of participation are given for the completion of each module, while certificates of completion are given for participating in a series of four inter-related courses–for example, a Bible Survey certificate after completing the four ST4T modules. After completing all eight modules, the Bible Institute offers a certificate of recognition. Other elective one-week modules include:

1. Morality and Sexual Purity;

2. Prayer; and

3. The True Gospel.

A typical class session covers two stories, with a break between the two. Each story is told twice, dramatized, retold by various students, and discussed using the five typical ST4T questions: What did you like about the story? What troubles you about the story? What does this story teach you about God? What does it teach you about man? What is your personal application of the story? Afterwards, analytical discussions include key terms and phrases, difficult concepts, cultural implications, and ministry applications. Finally, the story is told for a third time.

It should be noted that the schools in São Tomé and Príncipe are not necessarily designed for illiterates or for students with minimal education. The Oral Bible Schools are intended to offer an alternative teaching and learning style to the more formal academic program that students were struggling with. It was observed that some of the students who were failing the courses of the traditional Bible Institute are excelling in the Oral Bible

---

34. Stringer, *ST4T*.

Schools. Participants include youth, professionals, mission leaders, and senior pastors of large congregations.

"*Wir sind begeistert von der effizient des storytelling der Methodik der Oralen Bibelschule, da es Kerninhalte des Evangeliums in einer natürlichen Sprache tiefgreifend in Herz und Verstand pflanzt,*" Joachim Schultze said.[35] He was enthusiastic about the efficiency of storytelling, which is the methodology of the Oral Bible School. It deeply plants the core contents of the Gospel in a natural way in the heart and mind of a student. "*Unsere Hoffnung für die nächsten Jahre besteht darin, auch eine natürliche Reproduktion dieser Methodik im Umfeld der Gemeinden beobachten zu können.*"[36] The hope for the next few years is to be able to see a natural reproduction of this methodology in the community. He said that, personally, they as missionaries were challenged to pass on God's message naturally and authentically among their circle of friends. "*Wir sind sehr dankbar für diesen für uns neuen praktische Ansatz Gottes Wort weiterzugeben, und hoffen auch in Zukunft auf diese Art und Weise den hiesigen Gemeinden dienen zu können,*" Schultze said.[37] He said that they were very grateful for this new, practical approach to pass on God's Word. In the future, they hope to be able to serve the local churches utilizing this methodology.

"*Möge das Gottes Reich auf unseren Tropeninseln dadurch wachsen und ein tiefes Verständnis der Geschichte Gottes mit uns Menschen entstehen,*" Schultze said.[38] May the kingdom of God grow on our tropical islands, along with a deep understanding of the story of God grow among the people.

Brazilian Baptist missionaries Celso and Andreia Fonseca served in Senegal for ten years and participated in a two-year IMB-sponsored StoryTogether Oral Bible Storying project there. They now serve as visiting primary instructors for the Oral Bible Schools in São Tomé and Príncipe. "*Encontramos lá várias igrejas com pessoas cheias de sede de conhecer mais e estudar a Palavra de Deus,*" Celso said. "*Temos que dizer que nas vertentes mais carismáticas dentre os evangélicos a oralidade é uma realidade há muito tempo.*"[39] They found several churches with people thirsty to know more and with a desire to study the Word of God, he said. With evangelicals, orality has been a reality for a long time. "*Mas há uma diferença quando se usa a oralidade para pregações e histórias pessoais,*" he said. "*O que a Escola Oral da Bíblia trouxe de novo é a própria palavra de Deus entregue*

---

35. Joachim Schultze, email message to author, May 16, 2020.
36. Joachim Schultze, email message to author, May 16, 2020.
37. Joachim Schultze, email message to author, May 16, 2020.
38. Joachim Schultze, email message to author, May 16, 2020.
39. Celso Fonseca, WhatsApp message to author, February 28, 2020.

oralmente. Ficamos logo impressionados com a capacidade da maioria deles de recontar as histórias bíblicas logo que a ouvem e colocam dentro do coração após as perguntas de observação e interpretação."[40] There is a difference when using orality for preaching and for personal stories. What the Oral Bible School brings is the Word of God delivered orally. He was impressed with the ability of students to retell the Bible stories as soon as they heard it. Then they put it into their hearts after the working through questions of observation and interpretation.

Fonseca said that while going through the two-course survey of the book of Acts, the atmosphere was almost palpable. He said, "*A cada história, a compreensão crescia na sequência dos acontecimentos. Quando terminamos de contar a história da prisão de Paulo em Jerusalém, por exemplo, um dos participantes disse espontaneamente que ele sentia a história como se estivesse num cinema.*"[41] With each story, understanding grew in the sequence of events. When instructors finished telling the story of Paul's arrest in Jerusalem, one of the participants spontaneously said that he felt as if he was in a cinema. "*Logo as pessoas perceberam que eles não eram meros expectadores que sentavam para ouvir alguém dar a sua interpretação da Bíblia,*" Fonseca said, "*mas que eles estavam tomando para si essa responsabilidade. Nesse contexto o tempo é um fator fundamental que é altamente valorizado no propósito de explorar o texto audível ao máximo.*"[42] He said that students soon realized that they were not mere spectators who sat to hear someone give their interpretation of the Bible, but that they were taking this responsibility on themselves.

Fonseca said that he and his wife are constantly surprised by the fact that the Word of God has the power to transform people as they apply it to their daily lives. "*E acreditem, as aplicações que ouvimos as pessoas fazerem surpreenderam no fato de que nós não poderíamos fazer melhor do que eles mesmos,*" he said.[43] Believe me, he said, the applications they heard that the students made surprised them. They as instructors couldn't do better than the students themselves, he said.

One senior pastor of a major denomination came to class one evening and shared about something that happened just that day. He told of a woman he had been witnessing to for years. She never showed any interest at all in what he had to say. That morning, however, he shared the stories he had been learning in the Oral Bible School's evangelism course. "Not only

---

40. Celso Fonseca, WhatsApp message to author, February 28, 2020.
41. Celso Fonseca, WhatsApp message to author, February 28, 2020.
42. Celso Fonseca, WhatsApp message to author, February 28, 2020.
43. Celso Fonseca, WhatsApp message to author, February 28, 2020.

did she listen to what I had to say," the pastor said, "but she understood what I was saying. And not only did she understand, but she also responded." That morning, the woman received Christ as her Savior and Lord.

Oral Strategies in the Congo Basin Lead to an Oral Bible School in the DRC

For the IMB, the Congo Basin region is made up of the countries in central Africa whose waters drain into Africa's mighty Congo River or that are affected by it. The IMB began to focus specifically on the Congo Basin in 2015 under the leadership of veteran missionaries Jeff and Barbara Singerman. The Singermans are ardent advocates of Orality and Bible Storying. Jay and Kathy Shafto, with Orality and Bible Storying experience, then joined the team in April 2016. This author and his wife Carla joined as Orality and Bible Storying strategists in December 2016. Since then, the Singermans have moved on to broader responsibilities within the IMB's Sub-Saharan Africa affinity, and the Evans have moved to Angola as the IMB's country leaders. The Shaftos now lead the work in the Congo Basin region.

"The Congo Basin team uses an orality approach in all we do and teach," Shafto said. "Our initial training in Orality is called Tell His Story. It requires fifteen hours of instruction and is focused on evangelism. Everywhere we have held Tell His Story trainings, the participants have been active, and results have been amazing."[44] After holding Tell His Story trainings in three Baptist churches in the Sud-Ubangi province of the DRC, the head of the churches' denomination asked Shafto to introduce Orality in his Bible school. In October 2019, Shafto and a Congolese partner, Joachim Ndebe, went to the school to teach a two-week module using ST4T materials.

The Bible school has approximately 50 students, ranging from 30–60 years of age. It typically uses a traditional curriculum, offering such subjects as New Testament Survey, Old Testament Survey, The Epistles, Apologetics, Pastoral Counseling, Hermeneutics, Church History, etc. For their oral approach, Shafto and Ndebe chose to teach the first module of ST4T, consisting of twenty-one stories, to give an overview of the Old Testament and Gospels.

Each morning, they taught two stories from the ST4T materials. They then asked the standard ST4T questions about the stories. In the afternoons, all students went into the neighborhood two-by-two to tell the stories and start spiritual conversations leading to evangelism.

---

44. Jay Shafto, email message to author, February 28, 2020.

This was an aspect of their seminary training that had not been included in the curriculum. When they went into the neighborhood, they found people receptive, asking questions and responding to God's Word. One family said, 'You're from the seminary? This is the first time anyone has ever visited us from the seminary. We always wondered what you did over there?' Another group of young men were smoking marijuana when the seminarians approached and asked to tell them a story. 'You are willing to sit and talk with us,' one asked. "Yes, we are," they responded, and proceeded to share with them that day's stories. Two made decisions for Christ and another recommitted his life to Christ. As well, several villages where there was no church asked if the students would begin one.[45]

Shafto explained that the objectives of the orality-based course were to master twenty-one stories, tell those stories, record the number of contacts made and their responses to those stories, and learn how to lead a storying group. "After our departure, students were required to start a storying group individually or in pairs as part of the course requirements," he said.[46]

"The engagement of the Word of God was deep and personal," Shafto added. "Students themselves repented of sin and recommitted to applying God's Word to their lives, in addition to learning the stories. The practical aspect of the requirement to go out to tell stories was also impactful. One of the resident professors gave the testimony that if the church were to send him anywhere to start a church he would now know how."[47]

Shafto said the course gives practical experience in evangelism though the daily sharing of the stories, discipleship through the discussion questions and application after each story, leadership development by requiring every student to lead a story session with classmates under our supervision, and church planting through the starting of story groups in villages.

"*La formation permet aux pasteurs d'être des hommes de terrain, et s'investir dans la création des petits groupes dans des villages, pour permettre l'implantation des cellules et d'autres églises,*" Ndebe said. "*L'école biblique orale permet a nos pasteurs de faire revivre l'église, a faire transmettre les enseignements et les histoires bibliques des générations en générations comme nos ainés avaient fait qui avait entainer une croissance rapide au début de l'église.*"[48] The training allows pastors to be out in the field, investing in the creation of small groups in villages, leading to new church cell groups and the planting of new

45. Jay Shafto, email message to author, February 28, 2020.
46. Jay Shafto, email message to author, February 28, 2020.
47. Jay Shafto, email message to author, February 28, 2020.
48. Joachim Ndebe, email message to author, May 7, 2020.

churches, Ndebe said. He said that the Oral Bible School equips pastors to revive the church. They transmit the teachings of biblical stories in the same way that has been done for generations—from generation to generation, as elders had done, which led to rapid expansion of the church.

"*Les histoires biblique est un moyen simple et pratique de faire connaître aux Pasteurs les vérités de la bible et de comment le partager,*" Ndebe said. "*J'étais étonné de voir les étudiants qui ont fait trois ans d'études à l'école Pastorale, même le Directeur Général, dire que c'est une méthode qui nous a aidé de comprendre la Bible et aussi un moyen de le faire connaître aux fidèles de nos églises, pour que eux puisse le faire aussi aux autres.*"[49] He said that using biblical stories is a simple and practical way to let pastors know the truths of the Bible, as well as teach them how to share those stories and truths. He was amazed to see students who had done three years of study at a pastoral training school, even the Director General, say this is a method that has helped them to better understand the Bible and use it in the church to encourage the faithful in a way that they can reproduce it.

Shafto agreed. "Orality based teaching is life transformational," he said, "building the character of the pastors and giving a deep understanding of the Bible. The oral approach leads to high retention of Biblical narratives and is considered more useful and practical by the students and professors. This meets the school's goal of equipping pastors for real life ministry in churches."[50]

While firmly rooted in an Oral Bible Storying approach, the course took, and future courses will take, a hybrid path. "On several occasions, we came upon topics that required further study," Shafto said. "For example, baptism and the trinity. When these topics came up in stories, we took extra time to discuss them further and read together other passages that clarify that doctrine."[51] Shafto and Ndebe also discovered that some of the stories addressed false teachings prevalent in local cults and false churches. "We took extra time to specifically apply the story to the teachings being presented by these cults and the questions asked by people familiar with those teachings," Shafto continued, "This hybrid approach of story plus scripture verses will be taken to discuss other theological and doctrinal issues such as the Holy Spirit, the Bible, salvation, sin, family."[52]

Shafto and Ndebe intend to develop teaching modules to address a general understanding of the Bible, plus meet current needs in the

---

49. Joachim Ndebe, email message to author, May 7, 2020.
50. Jay Shafto, email message to author, February 28, 2020.
51. Jay Shafto, email message to author, February 28, 2020.
52. Jay Shafto, email message to author, February 28, 2020.

students' context. In no particular order, courses are to include Acts Part 1, Church Planting (Acts Part 2), the Epistles, Leadership from the Life of David, Tell His Story Evangelism, Cults, Prayer, Purity and Sexuality, and Assurance of Salvation.

Shafto said that hermeneutics is taught "along the way" rather than in a class of its own, with each story-discussion reinforcing the importance of understanding the passage in its context, the dangers and limitations of allegory, and the difference between interpretation and application. "The question, 'Where do you see that in the story?' uncovers most problematic interpretations," he said. "As more stories were learned, an understanding of theology in the scope of the biblical narrative began to emerge. Connections were made between Old Testament prophecies and their New Testament fulfillment. Themes that repeated themselves across multiple stories adding depth and nuance to doctrines."[53]

Mozambique's "Oral-Friendly" Theological Education Approach

Theological education for Baptists in Mozambique is at a crossroads right now. The challenge at hand is to develop and integrate basic, median, and superior levels of theological education for existing and future pastors of the Baptist Convention of Mozambique, while keeping in mind their geographic, education, and literacy backgrounds. Missionary Brian Harrell, IMB strategy leader for Mozambique, is working with the convention's theological education department to come up with a comprehensive and nationwide plan. "What a unique challenge we have," Harrell said, "reaching out to attend to the need of our geography and present context, while at the same time reaching forward to the emerging future of Mozambique."[54]

At present, there are over 500 congregations without pastors, while most of the potential leaders have little education, live far from existing centers of theological education, and are living a subsistence lifestyle similar to the lifestyle of those they lead. "At the same time, we recognize that the emerging reality of Mozambique is a move towards urban with the next generation of leaders being younger, more educated and with a greater need for bi-vocational training," said Harrell.[55] Adding to this is the expectation that the number of churches will increase, making it necessary to have even more pastors.

53. Jay Shafto, email message to author, February 28, 2020.
54. Brian Harrell, email message to author, April 6, 2020.
55. Brian Harrell, email message to author, May 12, 2020.

The desire is to a have a core curriculum that is foundational to all levels of theological education, and the Mozambican theologians came up with a list of fifteen courses they believe to be necessary for a pastor's education. "Given that, we talked about the possibility of a more oral approach at the basic level," Harrell said, "and the ability for the basic level to be given at distance through moderators in the field."[56]

Included in the fifteen courses to be developed include: Evangelism and Missions, Bible Geography, Devotional Life, the Worship Service, How to Teach the Bible, Introduction to the Bible, Christian Ethics and Leadership, Christian Education, Homiletics, and Practical Ministry.

"There is a desire that the Basic Level be given in an oral format as well as a more literate format," Harrell said. "This is an area in which we can lead in providing a framework for teaching the same content, but in an oral manner. This is an opportunity for us as a mission to make a contribution to the Convention through our experience in Orality. The end goal is that the Basic Level could be offered in both a literate and oral format, and that a multitude of national moderators would be equipped to do so."[57]

He said, "The basic structure that we are working towards is to use a Chronological Bible Storying approach foundation and then intersect with courses where they fit (perhaps in multiple places) in the CBS timeline."[58]

Harrell proposes what a five-day module would look like:

- Pre-work: Students are sent the passages in advance and, if possible, recordings of the 10–12 base stories for the week. Students should go to the module with a working knowledge of the stories.
- Day 1: Introduction, covering the nature of the Scriptures and basic rules for answering questions from the Scriptures. How this relates to culture and experiences, will be covered, and the necessity of allowing the Scriptures to speak for themselves. Subsequent modules would focus on specific hermeneutical issues that arise in stories: How to interpret Law, Prophecy, Psalms, Epistles etc.
- Day 1–2: Days one and two would also be a review of the stories using observational questions: Who, How, When, Where, What, perhaps Why (in terms of context not interpretation).
- Day 3: Day three would introduce interpretive questions that focus on basic doctrines. Questions like, "What do we learn about God?" will be recurring. Other questions will arise at the appropriate time within

---

56. Brian Harrell, email message to author, April 6, 2020.
57. Brian Harrell, email message to author, April 6, 2020.
58. Brian Harrell, email message to author, April 6, 2020.

the narrative: The Church, the Holy Spirit etc. Summaries of what is gleaned can be recorded or they can write down their observations at the end of the discussion. "I think it would be important to address the significance of our theological discoveries within our local context," Harrell said. "Theology should never be an abstract pursuit of propositions concerning the truth about God."[59]

- Day 4: Insert elements of the 15 core courses as appropriate. "For instance, in the second module, while discussing the Ten Commandments, this would be a great time to introduce Christian Ethics, and then revisit the discipline again at the Sermon on the Mount, providing an Old Testament/New Testament comparison," Harrell said.[60]
- Day 5: Develop practical application as appropriate to the module, re-record stories in the students' local dialects, and write observations from the week.

Harrell said,

> In the end, this is a bit of a hybrid approach that seeks to lay an oral foundation. In all likelihood, there is going to need to be some printed or written material in order to show work to whomever is responsible for theological education in context. I think though, that even testing could be done in an oral format, as I have seen my local national colleagues do with students who just struggle to write.[61]

Oral Scripture, Self-Theologizing, and Oral Bible Schools

The "Three-Self" principle for indigenous churches has been around for over a century: self-governing, self-supporting, and self-propagating. However, two prominent missiologists, Paul Hiebert and David Bosch, advocated for a fourth "self–that of *self-theologizing*. While somewhat controversial, the validity of self-theologizing is now emerging in the fields of missiology, Oral Bible translation, and Oral Bible Schools. Tom Steffen and William Bjoraker, in their book *The Return of Oral Hermeneutics*, argue that now is the time for this concept to once again step up and take its place in the world of hermeneutics, as it did prior to the canonization of Scripture. They say that truth from an oral perspective calls for

---

59. Brian Harrell, email message to author, April 6, 2020.
60. Brian Harrell, email message to author, April 6, 2020.
61. Brian Harrell, email message to author, April 6, 2020.

trustworthiness, while truth from a literary perspective calls for accuracy. They emphasized that truth requires more than propositional logic to grasp its essence. "All Scripture is Holy Spirit inspired . . . and invites us to find our story in the grand narrative," they said.[62] They call for the embodiment of Scripture resulting in the formation of theology.

Theology often emerges from an "aha" moment when segments of the grand narrative make a connection within someone, revealing a theological truth in the mind of the individual. Rarely is hermeneutics thought of when a Bible story is told and the five basic ST4T questions are asked, but that is exactly what is happening. Trainers are going through the process of interpreting Scripture, or at least leading students to do so. This is frightening to some, as expressed by leaders of the Oral Bible Schools in Benin, fearful that this can lead to heresy. Tellers of the Word and facilitators of the discussions afterwards walk a fine line while leading students to make accurate interpretations and applications. What is avoided is telling the listener what to believe. The desire is to allow students to draw their own conclusions after making discoveries found in the Bible story. Instead of theology being taught, it is caught!

There are no right or wrong answers, typically, to the five ST4T questions. Responses are based on self-perceptions—"This is what I like." "This is what I don't like." "This is what the story tells me." Etcetera. If an answer seems "off", trainers go back to the story—"What does the story say about this?" "What in the story makes you say that?" Sometimes it needs to be said that the particular story in question doesn't address the issues brought up by the students, but perhaps a past story has addressed it or a story in the future will. Naturally, responses to the five basic questions vary, depending on the listener. A child may have simple answers, while a pastor may have detailed and complex answers. Students answer based on their educational levels and experience in the Christian faith. These answers are the early formations of theology within an individual and community that don't have access to higher levels of theological education or would not be able to comprehend it. Every time a student answers the questions about the nature of God and the character of man, theology is expressed.

There are three basic types of questions that are asked in a discussion, understanding that answers become progressively more difficult for a student. The first are fact questions. If it can be ascertained that students have the facts of the story, it can be assured that they will most likely mull over it, even if subconsciously, and the Holy Spirit can work in their lives. This is why a retelling of the story is so important. One way to ascertain whether

---

62. Steffen and Bjoraker, *Return of Oral Hermeneutics*, 11.

students have the facts is to ask chronological questions: "What happened first?" "Then what happened?" "What happened next?" Their responses are the facts of the stories. The second type of question is a discovery question: "What do you discover based on what you just said, the fact that was expressed?" It must be remembered that making discoveries is a bit harder than just recalling facts. Finally, there are application questions, "Based on what you've discovered, what does that mean for you?" These responses are the most difficult to make. Teachers or trainers often desire to get to the application right away, and for individuals, oral-preference learners in particular, this may take days or even weeks to get to. Sometimes they may never be able to express in words an application, though one may be made and is evident in his or her life. However, trainers give students opportunity to express applications based on the stories they have heard and learned–both personal application and ministry application.

Interestingly, the process of these progressive questions and responses are, in many ways, hermeneutical processes. The five ST4T questions and the three basic types of questions are also part of a self-theologizing process. Self-theologizing is very apropos to the world of orality in general and to Bible Storying specifically. Self-theologizing has been manifested in most of the Oral Bible Schools reviewed in this survey. An additional important aspect is the use of linguistic techniques while leading story-crafting trainings, workshops and courses. These linguistic techniques are, in fact, hermeneutical techniques for the oral communicator. Basic linguistic techniques employed include contextual gaps, frames of reference, key terms, making explicit that which is implicit, etc. All contribute to how Oral Scripture is not only told, but interpreted as well, leading to the formation of theology.

However, beyond the questions asked by trainers and answered by students, the stories alone have the power to elicit the theology imbedded within them. Frequently in Orality and Bible Storying trainings, four consecutive stories from the book of Mark are used—Jesus Calms the Storm, the Demon Possessed Man, the Bleeding Woman, and Jarius' Daughter. After learning and processing these stories, participants, without prompting, frequently express a theological understanding of what they call "the power stories of Jesus"—Jesus has power over nature; Jesus has power over evil spirits; Jesus has power over sickness; and Jesus has power over death. While this may seem basic, it is, indeed, an expression of self-theologizing.

It cannot be over-emphasized how important it is for a student or an individual to discover from Scripture truth for himself or herself without being told what to believe. Sociologists indicate that truth rooted in the heart, rather than truth from the head–head knowledge so to speak–is what is truly believed, because it is experienced, rather than being implanted in the mind through instruction or teaching. Stories help one experience truth; thus, it becomes real. Students of Oral Bible Schools experience the stories they are presented with, and the emerging theology becomes truth for them. That truth is instrumental in the formation of a biblical or Christian worldview. Bible translation agencies now consider the product of Oral Bible Storying projects for bibleless peoples as First Scripture, therefore becoming the source from which theology emerges for those peoples. This self-theologizing is vital for the development and growth of the indigenous church. Floor suggests that from these Oral Bible translation projects, Oral Bible Schools be established, further developing and deepening a biblical theology within a people group.

Here is what one Baptist pastor in the DRC, Abraham Mudidi, said about self-theologizing. He is an Oral Bible Storying trainer and consultant, working closely with this author. "Theology by definition is an understanding of God–who he is, what he is, how he reveals himself, what he does, what he wants, etc.," Mudidi said. "It is the way people express in their own words what they have understood about God after processing the Bible, a Bible story. That is theology. So, nobody will ever hear God's story without getting a picture of who God is. Therefore, he will be able to express what he has learned about God by hearing the story; and that is self-theology."[63]

Mudidi reinforced the sociological and pedagogical concept that a story is experienced, and the experience results in truth realized. "Bible storytelling is a kind of journey," he said. "In fact, it is a journey.

> It picks you up, whether an individual or group, from somewhere and takes you to somewhere else, somewhere you didn't imagine before the narration of the story. During this trip, you are going to discover things about God, about people, or about His creation. At the end of the story, you have learned things that will bring you to some truths, or a conclusion about God himself or related to his action. The story has taken you from ignorance to what you now obviously know. You now have a different insight about God. This new insight gives birth to self-theology.[64]

He said that the Holy Spirit plays a major role in this. "The Holy Spirit, who is the Spirit of God and the Spirit of the Word of God, dwells in the narration of a Bible story," Mudidi said. "He is the perfect teacher. His role is

---

63. Abraham Mudidi, email message to author, May 15, 2020.
64. Abraham Mudidi, email message to author, May 15, 2020.

to reveal God to us. He will be revealing God to us during Bible storytelling. From His teaching in our heart comes self-theology."[65]

Concluding Reflections

There is a big mistake in assuming that Oral Bible Schools are only for the illiterate. This is just not so! Equally wrong is the belief that Oral Bible Schools are only for oral-preference learners or for those who employ a more oral decision-making process, thought process, or learning style. These are all valid and do, indeed, play important roles in whether to establish an Oral Bible School within a particular environment or circumstance. The real issue, however, is one of Bible literacy, or Bible illiteracy. People just don't know the Bible. The Bible and its contents should be at the core of all that is done by the church, from evangelism to discipleship to theological education. Biblically illiterate Christians result in biblically illiterate churches, and biblically illiterate pastors result in biblically illiterate discipleship. There is a deep need to integrate the ministries of the Church, with Bible content at the foundation of them all. These ministries should contain an integrated, comprehensive biblical narrative. Therefore, Bible stories speak to all levels of the missionary task of the Church and its members, regardless of the levels of literacy. At its very foundation, an Oral Bible School addresses the crisis of Bible illiteracy.

The intent of this chapter was to introduce the idea of Oral Bible Schools, survey the various approaches to them in Sub-Saharan Africa, and create an interest in them, with the possibility of establishing one. Illiteracy is not the criteria for such schools, but the desire to plant the Word of God in its narrative forms within a believer and create within him or her a theology grounded in the Word. Oral Bible Schools can be as simple as shepherds meeting around a fire in the mountains of Lesotho to a more academic institutional approach employed by many in this survey. What would it be like and what would the response be if churches established community Oral Bible Schools? Or if one was established within the church for discipleship and increased Bible knowledge? How about the methodology being applied in house groups or home cell groups? Or what about Oral Bible Schools being done on university campuses? The possibilities are unlimited. For resources and advice on Oral Bible Storying and Oral Bible Schools, write to tellhisstory@pobox.com.

---

65. Abraham Mudidi, email message to author, May 15, 2020.

Bibliography

Floor, Sebastian. Email message to author. April 8, 2019.
———. Email message to author. May 14, 2020.
Shafto, Jay. Email message to author. February 28, 2020.
Fonseca, Celso. WhatsApp message to author. February 28, 2020.
Harrell, Brian. Email message to author. April 6, 2020.
———. Email message to author. May 12, 2020.
Lovejoy, Grant. "Report on Tell the Generations Leader Training Program." Report [for private distribution only—not for publication] presented at Southwestern Baptist Theological Seminary, Fort Worth, TX, 2002.
———. "Tell the Generations Leader Training—Providing Theological Education for Oral Communicators: Southwestern Seminary's Role." Paper presented at Southwestern Baptist Theological Seminary, Ft. Worth, TX., January 26, 2001.
Mudidi, Abraham. Email message to author. May 15, 2020.
Ndebe, Joachim. Email message to author. May 7, 2020.
Nyamuke, Idore. Email message to author. March 29, 2019.
Schultze, Joachim. Email message to author. May 16, 2020.
Singerman, Jeffrey. *A Grounded Theory Study of the Perceived Effectiveness of Pastors Serving Oral Preference People in Benin, Africa*. PhD diss, Southeastern Baptist Theological Seminary, Wake Forest NC, 2018.
———. "Orality Observations Among Francophone West African Adults: Storying to Orality." In *Beyond Literate Western Models: Contextualizing Theological Education in Oral Cultures*. Hong Kong: ION/LCWE, (2013) 121–28.
Steffen, Tom, and William Bjoraker. *The Return of Oral Hermeneutics: As Good Today as It Was for the Hebrew Bible and First-Century Christianity*. Eugene OR: Wipf & Stock, 2020.
Stringer, Stephen, ed. *ST4T–Four Manuals in One*. Monument, CO: WigTake Resources, 2014.

7

Mining the Biblical Narratives for Individual and Communal Transformation

Bible Storytelling that Moves Beyond Proclamation to Deep Level Discipleship

Jennifer Jagerson

For the work of missions, the orality movement has provided an insightful framework by which to move forward with contextualizing the Christian message for a broad range of different cultures, addressing factors that had theretofore gone largely unacknowledged.[1] In the past, the medium of communication had been in many ways like the water in which a fish swims. Just as the water determines almost everything about the life of a fish, the manner in which we communicate, process, and authorize information colors every aspect of our social lives.[2] The results of engaging oral strategies over the past few decades seem to demonstrate the validity of many elements of the theory and the manner in which oral strategists have applied it.[3] Orality provides a way for the missional community to identify profoundly influential cultural dynamics that are critical for understanding and communicating with oral learners. It also provides helpful corrections to some of the cultural excesses and deficits of the West and points the way

---

1. Chiang et al., *Making Disciples of Oral Learners*; Steffen, *Worldview-Based Storying*. Chapters 1–3 provide the most extensive history of the modern-day orality movement to date.

2. Ong, *Orality and Literacy*, 29, 167.

3. Chiang and Lovejoy, "Extent of Orality"; Jagerson, "Resonance and Synergy," 14; Koehler, *Telling God's Story with Power*, 19–30.

A Reconsideration of Narratives

With the onset of the Enlightenment, western society increasingly marginalized narratives and their capacity to articulate valid, authoritative information.[4] This ran in contradiction to one of humanity's most fundamental, intuitive, and effective frameworks by which to interpret reality. Narratives are far more than the bedtime stories of childhood or the forms of escapism we imbibe with movies and novels. They are actually the mechanism for how we think about our own lives as individuals, in relationship with others, living with the cause and effect of circumstances along a timeline.[5] Moreover, cultural narratives accomplish a number of critical functions, such as: providing a unifying sense of norms for communities, establishing the roles of individuals within it, defining corporate understandings of meaning and purpose, casting vision for that which is worthy of effort and thought, and exhibiting the behaviors that are likely to accomplish it.[6]

Humans not only process our own reality through the lens of narrative, we use the stories of others, both fiction and nonfiction, to help make sense of the world by exploring characters as they face the challenges of life. These stories act as simulations that allow humans to experience challenging aspects of life and process what it means for their own choices.[7] Stories are inherently didactic, providing a moral interpretation of the kinds of things that happen in the world so that we can understand what happens in our own lives and communities.[8] Moreover, narratives that are deeply established in a culture play a profound role in determining how the members of that culture develop their own self-understanding, inform the development of new narratives (whether in agreement or opposition to existing narratives), and provide a framework by which to renegotiate old narratives in order to provide fresh understanding.[9]

---

4. Frei, *Eclipse of Biblical Narrative*, 81–82.

5. McAdams, "Psychology of Life Stories," 100–03.

6. Bruner, *Acts of Meaning*, 46; Hammack, "Narrative and the Cultural Psychology of Identity," 233; Wright, *New Testament*, 38–43.

7. Sugiyama, "Narrative Theory and Function," 239–40.

8. Ryken, *Words of Delight*, 21, 42; Osborne, *Hermeneutical Spiral*, 203.

9. Ricœur, *Time and Narrative*, 53–56; McAdams, "Psychology of Life Stories," 100; Hammack, "Narrative and the Cultural Psychology of Identity," 232–33.

Those working in the field of Narrative Psychology have developed a theoretical framework that understands narratives as a more appropriate way to approach addressing mental health. Rather than focus entirely on the problem that drives the client to seek help, these therapists focus on the narrative of the individual's life to put the problem in context and draw other aspects of life into the healing process. This might include the love and contribution of their families, careers and skill sets, friendships, and faith system.[10] A key concern is the manner in which an individual engages in what has been termed "narrative processing," which includes how they interpret negative events or challenges and integrate them into their sense of meaning and purpose.[11]

Studies have shown that individuals who tend to narratively process the events of their lives with negative interpretations, or "contamination themes" such as, "things always end badly for me," tend to have higher levels of depression and anxiety and lower levels of well-being and generativity.[12] Meanwhile, those whose interpretation of events resolve in what are called redemptive themes, where participants identify positive meaning and purpose even in negative circumstances, were found to have significantly stronger correlations with high levels of: life satisfaction, emotional stability, conscientiousness, sense of agency, generativity, maturation, and communion, which relates to their ability to establish a sense of community and belonging with others.[13] One of the goals for narrative psychologists is to support their client in identifying and rejecting negative schemas, or thought patterns, and draw upon resources such as their faith system to assert more positive interpretations for their lives. The ultimate goal is for clients to come to what are called "coherent, positive resolutions," where they are able to consistently interpret the meaning of the individual circumstances of their lives and integrate them into a broader, cohesive understanding of their life's meaning and purpose.[14]

These developments in Narrative Psychology provide helpful insights into the manner in which humans process information and develop

---

10. McAdams, "Psychology of Life Stories," 100.

11. Pals, "Narrative Identity," 1083; Hayes et al., "Avoidance and Processing," 115.

12. Lodi-Smith et al., "Narrating Personality Change," 680; Adler, "Living into the Story," 377.

13. Adler et al., "Variation in Narrative Identity," 478, 484; King and Raspin, "Lost and Found," 623; Lodi-Smith, "Narrating Personality Change," 687; McAdams, *Redemptive Self*, 14; Pals, "Narrative Identity," 1096.

14. Pals, "Narrative Identity," 1083; McAdams, *Redemptive Self*, 14; Maruna, Wilson, and Curran, "Why God is Often Found Behind Bars," 108; Lodi-Smith, "Narrating Personality Change," 680.

what they would call "narrative identity."[15] It seems to correlate closely with what we see in Scripture in terms of what it means to be an individual who chooses to live by faith in Christ. For example, in Ephesians 1–2, the Apostle Paul provides insights to help his audience reinterpret their place in the story of human history and the eternal realms in the context of being a sinners in a broken world who have been: adopted by the living God (Eph 1:4), saved by grace (Eph 2:8), seated with Christ in the heavenly realms (Eph 2:6), sealed by Christ's Spirit (Eph 1:13), and prepared for good works (Eph 2:10). Every aspect of their lives is meant to be reinterpreted according to that storied truth.

Taking all of these insights regarding narratives into view, it is no wonder that they are the most predominant genre in Scripture and, in fact, encapsulate the entirety of Scripture along the plotline where the problem of the fallen state of humanity culminates in the grand rescue of Christ's sacrifice.[16] It is this broader story and all of the shorter stories along the way that have established the biblical worldview in cultures and brought profound levels of transformation to individuals and societies alike.

Narrative is so fundamental to how we think, it is like the waters in which the fish swim. However, in the West, we have lost our sense of the power of the narratives and diminished their authority in favor of rationalism, propositional thought, and logic.[17] This includes the nature of how to *tell* stories in ways that deeply engage the listener as well as how to be the *listener* of a story and deeply interpret meaning. The purpose of this chapter is to explore the manner in which a particular oral strategy of Bible storytelling seems to have provided a way to richly re-engage the biblical narratives and mine them for the deeper purposes that we have been addressing. The Simply the Story (STS) method created a way to recapture the narratives of Scripture to support individuals and communities in rich, faithful interpretations of the divinely inspired author's intent and process their own stories in light of the truths that they find.

Bible Storytelling: Simply the Story

Oral strategists, initially with organizations such as New Tribes Missions (now ETHNOS360) and the International Mission Board of the Southern Baptists, have developed a number of Bible storytelling methods that

---

15. Adler et al., "Variation in Narrative Identity," 476–77.

16. Steffen, *Worldview-Based Storying*, 156–57; Steffen and Bjoraker, *Return of Oral Hermeneutics:* 94–95.

17. Frei, "Eclipse of Biblical Narrative," 20.

center around the telling, interpretation, and application of Scripture for oral learners so that they not only master the interpretation and application of biblical stories, but are trained to immediately pass on that skill to others for rapid transmission and proclamation of the Gospel.[18] One of the methods that emerged was Simply the Story (STS), which is unique in a number of key ways. In the early years of STS's implementation, reports by practitioners identified benefits that reached even farther into the deeper, more long-term goals of church planting, including profound levels of individual and communal transformation.

The Simply the Story method consists of five stages. Practitioners solidify the learner's initial, oral knowledge of the story with the first three stages: 1) tell the story, 2) have the participants retell the story to each other or have a volunteer share it with the group, and 3) lead the group through the story again to reaffirm accuracy.[19] This often leads to near memorization of the stories when combined with the final stages. The final two stages (Spiritual Observation and Spiritual Application) engage the process of interpretation and application. After introducing any necessary background knowledge from Scripture to understand the context of the story in the Spiritual Observation stage, the leader goes through each section of the story, choosing only a verse or two at a time, and asking the questions:

a. What did the character say and do?
b. What choices did he or she make? What *other* choices could they have made?, and
c. What is the short term impact or long term consequences of those choices?

It is a fairly simple set of questions that are asked over and over as the group progresses through the verses along the storyline, providing a culminating understanding of the cause and effect of the moral choices of the characters and whether they responded in right relationship to God.[20] All of this is meant to be done in a discussion format. The leaders are taught to be careful not to be the "sage on the stage," but to use the questions to draw out the learners so that they have the delight of finding treasures from the text for themselves.

While the Spiritual Observation questions are fairly simple and memorable, they are also profoundly well aligned with the literary conventions

18. Chiang et al., *Making Disciples*; Willis and Snowden, *Truth that Sticks*; Steffen, *Worldview-Based Storying*.
19. Miller, *Simply the Story Handbook*, 56–62.
20. Miller, *Simply the Story Handbook*, 63–69.

that narrative authors employ to communicate meaning. The choices of the characters in the context of many options, what their choices mean about each character as they move along the plotline, and the consequences of those choices as the problem of the story comes to a crisis and resolution, are meant to exhibit not only *what happened* in the narrative but the *kind of things* that happen in real life.[21]

The narratives of Scripture have the added component of divine involvement. God inspired the authors to put the information in the form of stories as much as he inspired the story's content. God is also a character in the stories whether he is mentioned or not, working to draw human societies and individuals to himself. The moral of the stories is always centered around whether the characters responded in right relationship to him. Finally, God is at work in the audience as they process the story, whether orally or literarily, using the stories to create simulations of experience upon which to understand how to respond to Him in the course of their own lives.[22] Critical to interpretation is engaging the dilemmas that the characters face on an affective as well as cognitive level, intuiting the significance of the problem of the story for them, and imagining the personal impact as they face their various potential choices.[23] By considering the different options a character has, the audience can better empathize with them as they face the tremendous temptations of life, such as falling into besetting sins, taking the easier road, or failing to rely upon God.

This in-depth level of engagement of the story is meant to lead towards personal application. For stage five, or Spiritual Application, of the STS model, leaders are taught to choose 2–3 of the lessons identified by the participants from the story during the Spiritual Observation stage. Then, for each one, they ask:

a. Does this problem still exist today?,

b. Do you know any examples of it in your local community?, and

c. Has it happened to you or anyone you know?[24]

These questions lead the audience to increasingly intimate interpretations of the meaning of the text in the context of group discussion.

Trainings for the STS method come in many forms, kept intentionally flexible in order to meet the demands of the wide range of circumstances

---

21. Resseguie, *Narrative Criticism*, 19–21; Ryken, "Introduction," 22–23; Ryken, *Words of Delight*, 20, 22; Osborne, *The Hermeneutical Spiral*, 203.

22. Sternberg, *Poetics of Biblical Narrative*, 159, 161.

23. Osborne, *Hermeneutical Spiral*, 220; Ryken, *Words of Delight*, 64–65.

24. Miller, *Simply the Story Handbook*, 70–74.

where it is taught across the globe. This includes anything from one to five-day workshops to Oral Bible Schools where individuals covenant with each other to meet on a monthly basis for days and even weeks at a time to learn upwards of 296 stories from across the metanarrative of Scripture.

Empirical Research

A number of Oral Bible Schools were established by local, indigenous evangelical church denominations in impoverished, rural farming communities in southwest Ethiopia. The goal was to equip their local pastors, some of whom were nonliterate, all of whom identified as oral learners, for proclamation of the Gospel and to use to teach their existing parishioners in their church settings in place of traditional sermons, and in some cases, for their small group ministry. A formal study was conducted to explore the impact of the Oral Bible Schools. It consisted of twenty-seven semi-structured qualitative interviews (twenty-six male, one female) with Oral Bible School graduates and five focus group interviews (with a total of forty-eight participants: 26 female, 22 male) with the parishioners who learned the STS method from them.[25]

The findings from the study revealed that the method was effective at meeting the objectives of oral strategists in terms of replication and proclamation of the Gospel. There were strong reports regarding its effectiveness for evangelism, providing a positive way to engage nonbelievers in winsome and powerful discussions about faith in Christ, and equipping oral learners who had theretofore been marginalized to the sidelines of their church to engage in dynamic ministry.[26]

What is perhaps just as interesting were the dominant themes from the interviews that related to the effects of the method regarding individual discipleship and deepening and sustaining a richer communal life for the churches involved. These results seem to have been based on several factors:

1. the divinely inspired biblical stories, which, though often quite short, are packed with a rich and profound surplus of meaning about the most intensely important information in all of human literature, making each story a treasure trove for the process of interpretation,

2. the genre of narrative, including the literary conventions that their authors used to convey meaning, which seems to have been a particularly accessible format of communication, and

---

25. Jagerson, "Resonance and Synergy," 7–8.
26. Jagerson, "Resonance and Synergy," 13–15.

3. the method in which the narratives were taught in terms of the pedagogy, which had elements that seem to have taken particularly effective advantage of the first two factors,
4. the synergy between the different stages of the method that, taken together, seemed to have an had exponentially powerful impact.

The critical importance of these results warrants further consideration.

One of the strongest themes in the research was the expressed importance of having the stories in "their heart pocket." This is how the STS training frames the process of memorizing the stories. One OBS graduate explained: "The first and most important change [from more traditional forms of teaching] is that it has helped ministers to deeply internalize the word of God, to communicate it easily and even made us walking Bibles ourselves." Another said: "We didn't know these lessons before, and they help put the word of God in our hearts." Interviewer: "What do you mean . . . you had already been to Bible college, so you already knew the Bible in so many ways, how is this different?" Participant: "Yes, I knew the Bible before, but the difference with this is that now, after studying the Word I don't forget it, it stays in my heart."

The ability to meditate on Scripture at any point in the day appears to have led to transformation that extended to behavior. As one participant explained: "As we meditate about the Word our rebellions against God will be changed to obedience and we feel the presence of Holy Spirit. If we learn the story of the Ark of Noah, I remember and meditate on the story wherever I go and be . . . I can't read and write but after those guys came and taught us God's word this way, I am still remembering and benefitting from them." A focus group member provided another example:

> It helps regarding my faith and regarding my thinking level and in my decisions . . . when Jesus teaches His disciples about the Law of Moses he said, "It is written in the Law, which says, don't commit adultery, but I say the one who looks after women in a lustful manner is committing adultery." Interviewer: "How does that help?" Participant: "First the Word is in my mind and I don't forget it. It keeps me to not think when bad thoughts come to my mind." Interviewer: "It helps you to keep your purity?" Participant: "Yes."

Memorization and internalization of the stories was often identified specifically as the *key* factor for the effectiveness of the method: "It is memorizing. If we don't memorize no matter how we do, other things, we don't understand it. We will be useful when we have it in our minds. The main thing is the mind." The importance of memorization was affirmed by literates and nonliterates alike. For example, one participant explained, "Previously, I used to just read and write. But now I memorize it and meditate on it in my head."

Along with memorization, the questions from the Spiritual Observation stage seemed to have born rich fruit. Participants seemed to have been able to master the questions so that they not only could participate in their groups, they were able to master the process of asking the questions to explore the stories on their own and for others. A common theme in the interviews was clear descriptions of this process, such as this explanation from a focus group member:

> After our pastor who is part of the Oral Bible School taught me how to read and study the Bible, I have seen changes in the way we understand the Bible. I remember once our pastor told me the story of Lazarus, Mary and Martha story . . . first of all it helped me memorize the story in my mind and it also made me certain about asking very important questions while I'm reading the Holy Bible. The first question, which I ask is who are the participants in the story, what were their actions . . . What did they do? What was another opportunity? . . . Different choices and another, yeah, and alternative choices that could have been made. Finally, it helped me to ask, what is context of the story?

The importance of the questions was often expressed as the participants spontaneously explained what they had learned from particular stories, such as here, where the participant twice highlights the question about what other choices a character could have made in order to explore the context of the story and come to stronger realizations about the significance of the choice they actually made (from 2 Kings 4:1–7):

> The woman whose husband is dead went to Elisha and shouted that creditors are going to take her sons away from her. Before she went to the man of God, she had different choices she could have made, but she decided to go to man of God believing God has the solution. Elisha, the man of God . . . asked her what is in her house. She told him there is nothing in the house except jars of oil. At this moment he could have said to her, "Go and beg from people or sell your kids." Elisha had faith, and so he commanded her to collect empty jars.

The recognition that both the woman and Elisha *could have made* other choices reinforces the model that the characters provide for what it means to turn to God in faith in the face of what might seem like more practical, secure, or lucrative options.

Participants consistently articulated the importance of slowing down and attending to the details of the stories, rather than, as several described it, going "roughly" through the text. An OBS graduate explained:

> Previously we used to just roughly go through the stories... For example, in the book of Genesis chapter 12, verse one it states about the calling of Abraham, in a land where no one hears the voice of God, the land of his father. I admire the fact that he heard the voice of God and he took the voice of God as a map. So some people, when they preach, they pass that part by just briefly stating that Abraham was called and I don't like the fact that they don't deeply show the situation that Abraham was in and what it meant to be called by God... this verse about Abraham has fully controlled my life. Because, I am always amazed and filled with wonder that I am worshiping and serving the God of Abraham that Abraham worshiped and served.

This process also seemed to create a sense of profound personal connection to the individual characters in the stories. As one OBS graduate reflected: "[I] was very much touched by Joseph's life, how he was persecuted, how God was with him and finally how God raised him and glorified him, and finally, how he rescued his family from the famine... I wondered how he went through such a difficult time and went to prison but still held on to righteousness."

The process of Spiritual Observation seems to have established the memorization of the stories and created deep levels of internalization regarding their content and meaning. Throughout their descriptions, the participants demonstrated rich levels of empathy towards the characters as they addressed the considerable challenges of life.

There seems to have been a correlation between the deep level processing of a character and the deep personal insights and transformation that the participants expressed for their own lives when it came to the Spiritual Application stage. As one focus group member articulated:

> One of the stories is Bartimaeus. This person is blind. When he heard Jesus is walking by the street. He shouted, 'Son of David, have mercy on me!' The disciples were telling him to not shout and call out to the Lord. He kept calling Jesus and then Jesus healed his eyes. When we apply this word to our lives, in the house of God I can pass through different challenges. People may reject us and say bad words while we are seeking for God.

> Calling and searching for God no matter how and what people say and do to us will bring us solutions to every problem of our lives. God opened the eyes of blind Bartimaeus. If I have any problem, I can ask God for the solution.

It is as though the biblical stories highlighted an aspect of life and modeled potential responses, at times even casting a vision, for the participants. In doing so, they highlighted challenging aspects of the individual's lives and brought them to the fore so that they could evaluate them in light of the perspective of Scripture. This included the ability to appropriately navigate theological concepts that can be daunting for personal application. In the example above, the focus group member appeared to have been strengthened in faith regarding a new capacity to trust God for good things, but this did not devolve into a form of the prosperity gospel. Through the story's depiction of complex human dynamics, she was able to navigate the complex reality of trusting for God's blessings in a fallen world for herself and find resolve to stand firm even when she might face difficult circumstances and opposition.

One of the OBS graduates explained the outcomes of studying the story of the Gerasene demoniac in Mark 5:1–20:

> In the story it tells that the guy had been suffering for a long time and that when Jesus came, the spirit tormenting the guy left and he became okay. When the people saw him dressed normal the people were amazed. And so, when I tell people this part of the Bible like a story, people who have lost hope in their life and are going through difficult situations get to compare themselves to the character and see that Jesus, who gave the guy new hope, will also give them new hope.

As seen with this example, the stories with strong representations of redemption seem to have empowered the participants to come to terms with areas of sin and shame, acknowledging aspects of life that often remain hidden because they are too painful and vulnerable to expose.

These redemptive stories seem to not only cast a vision but provide a character to identify with on a personal level. The character's life acts as a simulation to process the emotions of coming to terms with painful areas of failure. The audience is able to not only see, but on some level experience, how one can face their failure and come out on the other side with their relationship with God not only intact but improved. It demonstrates the counterintuitive truth that the ways of righteousness such as humility and repentance (in whatever storyline they are exhibited) are actually powerful choices of wisdom that, in the context of God's Kingdom, lead not only to right relationship with God, but to restoration beyond even normal levels of dignity to depictions of high honor. This potential for restored relationship, honor, and ultimately, belonging, seems to have dissembled the participant's fear of rejection and assuaged the pain of failure while providing an impetus for taking emotional risks. The participants often used the same language modeled in the biblical text to illustrate this journey in their own lives. They did not tend speak with shame about the sin that the stories they highlighted, but with a sense of freedom and victory that had real-world consequences of changed behavior. As a focus group member explained:

> A story changed the way I give love for my children. I used to give more for one, less for the other but that story changed me ... When Isaac got old and wasn't even be able to see, Isaac loved Esau more than Jacob and Rebecca loved Jacob more. Because Rebecca loved Isaac more, she did favors for him that brought great breakdown in the family. Because both the parents didn't equally share their love for their children that breakdown of the family happened. I took one lesson for my family, which is making a decision to love my children equally.

An Oral Bible School graduate explained, initially referring to the story of Christ's healing of Bartimaeus:

> ... many people knew him at the side of the road, but after being called by Jesus his place was also changed. So when Jesus calls you, your position will also change. The other thing is the opening of his eyes ... so when other people saw him, they asked, 'Is this not the man who used to beg by the side of the road?' but his story has been changed now. And so, when I apply this to my life, I see that the Lord can change stories. And the fact that he can open the physical as well as the inner eye ... as the Lord raised the person from the side of the road, he raises us today from different places, some of us may be raised from *chaat* houses, it can be from an *areke* [the local gin] house. From uncomfortable places and conditions Christ took us out. As he [Christ] got him [Bartimaeus] out from that place, he also took us out of useless places and appointed us to great positions and assignments. He made us his own people and changed our story ... I have seen a change both in me and the people I minister to. As I present all the story, all of it is kept in their mind. And when they hear this story, they are very happy and understood that the Lord can change people's story. And I have also heard them tell the story to others and preach the gospel. And so they testify to me that they have found a new thing. So I see the change between my

ministry before the [OBS] school and after the school in the life of the people I minister to and in myself.

This explanation encapsulates a number of themes that have already been addressed in terms of the importance of memorizing the stories, processing their content in detail using questions that draw deep attention to the characters, and then mining the revelations that emerge for deep levels of application for today. It illustrates how these different elements seem have a compounding effect, each building on the next to deepen and confirm the learning that takes place.

Another element that appeared to be a powerful part of this dynamic was the effectiveness of using discussion as the primary way to engage the text. An indispensable aspect of the discussion's effectiveness seems to have been the use of questions the directed the participants continually back to the text, offsetting any tendencies for the conversation to meander, become side-tracked, or base the interpretational process on opinion rather than the intended meaning of the author.

This dynamic seems to have created a training process for how to approach the text for meaningful interpretive insights in a pattern that allowed the participants to gain mastery over the process. This honored the intelligence of the participants by showing them that their leaders believed they could be trusted to mine Scripture for truth rather than having it fed them. This was heightened when the participants found spiritual truths that their pastors had not identified or when they were able to experience the joy of ministering their insights to others and seeing it impact their lives. As one focus group participant explained: "It's comfortable for us to learn in a group. The reason why it is convenient (comfortable) is because the teacher himself learns there and brother teaches brother. Whatever I have the others hear and I will also listen to what others say. Whatever we found useful we take it and we apply it . . . When one shares what he thinks is good and the other people think it is not, that is where we are able to discuss it."

This quote expresses another theme, which was that as oral learners, discussion was an intuitive, culturally natural way to learn. One OBS graduate described the importance of discussion when it came to using the STS method to teach his church, "the benefit of taking time and discussing helps for the word of God to sink in to the hearts of men. They will grasp it better. In addition, they won't be bored with it, and as people know more, they will have hunger to know even more."

The process of discussing with each other also appears to have cultivated rich relationships between members of the communities that engaged them. As one participant explained: "It has a benefit and that is we will learn from one another and if we don't know something we might learn from another person. When we came together from different places, we can find a new thing and love will increase." Interviewer: "For each other?" Participant: "Yes, love will increase for each of us and our knowledge will increase too. For this reason, it has a lot of importance." Another participant explained: "Discussion with the group is a strong side of the school . . . [it] helps us to see what we didn't see before and it also helps us to remember it for long. Interviewer: "Does that affect the relationship with other students in the school?" Participant: "It brought a spirit of learning from each other. It created also unity among us." Another said, "It has benefits, we will discuss the stories and get deeper understanding on it and we will pass on to others what has helped us and built us." Interviewer: "Have you seen that same impact when you use it in your church?" Participant: "Yes."

The community effort of sharing the stories seems to have provided them with common references for how to negotiate life, such as whether they were going to choose the way of Martha or Mary after Mary chooses Christ as the once necessary thing (Luke 10:38–42). These references seemed to take on a symbolic effect where complex aspects of life could be codified so that they could discuss significant daily challenges and commitments of faith in shorthand. It also seemed to have a unifying and bonding effect, not only because they knew the story itself, but because they had deeply mined it together and had rich discussions about highly personal, often vulnerable, applications that addressed issues at the very marrow of their lives. Take, for example, this explanation for how one Oral Bible School learned to handle rebuke in their community: Participant: "In the story in the gospel of Matthew, where Jesus was walking on water, and after that we discussed how the water was not able to sink him, as he came to the world as a human being. And how Jesus rebuked Peter by first holding on to his hands. And so, we saw how we should rebuke people by first holding on to them."

The discussions that lead to these revelations seemed to have a kind of synergistic energy where the nature of the agreement between participants empowered the individuals with special confidence and conviction by which to carry out the lessons that were learned. This seems to have resulted in a kind of corporate understanding that contributed to community transformation, not through the imposition of a law or legalism, but through the wholehearted conviction and rich, mutual agreement by the members.

Concluding Reflections

The remarkable nature of the transformative results of the STS strategy warrant further exploration and development. For example, there seemed to be a strong interaction between the different steps and the use of discussion that make the method exponentially more effective than the sum of its parts. This included a strong, synergistic relationship between the memorization of the story and the Spiritual Observation questions that led to deep levels of internalization of the story. Part of the reason the use of discussion seems to have been effective was because the questions were well crafted for interpreting the genre of narrative. The expressions of the participants seem to confirm what scholars from the fields of cultural psychology, philosophy, evangelical theology and biblical studies assert about the power of common cultural narratives or worldviews.[27] They also seem to correlate with the assertions of researchers in narrative psychology about establishing narrative identity. The participants seem to have come to "coherent, positive resolutions" about different circumstances in life by reinterpreting their stories according to redemptive themes by harnessing the lens of the biblical stories as a model for self-understanding.

Going forward, these findings might provide insight for the ongoing development of oral strategies, not only for narrative, but other genres as well. What questions might best draw out the author's intent for the epistles or the prophecies? How might the STS method be used to not only proclaim the Gospel among unreached people groups, but serve as the primary educational model to establish and sustain church plants over time? On the other hand, the STS strategy might inform hermeneutical strategies in the West, such as providing a literary version of the outlines that are commonly used with interpretation of Scripture when approaching narratives. It also has implications for how to go about equipping the saints, such as training lay people to study Scripture on more profound levels or to serve as small group leaders in western and nonwestern contexts. Is there, as Tom Steffen might suggest, a significant role for a form of oral hermeneutics that would enrich the study of Scripture across cultures and roles in the Body of Christ.[28] The testimonies of the profoundly unifying power of the STS process and the manner in which it seems to bring significant levels of individual and communal transformation provides a

---

27. Carson, *Christ and Culture Revisited*, 120; Hammack, "Narrative and the Cultural Psychology of Identity," 222–23; Ricœur, *Time and Narrative*, 58; Wright, *New Testament*, 65, 122–25.

28. Steffen, *Worldview-Based Storying*; Steffen and Bjoraker, *Return of Oral Hermeneutics*.

compelling case for the adoption of the method among oral learners for whom the strategy was created as well as literate learners in the West who have lost their sense of storied truth and how to engage it in order to learn how to interpret and tell their own stories.

Bibliography

Adler, J. M. "Living into the Story: Agency and Coherence in a Longitudinal Study of Narrative Identity Development and Mental Health Over the Course of Psychotherapy." *Journal of Personality and Social Psychology* 102 (2012) 367–89.

Adler, John, et al. "Variation in Narrative Identity with Trajectories of Mental Health Over Several Years." *Journal of Personality and Social Psychology* 108 (2015) 476–96.

Bruner, Jerome. *Acts of Meaning*. Cambridge, MA: Harvard University, 1990.

Carson, D. A. *Christ and Culture Revisited*. Grand Rapids: Eerdmans, 2008.

Chiang, Samuel et al., eds. *Making Disciples of Oral Learners: Lausanne Occasional Paper (LOP) No. 54*. Lima, NY: International Orality Network, 2004.

Chiang, Samuel, and Grant Lovejoy. "The Extent of Orality: 2012 Update." *Orality Journal* 1 (2012) 11–39.

Frei, Hans. *The Eclipse of Biblical Narrative: A Study in Eighteenth and Nineteenth Century Hermeneutics*. New Haven, CT: Yale University, 1974.

Hammack, P. L. "Narrative and the Cultural Psychology of Identity." *Personality and Social Psychology Review* 12 (2008) 222–47.

Hayes, A. M., et al. "Avoidance and Processing as Predictors of Symptom Change and Positive Growth in an Integrative Therapy for Depression." *International Journal of Behavioral Medicine* 12 (2005) 111–22.

Jagerson, Jennifer. "Resonance and Synergy: The impact of Oral Bible Storytelling in Rural Ethiopia." *Global Missiology* 3 (2017) 1–19.

Koehler, Paul. *Telling God's Story with Power: Biblical Storytelling in Oral Cultures*. Pasadena, CA: William Carey Library, 2010.

King, Laura A., and Courtney Raspin. "Lost and Found Possible Selves, Subjective Well-being, and Ego Development in Divorced Women." *Journal of Personality* 73 (2004) 603–32.

Lodi-Smith, J., et al. "Narrating Personality Change." *Journal of Personality and Social Psychology* 96 (2009) 679–89.

Longman, Tremper, III. "Biblical Narrative." In *A Complete Literary Guide to the Bible*, edited by Leland Ryken and T. Longman III, 69–79. Grand Rapids: Zondervan, 1999.

Madigan, S. *Narrative Therapy*. Washington DC: American Psychological Association, 2011.

Maruna, S., et al. "Why God is Often Found Behind Bars: Prison Conversions and the Crisis of the Self-narrative." *Research in Human Development* 3 (2006) 161–84.

McAdams, Dan P. "The Psychology of Life Stories." *Review of General Psychology* 5 (2001) 100–22.

———. *The Redemptive Self: Stories Americans Live By*. New York: Oxford University, 2013.

McAdams, Dan P., et al. "When Bad Things Turn Good and Good Things Turn Bad: Sequences of Redemption and Contamination in Life Narrative in Midlife Adults and in Students." *Personality and Social Psychology Bulletin* 27 (2001) 474–85.

McLean, K.C., and M. A. Fournier. "The Content and Processes of Autobiographical Reasoning in Narrative Identity." *Journal of Research in Personality* 42 (2008) 527–45.

McLuhan, Mark. *The Gutenberg Galaxy: The Making of Typographic Man*. Toronto: University of Toronto, 1962.

Miller, Dorothy. *Simply the Story Handbook*. Hemet, CA: The God's Story Project, 2019. http://simplythestory.org/downloads/PDFs/STS_Handbook_v6c_2019-12-12.pdf.

Ong, Walter. *Orality and Literacy*. 3rd ed. New York: Routledge, 2012.

Osborne, Grant. *The Hermeneutical Spiral: A Comprehensive Introduction to Biblical Interpretation*. Downers Grove, IL: IVP Academic, 2006.

Pals, Jennifer L. "Narrative Identity Processing of Difficult Life Experiences: Pathways of Personality Development and Positive Self-Transformation in Adulthood." *Journal of Personality* 74 (2006) 1079–09.

Resseguie, James L. *Narrative Criticism of the New Testament: An Introduction*. Grand Rapids: Baker Academic, 2005.

Ricœur, Paul. *Time and Narrative* (Vol. 1). Translated by K. McLaughlin and D. Pellauer. Chicago: University of Chicago, 1990.

Ryken, Leland. "Introduction." In *A Complete Literary Guide to the Bible*, edited by Leland Ryken and Tremper Longman III, 15–39. Grand Rapids: Zondervan, 1993.

———. *Words of Delight: A Literary Introduction to the Bible*. Grand Rapids: Baker Academic, 1992.

Steffen, Tom. *Worldview-based Storying: The Integration of Symbol, Story, and Ritual in the Orality Movement*. Richmond, VA: The Rainmaker, 2018.

Steffen, Tom, and William Bjoraker. *The Return of Oral Hermeneutics: As Good Today as It Was for the Hebrew Bible and First-Century Christianity*. Eugene, OR: Wipf & Stock, 2020.

Sternberg, Meir. *The Poetics of Biblical Narrative: Ideological Literature and the Drama of Reading*. Bloomington, IN: Indiana University, 1987.

Sugiyama, M. S. "Narrative Theory and Function: Why Evolution Matters." *Philosophy and Literature* 25 (2001) 233–50.

Willis, Avery, and Snowden, Mark. *Truth that sticks*. Colorado Springs, CO: NavPress, 2010.

Wright, N. T. *The New Testament and the People of God*. Minneapolis: Fortress, 1992.

Part 3
Horizon: Bible Translation

8

What Can We Expect from Oral Bible Translation?

John E. Stark

Oral Bible Translation as Bible Translation

ORAL BIBLE TRANSLATION IS Bible translation done orally. That is both an accurate and an oversimplified statement, but it sets the stage for this discussion. The goal of Oral Bible Translation (OBT) is to develop Scripture that delivers the complete Bible content in a way that can be maximally processed by the oral preference delivery language[1] community. OBT, both as an identified process and as an element in global mission strategy, is an emerging concept. In this chapter I show the process of OBT, place OBT into the historical stream of Bible Translation and provide an overview of how it is currently being implemented. I go on to detail the OBT process as it is approached by Spoken Worldwide, then look at some of the issues concerning Scripture engagement raised by OBT. The chapter closes with a challenge to us all to push our operational processes more deeply into the oral learning capabilities of the communities we seek to serve.

The OBT Process Overview

There are many variations of process among OBT practitioners. This graphic presents a generalized overview of the materials, people, processes and the individual steps that are widely utilized (see Figure 8.1) in OBT.

---

1. By "delivery language" I mean exactly the same thing that is widely understood by the use of "target language," the language into which the translation is being made. I simply find "delivery language" a more friendly phrasing of the concept.

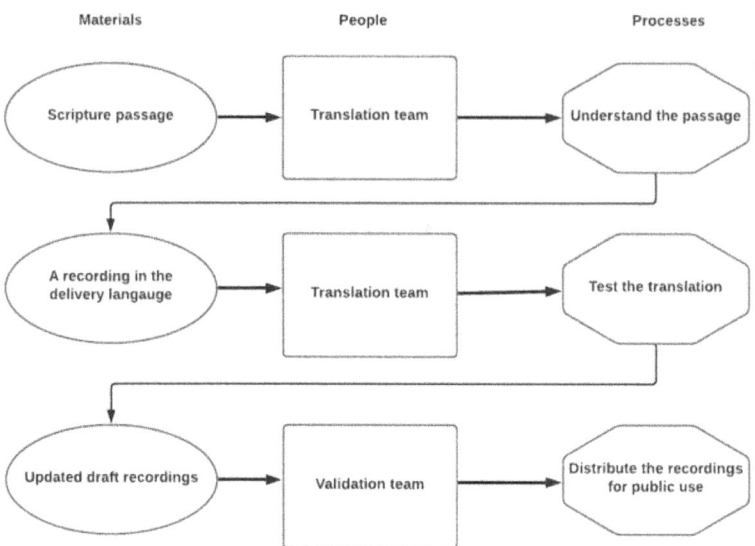

Figure 8.1 Key Elements of Oral Bible Translation

The Setting of Bible Translation

Bible translation can be traced as far back as the Septuagint, (Old Testament Hebrew into Greek) done in the third century BC, Jerome's Latin Vulgate in the fourth century AD, and a translation by Ulfilas into the language of the Goths in the early 400s AD.[2] While early translators such as Jerome and Ulfilas worked to make the content of Scripture available to the common person, with the growth of organized Christianity a belief developed that Scripture should be preserved in a "high" form of a few major languages, and that only those who were specially trained in reading and understanding the high language text could directly access the content of Scripture. Those with the special training would then "explain" what the Bible said to the bulk of the population.

This approach to using Scripture, i.e., access only by the specially trained, created an environment in which Scripture could exist in a single, stable form over centuries, while the natural process of human language formation and change created a population that would not be able to understand the written of the time Scripture even if given access to it. Their

2. See Gascoigne, "History of Bible Translations."

day-to-day speech gradually evolved into forms that were truly different languages than those of the ancient translations. In addition, Christianity expanded into areas where Hebrew, Greek and Latin, the languages of Christianity's geographic base, were unknown.

By the time of the Reformation, Martin Luther, John Wycliffe and others had revised the vision for widespread access to Scripture and once again there was a period in which the Bible in the language of the common person was widely available. Of course, at the time of the Reformation literacy was not widespread, and most people did not read Scripture for themselves. What changed was when their church leaders read Scripture in public; it was in a form that they understood without special explanations. This harks back to the time when Nehemiah once read the Scriptures to the people of Israel, "So the people went away to eat and drink at a festive meal, to share gifts of food, and to celebrate with great joy because they had heard God's words and understood them" (Neh 6:12 NLT).

Following the Reformation period, the stability of the written form of Scripture once again created a situation where common communication continued to change while the words of Scripture remained static and became an archaic representation of language. Christians in the modern era who share Jerome's view that 'ignorance of the scriptures'[3] is ignorance of Christ undertook many major language translations in the 19th and 20th centuries.

The modern acceleration of Bible Translation can be traced back to the work of Cameron Townsend and the founding of Wycliffe Bible Translators. Translators in this organization have been amazingly successful at producing written translations in a vast number of the world's languages.[4] This includes portions of Scripture if not a full Bible. It has only been in the past 10 years that the concept of Oral Bible translation has entered the global missiological discussion.

The Growth of Orality in Missions

Orality as a strategic element in cross-cultural missions has gained tremendous recognition and momentum since Chronological Bible Storying began to grow in the 1980s. The Jesus Film Project (JFP) and Faith Comes

---

3. Gascoigne, "History of Bible Translations," para. 18.

4. "Today there are over 1,500 translation projects currently in progress, with 518 language groups having the entire Bible and 1,275 having thee New Testament in the language they understand best." Wayback Machine, "Throwback Thursday: A Man with a Vision."

by Hearing (FCH) Bible recordings (as well as others) represent a step toward orality, but we are learning there is a unique element in how oral-preference communities exchange information. This requires the entire translation process from the first draft to final recording be focused on oral delivery. The JFP and FCBH recordings are both tied to original translation (film and text) that were created in a literate learning environment. Nonetheless, these processes have proven effective and have paved the way for a more deeply oral approach to Bible translation.

The author's first exposure to orality as a cultural pattern that should be incorporated in missions methodology came when I discovered Herbert Klem's *Oral Communication of the Scriptures*. I was part of a three-language cluster project in Nigeria (The Kambari Language Project [KLP]) at the time I discovered the book. It was clearly relevant as Klem wrote about the Yoruba people of Nigeria and his efforts to leverage an orality-based approach to communicate the Gospel. Encouraged by what I read, I led KLP to try oral drafting for passages of Scripture even though the end goal was a written text version of Scripture in each of the three languages.

By the late 1990s and the first decade of the 21st century, there was a professional organization focused totally on orality as a mission strategy—the International Orality Network (ION). Mission agencies focused on orality as well, operating on the level of Oral Bible Storying, StoryRunners and Spoken Worldwide being two examples.

The Orality movement grew using the Oral Bible Storying (OBS) philosophy, which I describe as close to, but not tied to, Scripture. OBS seeks to create audio material that is based on Bible content, faithful to the Bible message, and tailored to local spiritual needs. Many orality efforts pre-select a set of passages to serve as the source of the delivery language material. This set is often selected by missionaries with regional or local participation as to what they see as the most critical biblical content for a given language group. In other instances, the story set is pre-determined by the theological value set of the mission agency resulting in a single selection set used globally. A third approach (taken by Spoken Worldwide) is to work in conjunction with delivery language Christians and select individualized story sets that address locally determined needs. The OBS philosophy of "close to/based on Scripture" runs as a common thread through all of these content development approaches.

Mission strategists, seeing the value of orality, also began to see that a limited set of stories produced using OBS values was not providing the delivery language communities with access to the entire counsel of God, i.e., all of Scripture. Questions arose: Would it be possible to create an oral Scripture that was faithful to the full content of a passage of Scripture?

Could an Oral Bible Translation include everything in the passage yet add nothing to the passage?

This concern ran parallel to advances in technology that allowed developers to answer the question with "We think so." Over time the answer has become: "We definitely can create an Oral Bible Translation that includes everything in the passage yet adds nothing to the passage."

One of these technologies was the rise of cellular telephones and their increased power to include recording and sharing applications. These devices allow local people to utilize technology they already own and understand to create and share audio Scriptures.

Another technology advance was the creation of Oral Bible Translation software. This development grew from an idea proposed by Robin Green in her MA thesis at Dallas International University.[5] FCH undertook the development of the software (Render), and now offers training in using Render and basic translation techniques.

Other mission agencies have undertaken Oral Bible Translation at various levels and with a varied set of processes. The Seed Company, Youth With A Mission, Wycliffe and Spoken Worldwide come to mind. As I have been the Director of Oral Bible Translation for Spoken Worldwide for the past five years, that is where my most current experiences lay which form the basis for what follows.

OBT Adheres to the Historic Translation Values

Among all the agencies involved in Oral Bible Translation, the core values of translation are retained. Everything that is in a passage should be included, and nothing should be added. The nature of the translation should be clear, accurate and natural in the delivery language. These are common values embraced by all involved in both text-delivery translation and in oral translation. There is, as with all core value statements, a wide number of interpretations and implementations as people undertake real-world translation.

OBT: An Opportunity for Change

I felt the development of Oral Bible Translation as a discipline could serve as a platform for re-thinking the traditional process of translation while retaining the traditional values for the final product. To facilitate this re-thinking, I broke the translation process down into its simplest elements.

5. Green, *Orality Strategy*.

Anything less than this is no longer translation. Anything more is simply fleshing out the processes.

The Basic Elements of Translation

For an end product to be called translation it has to include moving information from a source language into a delivery language. For that to happen there are three key elements of translation:

1. The translators develop an appropriate understanding of the passage;
2. The translators express the content in natural delivery language words and forms; and
3. A series of processes are undertaken to ensure the passage accurately conveys the source message (see Figure 8.2).

Each basic element merits a fuller explanation. For the first element an appropriate understanding includes recognizing if the passage represents an historic, real-world event or fictional (but possible) event. Awareness of the characters (Pharisees, etc.), the setting, and other details are also necessary. The phrase "appropriate understanding" is a shorthand statement that represents the translation team's best efforts at understanding a passage the way the first group of people to hear it understood the passage. In text-driven translation this is traditionally achieved through biblical training and academic research by the translators. Oral translation projects vary in how this is done, but it must be done.

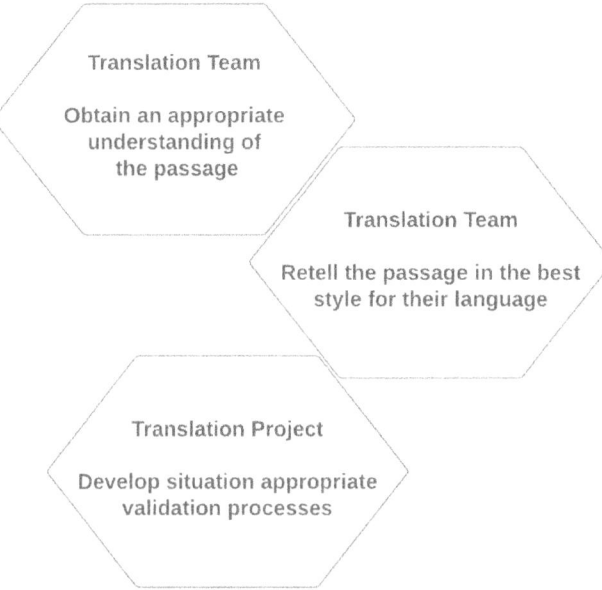

Figure 8.2. The Basic Elements of Translation

Much of what is needed for an appropriate understanding is available to Oral Translation teams simply by listening to respected versions of Scripture that exist in a lingua franca they are competent in. If multiple translations in the lingua franca are available, listening to the various translations of the selected passage expands the translation team's understanding.

I have been part of oral translations in which no lingua franca version existed to serve this role. In one instance, a single individual was bilingual enough to create a front translation for the oral translation team to use as a primary source. I have also been part of oral translations in which delivery language speakers have extensive theological education and are highly fluent in English. The variances between these two projects, the first in Botswana, the second in a major Middle Eastern language, illustrates the need to find individualized ways to reach the common core goal of an appropriate understanding of the passage.

As for the second element—express the content naturally in the delivery language—my experience in Nigeria with text-based translation along with my exposure to other text-based translation projects, the presence of published lingua franca Scripture remained a powerful force in shaping the final phrasing of the translation. In short, people expected the content of the delivery language Scripture to align verse by verse (as much as possible) to the lingua franca Scripture. The translation team, seeking to create a delivery language version of Scripture that would be accepted and used by their community, would by necessity, conform to this expectation and largely translate verse by verse. This can create awkward phrasing and a delivery language Scripture that is difficult for the local community to understand. As one man told me, "God speaks our language, but he does not speak it well." In cultures and communities that hold an expectation that holy, spiritual information should be reserved for specialists and not accessible by the common people, Scripture that is difficult or even impossible for most people to understand is seen as being appropriate. This, however, runs contrary to the values that drive most involved in translation work.

When the goal of translation is to make the entire counsel of God available to every person, the translation should be done in a way that is so natural in the delivery language that the community members are responding only to the content, *not* the presentation method. Oral Bible Translation allows translation teams to reshape the presentation of the biblical content into delivery language forms to a much greater extent than does test-based translation.[6] Here again, the two example projects mentioned earlier represent variations in how this value is achieved.

In Botswana there was very little awareness of Scripture and once the translation team had an appropriate understanding, they would automatically retell that content in their natural forms. In the Middle Eastern project, the translation team has a high level of biblical awareness and exposure to Scripture in multiple major languages. The need for naturalness in this instance required helping the translation team recognize full passage translation as a legitimate method of translating Scripture.

In text-based translation, there is a widely accepted sequence of exegesis, drafting, community testing and consultant review. The consultant review, usually accomplished through written back-translation of the delivery language text, occurs after the translation team has done their best effort at appropriate translation.

Oral Bible Translation is an emerging process and multiple approaches exist between various agencies to ensure passage accuracy. Many projects look to consultant input early in the drafting process to allow the initial recordings to be as close as possible to the final product. At Spoken, our

---

6. In text-based translation, some teams have utilized "verse blocks" in place of "verse-by-verse" translation to allow the translation to achieve greater naturalness at the discourse level of translation. That is a work-around that addresses, to a limited extent, the challenge of variations in presentation of information between the source and delivery language.

consultants operate as mentor/trainers, working with the translation teams to develop testing and quality control processes that maximize delivery language community participation and also ensure the final result is a quality translation. In Botswana, this included both oral and written back-translation that was reviewed by a consultant. In the Middle Eastern project, respected Christian leaders from the delivery language community formed a review committee that processed each passage.

Training in OBT

To provide a greater understanding of the Oral Bible Translation process, a typical Spoken training process follows. While these elements are in common with others doing Oral Bible Translation, each organization will package the overall process differently. These similarities and differences from organization to organization will not be isolated and itemized here.

A high value in Spoken is to train in a way that models the potential of the oral learners. We do not prepare outlines and lectures, but rather engage in a series of intentional conversations and practical exercises. Our training becomes a group of friends sharing experiences with the leader functioning to set discussion direction and keep input from the group relevant to the session purpose.

The first step in an OBT training session is to help those present become comfortable processing entire passages as a single translation unit. In order to start from known and comfortable content, I ask the participants to tell us stories. Depending on the people in the room, we may start with folktales from their own backgrounds. If I feel the group needs an example to get them started, I often tell the African explanation of how the tortoise got the design of cracks in his shell. It normally takes very little time to transfer the expectations of the participants from sitting in a lecture to taking part in the discussion.[7]

As the discussion progresses, there comes a point when it is appropriate to introduce the idea of translation by asking one person to retell another person's story. We can then discuss the retelling. Was everything from the original story included in the re-telling? What was the same? What was different? Was anything added in? At this point we are learning the translation value of faithfully replicating content as well as some of the key

---

7. During an OBT training session in Togo, one of the participants mentioned that he did not like my teaching. He could not find Point A, Point B and Point C to write in his notebook. Another participant asked him if he had learned anything. The reply: "Yes, I have learned a lot, but this is not proper teaching."

tools involved in community testing and reviewing material for appropriate presentation of the content.

The next step involves telling real events. We repeat the process of telling each other stories, this time focusing on things that have actually happened to us or that we know about. After some time, we move into retelling each other's story. Again, we return to: How did they do? We talk about the difference between real events and those that could have been real but were made up, and those that are in the realm folktales where animals behave like people. The goal is to think about the nature of the source, and how that affects the translation process for each story.

As the discussion moves to retelling, and doing that well, I began to ask questions like: Who are the people (characters) involved? Where do the events take place? What happened? How did the people feel?

The team discusses the difference between emotions that are explicitly expressed in the original story, and those that are implied in the original telling, and those that are supplied by the listener in order for the story to make sense. For narrative passages, the quality paradigm becomes: People, Places, Events, Emotions.

As our training discussion moves through the quality checking paradigm of People, Places, Events, Emotions, we begin to talk about variations between the original and the retelling, asking how those variations affect the listening experience. Do they change the content? Does that make the story easier (or harder) to understand? Does one form of the story make it easier for others to retell it well? The learning point here centers on the priority of faithfulness to content over retaining the narrative shape of the source.

Each of these discussion cycles touches to some degree on the primary elements of translation. We are

1. developing skills in gaining an appropriate understanding of the source,
2. learning to prioritize natural delivery language patterns over source language patterns while retaining content faithfulness, and
3. experimenting with quality control processes.

Because each learning session is a genuine discussion, each one is unique. I do try to have in my head some starter illustrations that help participants capture a concept and practice it within small "retelling groups" of participants. In all my training experiences there have been very few mother tongue English speakers, and even those have had a strong functionality in a second language. This reality allows the retelling groups to experience actual translation and see how the concepts under discussion play out. One of my favorite starters for the concept of content prioritized over source shape is an Irish limerick I made up for a session in New Mexico. It goes like this:

> The God of heaven is great.
>
> His blessings are neither early not late.
>
> He spends all his time
>
> With my best on his mind.
>
> All I have to do is wait.

Using this as a jumping off point, I ask the participants to form groups and translate this retaining both the shape and the conceptual content. This objective has never been achieved, and I suspect it is impossible to retain both shape and content. I do not let the participants keep trying to the point of frustration, but once it is apparent, they have realized the difficulty involved, we back out of the exercise and talk about how all languages have phrasing patterns that help the speakers quickly retain information. We talk about what that phrasing looks like in their languages, and everyone is quick to provide examples. The next step is to take the content of the limerick and express it in the natural phrasing patterns of their own languages.

Once participants have their own content-accurate translation of the limerick, they share those and provide the room with a back-translation, using English words within their own language phrase structures. Once again, we have practiced appropriate understanding, natural phrasing, and content verification, this time introducing the translation tool of Back-Translation.

By now the group is usually ready to try Scripture translation. Especially in the translation training phase, seeking passages that allow for early, easy wins in the translation process is important. The idea here is to select passages that are basic narrative, told in a straightforward chronological pattern with location features and characters that are as common as possible to those found in the delivery language community. For instance, Noah's flood would not be a good first story for Kalahari Desert groups since ankle-deep water is all they know in their daily existence. Stories about shepherds would be very common.

Early passage selection seeks to avoid many of the theological terms and special characters of Scripture. The parable of the Good Samaritan is harder than that of the Prodigal Son. The Good Samaritan[8] introduces the law of Moses, Jerusalem, Jericho, priest, Levite, Samaritan, all elements of Scripture that need to be understood in their original audience context to allow the translation team to gain an appropriate understanding. The

---

8. Luke 10:25–37.

Prodigal Son[9] deals with family disharmony, patron-client, honor and shame, restoration and lack of restoration. Other than some cultural details about how early inheritance is handled, the passage consists of events entirely plausible in my acquaintances of cultures.

This approach to Oral Bible Translation training allows the content of the discussion to bring up specific learning opportunities. It models a "learn while doing" approach that can be carried out of the training session and replicated locally by the training participants. One example is an event from a training I led in Togo.

The Togo group chose Jesus' first miracle[10] as one of their early translation passages. After all, weddings are common events nor are there theological terms or special historical characters. Then the question came up as to the nature of the miraculous wine. Was it actually alcoholic? That led to a discussion of how to solve questions by looking first at the passage itself. In the context of a wedding, guests would expect wine to have an alcohol content. When the master of ceremonies declared it the best wine, he would not likely have done so if it were only fresh grape juice, and other such internal clues. Some of the older pastors in the group refused to believe the wine had alcoholic content. After all, Jesus made it and Jesus would not produce anything alcoholic.

Others in the room took the position that as an historic event, it must be faithfully translated, and that the passage itself only makes sense if the wine is alcoholic wine. I have to admit that as the discussion facilitator I lost control of the room at that point. It simply seemed wisest to let the group proceed through their own disagreement and resolution process. At the end of the allotted time, I restated the translation principles of faithfulness to historic reality, utilizing context to resolve questions, and seeking a "what did the original audience understand" answer. Then I declared the discussion (and that learning session) closed for the day.

After the period of initial training is over, project specific questions follow: How will we ensure the translators have an appropriate understanding of the passage? How will we endeavor to prioritize delivery language naturalness while maintaining content faithfulness? How will we establish specific validation processes that work in this specific community? The questions are answered through dialog with local Christians and Spoken consultant trainers.

In summary, the Oral Bible translation process has four key process features that are common across all the projects I am aware of:

9. Luke 15:11–22.
10. John 2:1–11.

internalization, multiple oral drafts, community testing, and validation processes. Internalization is the process of enabling the translation team to gain an appropriate understanding of the source passage and re-express that content in natural delivery language forms.

Multiple oral drafts are developed and recorded as the passage moves through each of the validation cycles. In a validation cycle, each passage is recorded and reviewed within the translation team or in public testing. The "best" recording at the end of that cycle becomes the material which is used the next validation cycle.

Community testing typically refers to the validation cycles that expose the current best draft to a specific audience comprised of people who were not part of producing the translation draft. Questions are asked that enable the translation team to evaluate and update that draft for the next validation cycle. Two classes of questions are often used. The first class of questions (called translation questions or content questions) focus on the content of the translation and seeks answers that are directly from the passage. Some examples are: Who was involved? Or more generally: How many people were mentioned? Where were the people when these things happened? Where was the man going when he left Jerusalem?

The second class of questions (called understanding questions or response to passage questions) ask for replies that are not directly content from the passage but represent how the testing group is processing what they are hearing. Some examples include: Do you know of similar events that have happened in your community? Is there a person in the story that you identify with? Which person/people behaved badly/who behaved properly? Why? When asking targeted questions seeking a response to the passage, the translation team is looking for responses that fall within the generally understood message of Scripture, not a specific doctrine or teaching commonly associated with that passage.[11]

The final process stage is that of moving the passage through a locally determined final evaluation and validation process to establish if the work is acceptable for teaching and Christian training.[12]

---

11. When asked about the story of Jesus sending demons into a herd of pigs (Matt. 8:32), a group in Indonesia explained it had to be a miracle because "The pigs all drown. We know pigs are really good swimmers."

12. For a helpful resource, see Wendland, *Orality and the Scriptures*.

How Scripture in OBT is Used by Oral Communities

One of the challenges the developing Oral Bible Translation team faces is understanding how oral-preference societies will make use of Oral Bible passages. The question here is not about the purposes for which Oral Bible material will be used.

No doubt Oral Bibles will be used for evangelism, individual and group discipleship, and personal reflection on God's message to mankind. These are the same purposes text-based Scripture fills in our world. However, I don't think oral societies will be conducting a lot of word studies or building systematic theologies defined and defended by a package of selected verses. At least, I have not seen any indication of these methods of Scripture interaction during my years of working with oral communities.

What I have seen oral communities do is process passages as an entire passage and do so in a group setting. Gathering in a home or a community location and talking about the events of the day and the happenings in each other's lives is not only common; it may be the defining activity of oral communities. From what I have seen, this is also the way they primarily process oral Scripture: "Let's listen to a passage (from a player or a phone or even a human storyteller) and talk about what we hear."

During our work in Botswana a training participant asked if he could take the day's passage and tell it to his sister living a few miles outside of our training site. We arranged for transportation, and he told his family the translation passage of the day—The Prodigal Son.

During the story telling, the mother of the house, her children, and extended family were packed into a small block and mud room. The rustling sounds indicating lack of attention began to die down. By the end, the room enclosed a silence that seemed tangible to the touch. After a few moments, the mother spoke. "This is our story."

She went on to explain that her oldest son had sold the family's farm plot without any discussion or permission. As a result, they had no place to graze their few cows and had to sell them. There was very little opportunity to generate the funds the family needed for day-to-day life. In the meantime, they were aware of the way the son had gone off to a bigger city and was leading a life similar to that of the younger son in the story. Then she looked across the room and said, "When he comes home, what are we going to do? Will we welcome him as the father did, or will we behave like the older son and seek to repel him from us?"

I also know that oral learners carry the passages with them in their thoughts, rejoicing, reflecting, and applying what they draw from the Scriptures. For example, one villager said, "I have to walk six miles to catch transportation to town, six miles through a region where elephant herds roam free. Elephant herds are dangerous, but I think of my Bible passages and know God will protect me."

These two illustrations represent many such stories heard from Oral Bible translators and the people they serve. The Bible interaction processes we have developed in our Western Christianity serve us well but are unlikely to be the processes that ignite widespread Bible interaction among oral-preference communities. Learning more about the oral processes of Scripture engagement will enable Oral Bible translators to more effectively shape their translations for naturalness and ease of use within the delivery language community.

A second role for Oral Bible translations is to serve as a transcribable source to start the process of text-delivery translation when local communities develop churches and seek to engage in Christian practices that are common around the world. A third role for Oral Bible translations is to fill the primary source function in other Oral Bible Translation projects within the same linguistic and/or geographic grouping. The concept of using a major language Oral Bible translation as a source "text" places OBT into the conversation of the "Gateway languages" mission strategy discussion. Well-constructed Oral Bible translations in majority/lingua franca languages have the potential to provide other OBT projects with a deeper, appropriate understanding of Scripture.

How Oral Can We Go? Incarnational Mentoring

As far as I know, every active Oral Bible Translation project has a literate element active within it. That is to be expected since the starting point, the source, is a written document, and all the "appropriate understanding" materials exist in written form. However, over the years oral- preference learners have consistently exceeded my expectations of what they can do and do well. I have begun to ask myself, "How oral can we go with Oral Bible Translation?" I think the answer lies in Christ's incarnation.

The Incarnation

For Christians, the incarnation is the world changing truth of Christ stepping into humanness. Fully God and fully human, Jesus became like us to allow us to become like Him.

For years incarnational ministry was, and still is, a much-discussed topic in missions. How do we, who know Jesus, become more like those who don't know Jesus for the purpose of helping them become like him? Since my mission experience has been in the area of Bible translation, I have been thinking about what incarnation in Bible Translation would look like.

In all my years of Bible Translation, translation was a processing of going to the area where a language group lives, then asking them to learn to read and write in order to participate in the process of Bible Translation. Another way to say this is that we were crossing the incarnational barrier of language and asking the people we were among to cross the incarnational barrier of learning style.[13] In short, we have been doing partial incarnation while asking the groups we work to do the other half of the incarnation process (see Figure 8.3). This has created a situation where the total burden of incarnation has been distributed between the two groups and a "meet in the middle" pattern has developed.

What would it look like if we, the ones bringing a new message, took on more of the burden of incarnation and sought to cross both the language barrier and the learning style barrier (see Figure 8.4)? What are the key differences between a literate approach to teaching/learning and an oral approach to teaching/learning? I came up with three key differences:

1. the source of new information,
2. the delivery method of information, and
3. the distance from moment of learning to moment of using a new concept or piece of information.

Could I as a trainer, can we as a community of mission workers, learn to make a person the primary information source as opposed to the archived text source of books and internet we depend on? Can we move from "Go read this" to "Let's talk about this"? And can we make the doing of something simultaneous with the learning of that topic? In short, can we be more orally incarnational in our processes of helping others translate the Bible?

---

13. I am aware of, and believe in, the value of the societal benefits of literacy, both mother-tongue and national language literacy. I fully support missions that choose to invest in delivering this benefit. Having spent 30 years in literacy/translation work I do not regret any of it.

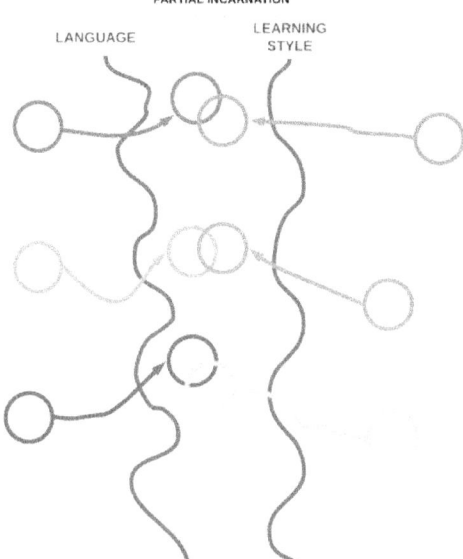

Figure 8.3 Partial Incarnation

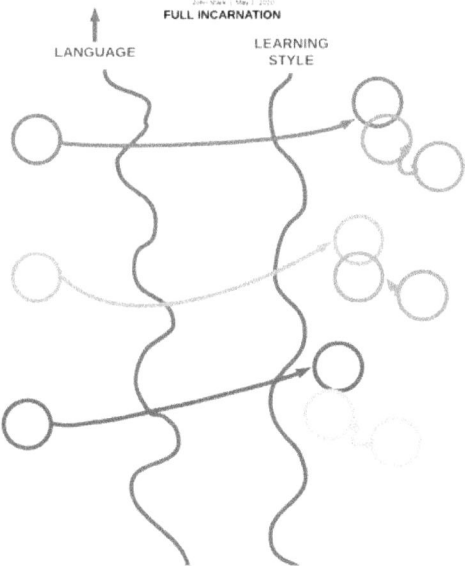

Figure 8.4 Full Incarnation

Following is one example where oral learners exceeded my expectations of what they could learn and do. Since there is a degree of reading skill in most communities due to globalization and development, a portion of the communities where I have worked could read. In Nigeria the Kambari Language Project had recently completed a small-scale printing of the translated Gospel of Luke. In a tiny rural church, a 19-year-old stood up in an evening service to "say my memory verses." He had received a copy of Luke two weeks earlier. He started into his recitation at Luke 1:1. At the end of chapter 7 the pastor intervened and asked the young man for permission to continue the other aspects of the evening service. That he could read was a result of globalization. That he could memorize on a scale that was beyond me was a result of his oral background.

In Spoken Worldwide, we have used the oral learning skills of communities to implement Pastor Development programs that create and utilize 300 Bible-based stories for locally relevant missions work. Can that same learning power transfer into Oral Bible Translation? I believe it can.

In oral learning a person or people serve as the source of new information. The delivery of new information occurs in conversations, and those conversations happen at the time that a given piece of information is needed in a real-world activity. To train oral learners in translation, the information source has to be someone who is available, who can talk them through what they are undertaking, and can recognize the learning points that are needed at the moment of doing the work. This real-time, situation-focused immediacy cannot be delivered via pre-prepared content.[14] Building translation capacity in oral communities becomes a process of intensive and extended interaction, interaction that the literate world labels mentoring.

The primary role of a translation consultant has been, traditionally, to review the translated passage and ensure it conveys the same message the source translation conveyed to the original audience. Moving the consultant interaction forward in the process allows the translation challenges to be resolved early in the drafting stage. The quality insurance steps become an integral part of the translation. The early drafts can be created with the functional goal of the consultant already accounted for in the overall translation process, ensuring the translated passage conveys the same content as the original.

Qualified consultants (or developing consultants in mentorship) should be holding intentional and frequent conversations with a few key individuals of the translation team. Those conversations should be centered on

---

14. While pre-recorded video may bypass the requirement of being able to read, it still falls far from the immediacy of live interaction at the moment of doing a given process.

covering the translation issues in the upcoming translation passages. These individuals in turn carry the conversations to the translation team. Often called translation advisors, (TAs), these people have built-in potential to become translation consultants. Spoken sees these as developing consultant/trainers who not only work with their own projects, but as they gain experience, also move into working with nearby languages. As they begin to divide their time between projects, someone in the original group will need to step into a learn-by-doing role that is opening up in the first project.

Within a few years, geometric growth should produce a large number of people capable of leading translation projects that produce high quality Scripture content. Those who commit to the process of developing themselves as consultant/trainers also commit to training others. The model made famous by Frank Laubach, "Each one teach one"[15] becomes each one teach two (or more).

In summary, the goal is a highly accurate expression of Scripture in the intended delivery language. To ensure that, a qualified consultant works closely with one (or more) individuals in a translation process to that ensures both naturalness and content quality in the translation. In the process, the participants begin to replicate themselves in the first project, and also begin work in a second project, always training others into the same roles.

This process is highly aligned with the natural learning of oral communities. The source of information is a known and trusted individual. The process of information transfer is conversational, and the moment of interaction with the information is at the time it is needed. When a person learns in the way that is natural to their community, that person is confident they can in turn transfer the learning to others.

Given the linguistic situation of today's world, multilingualism, mass media, global languages and widespread literacy efforts, there are very few purely oral situations. Given the complexity of our human nature, very few of us are purely literate. Our realities become more of a fuel gauge model with individuals and societies falling somewhere on a graduated scale between the two extremes, sharing to some extent features of both literate and oral skill sets (see Figure 8.5).

---

15. See Laubach, *How to Teach One and Win One for Christ*.

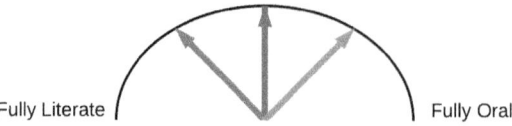

Figure 8.5. Literate vs. Oral Fuel Gauge

The challenge before those of us who are starting from a highly literate launching point will be to avoid the more comfortable and easier-for-us approach of pulling the delivery language community into our world and ways. We need to take on the higher-effort, less comfortable path of both becoming as oral as possible and providing our oral-preference colleagues an operational environment that validates the skills and processes of their side of the literate-oral continuum. I trust many of us will make a sincere effort to do just that.

Bibliography

Gascoigne, Bamber. "History of Bible Translation." HistoryWorld, 2001, http://www.historyworld.net/wrldhis/PlainTextHistories.asp?historyid=ac66.

Green, Robin. *An Orality Strategy: Translating the Bible for Oral Communicators*. MA thesis, Dallas International University, 2007.

Klem, Herbert V. *Oral Communication of the Scripture: Insights from African Oral Art*. Pasadena: Wm. Carey Library, 1982.

Laubach, Frank C. *How to Teach One and Win One for Christ: Christ's Plan for Winning the World: Each One Teach and Win One*. Grand Rapids: Zondervan, 1965.

Stark, John E. "Oral Drafting: A Technique for Naturalness in Translation." Paper presented at Bible Translation 2001, Dallas, Texas, October 18–20, 2001.

Steffen, Tom, and William Bjoraker. *The Return of Oral Hermeneutics*. Eugene, OR: Wipf & Stock, 2020.

Wayback Machine. "Throwback Thursday: A Man with a Vision." January 23, 2015. https://web.archive.org/web/20150123172201/https://www.wycliffe.org/stories/details/throwback-thursday-a-man-with-a-vision.

Wendland, Ernst R. *Orality and the Scriptures: Composition, Translation, and Transmission*. Dallas: SIL International, 2013.

9
Are We Telling Faithful Stories?
The Need for Evaluating Bible Stories

Don Barger

EVERY GOOD MISSIONARY STRIVES to communicate the gospel clearly to those who hear the message. To that end, many missionaries spend years learning one or more languages to enable them to clearly communicate gospel fluency in the heart language of those who are to hear the message. Missionaries go to great lengths in order to speak in the heart language, but are these enough? Even after such efforts to learn the language, sometimes, the message is still not clearly communicated. Appropriate communication involves not only using the right words, but it also requires clarity in delivery. The message is most clearly communicated to oral preference learners utilizing oral methods.

In the broad field of missiology, Chronological Bible Storying is a relatively young discipline. Using narrative to communicate with primary and oral preference learners is a model older than the Bible. Stories have been used to communicate the truth for centuries. Jesus used oral models when He told narratives and parables to His First-Century Palestine audience because this is how many people learned.

The challenge of communicating in the vernacular is not merely choosing the right language but also the appropriate communication style. Effective communication requires the utilization of models designed to limit misunderstanding and syncretism. Communicating in the right language is only part of the solution. Utilizing the correct learning style (oral versus literate) is also critical for missionaries. The purpose of this chapter is not to convince readers of the efficacy of using Bible stories, but instead, it is to present the challenge of crafting and telling good Bible stories. How can stories be evaluated to ensure they are told accurately and without embellishment. How can Bible stories be assessed for faithfulness? What tools are used to evaluate Bible stories? Can existing testing and checking methods in textual-based Bible translations be incorporated into an evaluative system for crafted Bible stories?

In many cases, Bible storying models lack the rigorous checking, testing, and consultation required by textual Bible translation. Currently, there are no agreed upon best practices for checking stories among mission agencies. This chapter will explore and describe the factors involved in the testing, checking, and consultant checking Bible translations and propose a model for checking Bible stories and story sets based upon the best practices of written Bible Translation consultation.

Written Bible translations are tested for clarity, accuracy, and naturalness. With careful tweaking to the testing process used in Bible translation, these same areas may be utilized to evaluate Bible stories. A few questions to consider for the evaluation of Bible stories may include:

- What should be tested in Bible stories?
- How should Bible stories be tested?
- Who is the right person (or people) to test Bible stories?
- What is the role of Bible story consultants?
- What are the core standards for assessing Bible stories that can be agreed to by individuals and agencies involved in Bible storying?

Bible storying is not a panacea to answer all problems related to clear evangelistic presentations, discipleship for new believers, training for leaders, or planting new churches. Bible Storying does open many doors for clear communication with oral preference learners and provides opportunities for ministry involvement previously closed due to preferred or necessary learning styles. While storying solves many problems missionaries face for clearly communicating with oral preference learners, these advancements will be of limited value if the stories are not told accurately and understood by the intended audience.

With all the benefits of storying, care must be taken that stories are not developed haphazardly. If stories are not carefully crafted and naturally told, they may create more problems than they solve. Poorly crafted stories may unintentionally introduce extra-biblical material to stories, leave out crucial portions of the story, miscommunicate fundamental biblical principles leading to syncretism, or not be understood in the receptor language due to poor story structure and word choice. The most compelling stories are told naturally, birthed from within the culture, clearly communicate to the receptor culture, and retold by those who hear the stories.

The Problem

A critical missing piece from many Bible storying projects is testing and assessment. Katharine Barnwell teaches that good translations should be accurate, clear, and natural.[1] These same criteria apply to Bible stories. Evaluation can help local partners determine what is acceptable in their Bible storytelling.[2] While story crafters should test their own Bible stories, they may also benefit from an objective evaluation of stories by utilizing an outsider as a part of the story assessment.[3]

Significant training efforts are available for basic Chronological Bible Storying techniques, but advanced storying practitioner and consultant training are also required. Many missionaries receive training on oral models and immediately begin to create stories for the people group. Instead of working with mother-tongue speakers to create a set of stories explicitly designed for the worldview of their people group, eager missionaries sometimes look for the quick answer and simply translate the sample stories they received in training. According to missionary strategist David Olson, less than ideal models are the current reality for most cross-cultural Bible storying occurring today.[4] In Olson's opinion, many people are using stories with little or no testing. Less than ideal models range from creating the stories themselves to translating stories from a language of wider communication. These non-worldview specific stories often lack the naturalness needed for replication throughout the receptor people group. Contextualized stories communicate better than generic stories. Without testing and evaluation, missionaries may falsely assume their stories are communicating.

A need exists to develop teams able to provide training for self-checking and consultation for story set development and checking of story sets. In recent years, positive shifts in storying methodology have led some to a movement away from missionaries crafting stories in English and translating them into other languages. Many new efforts now focus on training and coaching mother-tongue speakers of languages to craft stories. This shift has improved the naturalness of the telling and repeatability by those hearing stories. Even still, more training is needed to ascertain scriptural fidelity and to encourage the widespread practice of the emphasis on mother-tongue story crafters along with the development of checking processes and story consultation.

1. Barnwell, *Bible Translation*, 24.
2. Janet Stahl, personal communication with author, January 23, 2020.
3. Tuggy, "Test My Own Translation?," 14.
4. David Olson, personal communication with author, January 23, 2020.

Textual-based translation projects undergo a thorough checking and consultation process to produce accurate translations. Katharine Barnwell wrote, "The aim of translation is to communicate a message, to communicate that message in the natural language of the people in a way which everyone can understand."[5] If the Bible story aims to communicate a natural message into the vernacular to the intended audience, these translations must be tested to ensure this goal is accomplished. Bible storying projects share the same aim of natural communication of the story. Many of the same models used for testing written translations may be modified and used for Bible stories.

Solutions Found Within Existing Models

When looking for models for consulting and checking oral Bible storying projects, it is beneficial to understand how textual Bible translations are tested and consulted. What models are used to ensure that Bible translations are correct in form and not heretical? It is possible to technically translate correctly but to miss the meaning entirely. Agreed upon translation standards are beneficial to obtain good translations. Most organizations involved in written Bible translation are members of the Forum of Bible Agencies International (FOBAI) and have agreed to a set of standards for Bible translation.[6]

A significant contribution of FOBAI is mutually agreed upon basic Bible translation procedures and principles. Established procedures and guidelines ensure that each member organization uses similar models and terminology and greatly facilitates cross-agency cooperation. While this level of cooperation exists for written Bible translations, no such cooperation or agreement exists for those entities and individuals involved in Bible storytelling. Without this high-level cooperation, there is not widespread agreement on methodology or even terminology. This lack of cooperation creates confusion and makes consultation of stories difficult. The establishment of agreed upon testing and consultation models should be a priority for Bible storying agencies.

Instead of developing an entire system for checking Bible stories from scratch, a better model is to evaluate consultation models and tools utilized for textual based translations and adapt them for oral projects. Many of these models and tools transfer very well for evaluating storying projects. Scholarly

---

5. Barnwell, "Testing the Translation," 425.

6. For a list of organizations belonging to FOBAI, visit http://forum-intl.org/membership/members.

research on Bible translation consultation, based upon many years of praxis, is widely available. Articles from *Notes on Translation* and *The Bible Translator* and many books on the subject have provided translators with helps and best practices for over half a century. Bible storying practitioners have much to learn from this scholarship and experience.

Bible storying is simply the oral rendering of the biblical text in a narrative format. Many Bible storying practitioners call this process of moving (or jumping) a story from the written text to a narrative as "crafting stories." As previously mentioned, most textual Bible translators follow agreed-upon models of translation principles and techniques. While not universally accepted, various models have similarly been developed by those involved in Bible story crafting. The Orality Movement continues to learn from those engaged in traditional textual translation, particularly concerning tools for checking accuracy and intelligibility.

Before proposing a path towards developing best practices for testing crafted story sets, it is beneficial to examine a few less than best, but unfortunately, widespread practices. Often stories do not birth from within the people group. They are frequently chosen, crafted (or translated) by someone outside of the group, and even predominantly told by outsiders. These errors occur for a variety of reasons. First, the outside team may be beginning the work, and creating stories with mother-tongue speakers may not be possible. If there are no local partners to help select and craft stories, the outsider stories are sometimes the only option. Second, occasionally missionaries choose to craft the stories themselves out of convenience. The missionaries speak the language, and they believe it is faster just to craft the stories themselves. Third, it is not uncommon for missionaries getting started in Bible storying to simply use proven stories from an established set of stories used in a bridge language and translate them into the receptor language. There are probably many other reasons for not using people from the people group to craft stories, but these are the most commonly observed by the author.

While these less than best practices usually result in obtaining stories quicker, it is debatable as to these stories' long-term usefulness. Each of these shortcuts bypasses a critical step in creating clear, accurate, and natural stories. The lack of empowering mother-tongue story crafters is not present. Stories are not developed from within the receptor group. For some missionaries, crafting stories is seen as the end goal. The development of a set of stories quickly usually comes with the cost of not crafting clearly and accurately, which may be retold naturally throughout the people group. For some, faithful stories are not a vital part of a comprehensive scripture resource and church planting strategy. Viewing the development of mother-tongue story crafters who craft and tell worldview-specific stories is a better approach to developing a comprehensive plan.

When shortcuts such as those previously mentioned are utilized, a Bible storying paternalism often develops. New stories come from the outside missionary team and do not originate from within the culture. A reproducible model of storying focusing upon the development of national story crafters must emerge. This emphasis does not signify that there is no role for expatriate missionaries in Bible storying. On the contrary, there is a significant role to be fulfilled by outsiders.

In many cases, the Western missionary's role is better served as that of a trainer, coach, encourager, and story consultant. These roles may also be filled from within the culture, but most projects will initially require an outsider to fill these responsibilities. This new "facilitator" role requires a different type of preparation and training. A new missionary ethos focusing on empowering mother-tongue crafting will result in better stories. New training models should be developed to facilitate foreign missionaries' ability to understand the importance of empowering partners and local churches as they craft worldview-specific stories.

External assessment and consultation may help a story crafting team determine if the stories are clear, accurate, and natural. These three assessment areas used to determine whether a textual translation is a good translation are also useful when evaluating Bible stories. In addition to these three areas of assessment, a fourth area to be evaluated for Bible stories is retellability. Are Bible stories able to be retold by the intended audience? Even if crafted clearly, accurately, and naturally, stories are not useful if they cannot be retold.

While stories are not a translation from one language to another, crafting stories falls within the realm of jumping the truths of a story from one language into the vernacular of another in a narrative format. Borrowing from written translation models, one solution to be considered for Bible storyers is interagency cooperation, like what FOBAI provides for organizations involved in written translation. Best practices may be shared among different agencies allowing for cross-agency consultation of Bible stories. Testing and consulting stories should involve the four areas of:

1. Is the story clear?
2. Is the story accurate?
3. Is the story natural?
4. Is the story retellable?

Additionally, a review of Barnwell's ten ways to test a translation would also prove beneficial to anyone interested in testing Bible stories.[7]

Challenges of Testing and Consulting Stories

All story crafting teams should desire testing and consultation of stories. It is imperative that stories be crafted and told in such a way as to convey the biblical message faithfully. Testing helps ensure that stories are faithful to Scripture. Unfortunately, many teams do not include testing or consulting stories as part of their workflow of creating stories. Some teams believe it possible to speed up the development of stories by skipping testing and consultation. This shortcut may speed up the process, but it usually results in inferior stories. It is worth the extra time at the beginning of the crafting process to prepare good stories.

While most teams strive for clear, accurate, natural, and retellable stories, they do not recognize the added value of testing and consulting. These teams assume that they have crafted good stories, but they do not complete the steps to confirm. A clear understanding and rationale for testing should be established early in storying projects. Lack of testing is another argument for widespread, inter-agency collaboration on the development of storying best practices. Without an agreed-upon standard of best practices for Bible story crafting, it is difficult to establish a plumb line to consult stories. A simple set of agreed-upon standards is needed among storying practitioners and mission agencies.

Another challenge for implementing a strategy of consulting and testing Bible stories is the lack of trained consultants. A backlog of story sets awaiting consultation exists due to the lack of qualified consultants. Teams grow weary of waiting for consultants and move forward using their stories without consultation. Clear guidelines for who may be utilized as a consultant helps create paths for those who may assist in this area. These guidelines must encourage the development of non-western consultants. Story consultants need many of the same skills possessed by translation consultants, but the roles are not interchangeable. Due to the nature of working with oral learners, extensive previous experience working in oral cultures is necessary.

Ideally, consultants working with Bible story-crafting teams interact with the team throughout an entire project. Storytelling models such as StoryTogether, OneStory, or Oral Bible Storytelling, incorporate consultation throughout the crafting process and training. As the stories are developed,

---

7. Barnwell, *Bible Translation*, 180–88.

they are tested, consulted, and refined. Most storying efforts do not incorporate testing and consulting as a part of the crafting process. A simple, reproducible model of consultation and testing is needed for these projects.

Third-Party Consultations

Third-party consultations usually involve bringing in an outsider to help with the assessment of the story-crafting project. Usually, this person does not speak the receptor language but has worked with people of similar cultural backgrounds and speaks the language of wider communication. The purpose of third-party consultation is to bring a new and refreshing perspective to a project and provide an unbiased evaluation of the crafting process and stories.

Increasingly, donors are asking for third-party consultations before they will consider funding storying projects. Mark Overstreet writes, "Evaluations provide the data each partner seeks to confirm areas of progress and correct areas where more attention may be needed. Each third-party assessment measures a program's impact in areas of ministry and humanitarian content."[8]

Funding should not be the primary motivation for evaluating the effectiveness of storying efforts. The desire to communicate the Bible's message clearly, naturally, and accurately should be motivation enough, but increasingly, funding is making third-party assessment a necessity.

Based upon an adaptation of Barnwell's definition of the function of a consultant in written translation projects, the role of a consultant in a Bible storying project is to help story-crafting teams succeed in the task of producing a good, quality Bible story that meets the needs of the community for whom it is designed.[9] The consultant seeks to encourage, support, train, guide, and help story-crafting teams in every way possible. Outside consultation can assist missionary strategists and story crafting teams to identify areas where stories may miscommunicate. Consultations may also assist in using best practices encouraging reproducibility by using consistent themes and key terms throughout the set.

---

8. Overstreet, "Fruitful Labor," 2.
9. Barnwell, *Handbook*, 5.

Onsite Consultation Model

Third-party consultants must be adequately prepared for onsite consultations. A challenge outsiders face is the lack of understanding of the local customs and cultures. Arriving from the outside may create tension between the team who crafted the stories and the consultant. Intentional preparation may serve to mitigate some of the challenges outsiders face.

The following is a sample plan for conducting an onsite consultation. It should be noted that this is an ambitious plan. Rarely will circumstances line up as neatly as presented below. Even though most storying projects will not be as clean as presented, it is good to approach each project with a plan. The following steps will assist a consultant to prepare for an onsite consultation and minimalize challenges.

Preparation for the Onsite Consultation

1. Study the worldview and culture of the people group.
2. Request copies of the stories in audio and transcript form (if these exist).
3. Request copies of back translations. If these do not exist, attempt to have the facilitator provide a copy of at least three back translations of stories at least one month before arrival onsite.
4. Ask the team leader to describe the circumstances behind the story set. These questions may include:
   a. How were the stories crafted?
   b. Who crafted the stories?
   c. How was the story crafter trained?
   d. What has been the reception of the stories within the community?
   e. How are the stories currently being utilized?
   f. Describe the key terms used in the story set.
   g. What redemptive thread does the story set follow?
5. Encourage the crafting team to arrange for people to help test the story before arrival for the onsite consultation.

Onsite Consultation

1. Meet the story-crafting team. Keep this interaction low stress and assume the role of a learner.
   a. Focus on hearing their story.
   b. Inquire how the stories were crafted and currently utilized.
   c. Ask for success stories and celebrate these.
   d. Ask if the crafting team has any questions. Assure the team that your role is to help their team.
2. Ask the team to tell you some Bible stories.
   a. Observe how they tell stories.
   b. Ask a bilingual member of the team to do an on-the-fly back translation for you as the story is being told. Ask them to do the best they can but without interfering with the naturalness of how the storyteller is telling the story.
3. Inquire with the team about their previous exposure to testing Bible stories.
   a. Ask about how the team tested stories for accuracy, naturalness, clarity, and retellability. Explain and model additional tests that may benefit the team.
   b. If back translations were not previously available, ask the team to provide back translations of the stories. This may need to occur after hours. Be prepared to model this process at various times.
4. Visit storying sessions.
   a. Observe how stories are used.
   b. Observe the ease with which stories are retold.
   c. Observe if the stories are told without teaching and exposition.
   d. How is the post-story dialogue handled?
5. Attempt to interview someone who has learned the story second-hand.
   a. Ask the circumstances of how they were told the story. Allow the interviewee to control the flow of the conversation.
   b. Ask them to retell the story. Record the retelling.
   c. Back translate the story to the language of wider communication.

d. Anchor and check the story with the source text.
6. Provide initial observations for the story-crafting team.
   a. Focus on the positive aspects of what you observed.
   b. Focus on team building, affirmations, and clarifying training processes instead of criticism and pointing out errors.
   c. Allow the team to ask questions.
7. Meet privately with the story facilitator.
   a. Allow the story facilitator to ask you questions.
   b. Encourage the story facilitator in best practices.
   c. Set a time for a follow-up meeting to discuss observations.

Post-Onsite Consultation

1. Review the redemptive thread and overall story choices based upon worldview documentation.
2. Identify areas where the team is doing well.
3. Identify problems with clarity, accuracy (including story cohesion and key terms), naturalness, and retellability.
4. Prepare a written report for the story facilitator, including both affirmations and problem areas. Make suggestions for assisting the team grow in their ability to craft stories. Encourage testing throughout the process. Share a copy of the report and suggestions with the sponsoring agency.
5. Follow-up the written report with a phone call. Intentionally allow the story facilitator to ask questions.
6. Offer to continue to be a resource for the story facilitator and the crafting team.

This list of plans for conducting an onsite consultation is very Western. When preparing non-Western consultants, modify the presentation of this model to an appropriate learning style. Throughout the consultation process, the importance of developing and encouraging local teams of storycrafters cannot be overstated. Janet Stahl rightly points out,

> There is much for the teams to learn and the best way to do it is through practice and experience. However, our agendas as

missionaries wanting to make progress in completing stories, in completing projects, in evangelizing and discipleship . . . can sometimes get in the way of the team building on what they learn and improving their competency as Bible storytellers.[10]

The overall consulting process should be as simple as possible. It should not be an onerous process. It certainly should not shame the crafting team or the storyteller. The process should be affirming and redemptive for the story facilitator and the crafting team.

Testing a Bible Story

Clearly communicating a natural and retellable story within the receptor people group is the goal for Bible storytelling. Measuring the achievement of this goal requires intentionality, accountability, and patience. Several tests performed for testing written Bible translations may be modified for testing Bible stories. Refer to Barnwell's book, *Bible Translation*, for examples of the written Bible testing models.[11] Each of these tests begins with an uninitiated speaker hearing the Bible story several times. In each of the tests, it is imperative to use people who do not know the Bible story. The testers should not have previous knowledge, which may influence their understanding of the story. Their uninitiated responses are crucial for testing.

The following tests are adaptations by the author of written Bible translation tests. These suggested adaptations may be applied to Bible stories to accomplish similar goals as their written Bible translation equivalents. As with written translation testing, it is important to carefully explain to the testers that these tests are designed to test the Bible story and not the person doing the test.[12] If this is not clear, the testers frequently will not be candid in their evaluation. When possible, it is best to conduct these tests in the village where the stories will be utilized.[13] As with textual based Bible translation tests, maintaining a comfortable and familiar environment for the tester is essential.

---

10 Janet Stahl, personal communication with author, January 23, 2020.
11 Barnwell, *Bible Translation*, 182.
12 Barnwell, *Bible Translation*, 183.
13 Barnwell, "Testing the Translation," 425.

Method: Tell the Story Again Test

The tester tells the story to people representative of the receptor language. Some advocate playing the story from an audio recording to have the same story told the same way to each of the testers. Benefits are achieved using an exact retelling of using the same story, but the story's oral telling is a far superior model compared to an audio recording.

Process:

a. Tell the story to the person.
b. Ask the person what happened in the story. Attempt to have the person tell the significant themes of the story and the big picture. This helps them remember the story but may also reveal gaps where the story is unclear.
c. Tell the story again.
d. Ask the person to retell the story. If the person allows recording the story, do so.

Observations:

a. Listen to the story to ascertain if the words used in the story were unclear and changed in the retelling. Hearers might be reluctant to identify words that are unclear. Ask questions to ascertain if the hearer understood the story. Ask questions about different words to test understanding.
b. Note common places in the story where retellers struggle. Note common places where the story is told inaccurately, or information is missing.
c. Take note of how the story was retold. What mannerisms or expressions were used?
d. If you recorded the story, compare recordings to identify common errors in the story.
e. Did the person forget, add, or change something in the story?

Tests for:

a. Clarity.
b. Naturalness.
c. Retellability.

This test can be performed with an individual or a group of people. With more introverted people, the group setting may encourage more discussion about unclear points and facilitate the retelling of the group. Do not have someone retell the story if they have heard the story told by someone else in the group.

Method: Summarize the Story

Another method for testing the clarity of a story is by asking summary questions about the story. This method is excellent for testing if the story is clearly communicating what is happening in the story. Have the person listen to and interact with the story. Ask questions about the story to ascertain if the hearer understands the overarching theme of the story.

Process:

a. Tell the story.

b. Ask the person to explain the main point of the story.

c. Ask the person to summarize the story in his or her own words. This model can begin with a high-level summary but end with the tester adding as many details as he or she remembers.

Observations:

a. When listening to the summary, determine if the main point of the story was accurate? If it was not accurate, note inaccuracies.

b. Did the summary of the story cover all the main points of the story? Were parts of the story left out?

c. Is there a mismatch between what was told in the story and the summary?

Tests for:

a. Clarity.

b. Naturalness.

This test can be performed with individuals or groups, but as with the previous test, it should only be done with people who have not heard the story. Compare the answers from several different testers. Identify patterns of misunderstanding and gaps in the story. This test helps determine if the meaning of the story is clear. If gaps appear in the story, the situation may indicate that the story was not clear or natural.

Summarizing the story can be accomplished using a freely told phrase-by-phrase, oral rendition of the story. This model is another borrowed tool from written translation models. Using a freely told oral version instead of the word-by-word version improves naturalness. Barnwell describes a freely told version as,

> a version that someone speaks out of his own head. It is not a translation; it is the speaker's own natural way of speaking. It is not a version that has been written down and read. Freely told versions can help you very much to improve the natural style of your translation. This helps not follow the grammatical style of the source text. Freely told versions may leave out details. This is ok, continue telling the story to work on the accuracy and adding in missing details.[14]

The purpose of this test is primarily naturalness and clarity. By encouraging the person to use their own words to tell the story and not try to memorize the tester's words, better terms and phraseology may be discovered.

Method: Question and Answer

The question and answer test are beneficial for determining whether the story is clear and accurate. When utilizing this test for written translations, the text is read out loud prior to asking the questions. For the Bible storying test, tell the story instead of having the story read. It is beneficial to have several questions prepared prior to the session but remain flexible to ask questions arising naturally from the responses. Lithgow advises testers to "keep asking simple questions to ensure that he is comprehending clearly the main points of the translation."[15] Continued dialogue about the story assists the tester to ascertain understanding. Barnwell instructs the tester not to ask yes or no questions, if they like the story, or opinion questions.[16] Ask short, factual questions.

Process:

a. Tell the story twice with culturally appropriate transitions between the tellings.

---

14. Barnwell, *Bible Translation*, 113.
15. Lithgow, "What to Ask," 21.
16. Barnwell, *Bible Translation*, 183.

Ask questions about the story. Focus on explicit questions requiring a factual answer. Record the responses if appropriate. Examples from the Demon-Possessed Man story may include:

1. Where did Jesus go?
2. How did Jesus get there?
3. Who did Jesus find when he arrived?
4. Why was this person there?
5. What was the person doing when Jesus arrived?
6. What did the person say to Jesus?
7. What did Jesus say to the person?
8. Where did the demons go?
9. What happened to the demons?

b. Repeat this process with several people.
c. Compare answers provided by different testers.

Observations:

a. Are there questions consistently answered inconsistently? This may indicate a lack of clarity or the story may contain inaccuracies.
b. Sometimes inaccurate answers are due to poorly worded questions and do not represent problems with the stories. If a question is answered inaccurate, test the question to make sure that it is communicating clearly.

Tests for:

a. Accuracy.
b. Clarity.

Method: Which Story Communicates the Message?

This test is useful when there may be multiple ways of saying the same thing in a language or when the crafting team is uncertain which word or phrase communicates clearest. The stories are told to people representative of the receptor audience and asked questions to ascertain which is best understood. This test helps the crafting team to determine which version of the story communicates with the most clarity.

Process:

a. Explain to the person who will hear the story that you will tell two different versions of the same story and that you would like to know which story communicates the clearest.
b. Tell both versions of the story.
c. Ask: Which version is most comfortable to understand?
d. Ask: Why is one version better than the other version?
e. Allow for a free flow of group discussion (when performing this test with a group).

Observations:

a. Do not ask which version of the story they like the best. Ask which is understood the best. Which is the better story?
b. Attempt to ascertain why one version of the story is better than the other version. Was a word or phrase used in one version that makes the story unclear?
c. Do not just tell a version of the story and ask if they understood the story. This will almost always result in an affirmative answer. This does not answer the question of which is the best version of the story.
d. This test may be performed with individuals or with groups. If performed in a group, allow the group to discuss their opinions freely. Record this session if culturally appropriate.
e. Vary the order of the storytelling between testing groups.

Tests for:

a. Clarity.
b. Naturalness.

This test offers many benefits to the story-crafting team. When disagreements between members of the story-crafting team occur, it is sometimes difficult to arrive at a consensus as to which is the best version of a story or which word or phrase best communicates. The members of the crafting team can engage in rigorous evaluation of the story through the community testing. This interaction minimizes the need for direct confrontation with other members of the crafting team.

Method: Oral Back-Translation

Back-translations are invaluable for translators and story-crafting facilitators. They are also beneficial for story-crafting teams as they check their own stories. Back-translations allow non-native speakers to interact with the receptor language and may be performed orally or as a written transcript. Both models have advantages and disadvantages. Back-translations require working with a tester fluent in both the receptor language and the language of wider communication. This test deals with the process of performing an oral back-translation.

Process:

a. Record a clean telling of the story.
b. Play the story entirely for the person performing the back-translation. This person should be a representative of the receptor people group unfamiliar with the story.
c. Ask the person if there was any part of the story they did not understand.
d. Play the story in its entirety a second time.
e. Walk the person through the major themes of the story allowing them to tell as much as possible.
f. Ask the person to play the story phrase-by-phrase and translate what is said into the language of wider communication. This translation should be as literal as possible. This is not a summary of what was said. This is a phrase-by-phrase back-translation of what was actually said in the story.
g. Record the entire session on a second recorder. This recording will capture the original story and back translation.
h. Compare the back translation to the source text.
i. Review accuracy errors identified with the story-crafting team.

Alternative Process: When the story facilitator is observing the crafting team, it may be an interruption for the stop and go, phrase by phrase recording. If this is an early back-translation test, it may be useful to have a bi-lingual person provide an on-the-fly back-translation as the team is working out early versions of the story. This is not a substitution for the oral back-translation, but this modification can help a story facilitator or consultant gain insight otherwise inaccessible during the crafting sessions.

Observations:

a. Back-translations are a useful test for checking the accuracy of the story compared to the source text.
b. Not all errors identified in back-translations reflect an error in the story. Errors in the back-translation are common. Test the apparent errors to ascertain if the problem is with the back-translation of the story.
c. Recordings of back-translations are provided for the outside consultant. These recordings allow the outsider an ability to interact with the translation without speaking the language.
d. The use of back-translations by the consultant does have limitations. Beekman argues that "comments on back-translations are often fifty percent or more irrelevant."[17] The translation facilitator already knows answers to some of the questions because of cultural background, not apparent to an outsider of the culture, and can quickly address some of the concerns raised by the consultant.
e. This test requires two sets of audio equipment. One is used for playing the story, and the second is used for recording the back-translation. A small set of external speakers is helpful for this test.

Tests for:

a. Accuracy.
b. Clarity.
c. Natural.

Back-translations are a powerful tool for story-crafting, testing, and checking by the crafting team. Recordings of back-translation sessions should be shared with the consultant allowing interaction with the receptor language without understanding this language. While errors in the story must be corrected, this a delicate process requiring cultural sensitivity and wisdom. Janet Stahl offers a word of caution when using back-translations. She writes,

---

17. Beekman, "Back-Translations," 17.

Too often, checkers or consultants can quickly focus on details because it can be fairly apparent to a Bible scholar if detail is missing or added. Sometimes the confusion may be more difficult to identify because the story-crafting team don't know what they don't know, and the check comes from a very different cultural background.[18]

The goal of testing is to refine the story, making sure that it communicates clearly to the audience. Evaluate the story for additions, deletions, or misrepresentations from the source text. Note if the back translation is just the story or whether the back-translation reveals that teaching or explaining occurred during the telling of the story.

Another benefit of back-translations is the ability to identify issues of intra-story cohesion within a set of stories. Key terms used throughout the story set should remain the same. The examination of back-translations from each story in the set helps the crafting team, facilitator, and consultant identify problems with key term changes.

Oral back-translations are extremely valuable for Bible storying projects. Orally conducting the entire method models a process reproducible by facilitators and consultants who do not come from a print-based world. It helps create models that not only lead to mother-tongue story crafters but also opens up the role of story consultant to people who do not prefer print-based solutions.

Method: Transcripted Back-Translation

Transcripted Back-Translations may be created using the recordings produced with the oral back-translations. These transcripts allow further analysis of the story and comparison to the source text. This may be incredibly valuable for new facilitators and consultants. The transcripted back-translation allows the facilitator and consultant to evaluate a story paralleled to a bridge language source text. Experienced facilitators are often capable of evaluating stories by listening to an oral back-translation of a story, but the transcripted back-translation is invaluable for learning the process.

For traditional text-based translations, written back-translations may be required by some consultants. For storying projects, the use of written back-translation should be considered optional. The team must consider if the added benefit of the transcription is worth the time needed to create the transcript.

---

18. Janet Stahl, Personal communication with author, January 23, 2020.

Process:

a. Prepare a transcription of the story as modeled in Figure 9.1.
b. Evaluate the transcript as compared to the source text.

Observations:

a. Adding the timestamp of the audio recording is beneficial for reviewing the recording with the story-crafting team.
b. Consult translation helps and commentaries for evaluating translation choices.
c. Add areas for follow-up with the story-crafting team in the "Comments Column."

Tests for:

a. Accuracy.
b. Clarity.
c. Natural.

Figure 9.1 is one example of a transcripted back-translation, but there are many alternatives. The transcription may be as simple as writing out the back translation on a piece of paper, adding the information into a Word file, or creating a template in Excel. The mode for how the transcript is created is not essential. Avoid allowing the form to overly complicate the model.

The ability to compare the transcript of the story to the written source text is valuable to the translation consultant. This process allows for checking the story against the biblical text. This practice is one of the most beneficial accuracy tests for Bible stories because it allows the facilitator and consultant to see the story alongside the biblical test.

For new story facilitators and new translation consultants, this model is invaluable. Brian Kelly, International Oral Translation Services Coordinator for SIL, describes accuracy as "Fidelity or faithfulness to Scripture. Is the translation faithful to what we see in the source text? Instead of using exegesis as the term, we describe the process as becoming as intimate as possible . . . people characters, and motives . . . background, context that is happening."[19]

When producing back-translations, precisely record what is said in the written transcript. Avoid cleaning up the written version of the back translation. While the back-translation is recorded phrase-by-phrase from the story,

---

19 Brian Kelly, personal communication with the author, January 29, 2020.

the transcribed back-translation should be preserved word-for-word from the oral back-translation. Refrain from changing the grammar or word order. If the person performing the oral back translation did not know the word in the language of wider communication and used an indigenous word, write out the indigenous word in the transcribed back-translation.

Transcripted back-translations are also helpful when helping non-storyers understand the meticulous checking and testing that occurs for Bible Stories. Gatekeepers in existing churches sometimes do not believe that stories are accurate. This example helps them understand the meticulous process of checking Bible Stories. Another audience who may benefit from the transcription are missionaries who use storying but are not convinced of the benefits of checking Bible Stories. Leading them to test stories they use with a back translation can help them see where their stories need improving.

Figure 1 – Transcripted Back Translation

Time Stamp	Transcript	Scripture	Comments
0.00	One afternoon, Peter and John went to the temple to pray	Acts 3:1 Now Peter and John were going up to the temple at the hour of prayer, the ninth hour.	
0.05	They met a man who had been paralyzed since birth	Acts 3:2 And a man lame from birth was being carried, whom they laid daily at the gate of the temple that is called the Beautiful Gate to ask alms of those entering the temple.	
0.08	This man was taken to the entrance of the temple each day where he begged as people went in		
0.14	He saw Peter and John and asked them for money	Acts 3:3 Seeing Peter and John about to go into the temple, he asked to receive alms.	
		Acts 3:4 And Peter directed his gaze at him, as did John, and said, "Look at us."	Not in the story
0.22	He looked at them expecting them to give him something	Acts 3:5 And he fixed his attention on them, expecting to receive something from them.	
0.28	Peter said, "I don't have any money but what I do have, I give to you....	Acts 3:6 But Peter said, "I have no silver or gold, but what I do have I give to you. In the name of Jesus Christ of Nazareth, rise up and walk!	"in the name of Jesus Christ" is missing from the story
0.33	get up and walk!"		
0.38	Peter took him by the hand and helped him get up.	Acts 3:7 And he took him by the right hand and raised him up, and immediately his feet and ankles were made strong.	
0.42	The man was completely healed		
0.47	He got up and started jumping up and down and praising God.	Acts 3:8 And leaping up, he stood and began to walk, and entered the temple with them, walking and leaping and praising God.	Ask where the man went when he was healed.

Table 9.1 Transcripted Back Translation

Finally, another benefit of back translations is the accountability for the story-crafting team. After spending hours or days crafting a story, there is a temptation to accept the story as good enough when there are still areas needing improvement. The back translation is a way to submit work to an outsider who can provide unbiased feedback for the story.

Method: Storying Group Testing

A test proven beneficial for written Bible translations is the "Trial Version" test.[20] This test is conducted after other tests have been performed and can help make final revisions to a translation prior to publication. Performing the trial version test involves sending the translation to stakeholders with a request for feedback. Church leaders are ideal candidates for testing a trial version. An adaptation of this test is beneficial for Bible Stories prior to the wide dissemination of stories.

Bible stories that have gone through initial testing and checking can be further tested in storying groups made up of people from the receptor language. Before telling the stories, the tester explains to the group that these stories are being developed for use in their language and that feedback is needed. Explain the goals of clarity, accuracy, naturalness, and retellability for the translation.

Process:

a. Explain the goals of the translation to the audience.

b. Ask the audience to share feedback for the purpose of improving the stories.

c. Tell the story.

d. Ask if there is anything about the story that is confusing or that they did not understand.

e. Retell the story scene by scene. Elicit help from the audience by asking questions like, "Does anyone remember what happened next?"

f. Help the audience internalize the story. Consider having the audience act out the story as the story crafter narrates the story scene by scene (or use whatever techniques are appropriate for the culture).

g. Tell the complete story again.

h. Have members of the audience attempt to retell the story. Always tell the complete story again if errors were introduced during the retellings.

---

20 Barnwell, *Bible Translation*, 186.

Observations:

a. Allow participants to talk about the story as they need. Do not rush to the next part of the process if the audience is still internalizing the story.
b. Make a note of where the story bogs down and becomes difficult to retell.
c. A modification of this approach is performing one of the other testing models with a second-generation hearer of the story. As someone learns the story in the group, ask them to share the story with someone else. Test the third person's version of the story to see if it has changed from the original story.

Tests for:

a. Clarity.
b. Accuracy.
c. Naturalness.
d. Retellability.

The storying group testing is beneficial when stories are in final revisions. At this point, the story has already been tested for clarity, accuracy, naturalness, and retellabilty. This test will help the story-crafting team polish the stories and sound like they were birthed from within the receptor language.

Summary of Testing Methods

Story testing is performed to make sure that stories are accurate, natural, and clear in order to be retold throughout the receptor language. Stories lacking clarity and naturalness are unlikely to be retold. Testing unveils defects in the stories which may inhibit reproduction. Errors introduced through the story-crafting process are highlighted through the testing of stories. Testing does not guarantee that there are no errors. Testing highlights and minimalizes the possibility of errors. Incorporating story testing models into the crafting process results in better stories. Testing stories also make the external consultation because many of the issues typically identified in an external consultation will already be addressed in the crafting phase.

Each of the models for testing described above addresses different outcomes for what is being tested (see Table 9.1). A good story must contain each of the characteristics. Each test examines the different categories evaluated. Unfortunately, no one test answers all the questions necessary for ascertaining if a story is clear, accurate, natural, and able to be retold within the receptor people group. It is the use of a combination of tests that contributes to the necessary refinement of the story.

Concluding Reflections

Storying practitioners must learn from the translation principles established by Bible translators. Bible storying shares many commonalities with Bible translation. Many of the tools used by translators for checking and testing translations are also beneficial for testing stories. Roles such as translation teams, translation facilitators, and translation consultants find similarities with story-crafting roles such as crafting teams, story facilitators, and story consultants. Storying practitioners owe a debt of gratitude to Bible translation missionaries who paved the way for storying by developing a robust and reliable model for communicating God's Word to people in the vernacular.

Several systematic approaches to Bible storying have emerged over the past twenty years. These models of storying incorporate best practices for crafting, testing, and consulting Bible stories. The inclusion of outside consultation and story testing in Bible storying projects will significantly improve Bible stories' quality. Refining these two areas will be facilitated by mission agencies cooperation in adopting agreed upon best practices for story crafting, story testing, and the adoption of guidelines for developing story consultants.

Table 9.1. Summary of Tests with Testing Goals

Test	Clarity	Accurate	Natural	Retell-ability
Tell the Story Again	X	X		X
Summarize the Story	X		X	
Question and Answer	X	X		
Which communicates the message?	X		X	
Oral Back-Translation	X	X	X	
Transcripted Back-Translation	X	X	X	
Storying Group Testing	X	X	X	X

Bibliography

Barger, Donald. *Toward the Development of a Bible Storying Evaluation Method Utilizing a Synthesis of Bible Translation Consultation Methods*. PhD diss., Mid-America Baptist Theological Seminary, 2020.

Barnwell, Katharine. *Bible Translation: An Introductory Course in Translation Principles*. Dallas: SIL International, 2017.

———. *Handbook for Translation Consultants*. Dallas: SIL International, 2009.

———. "Testing the Translation." *The Bible Translator* 28 (1977) 425–33.

Beekman, John. "Back-Translations: Their Use and Limitations in Checking Translations." *Notes on Translation* 28 (1967) 16–17.

———. "Three Focuses of Consultation Procedures." *Notes on Translation* 81 (1980) 2–14.

Lithgow, David. "What to Ask in Translation Checking." *Notes on Translation* 42 (1971) 21–23.

Nida, Eugene. *Towards a Science of Translating: With Special Reference to Principles and Procedures Involved in Bible Translating*. Leiden: E.J. Brill, 1964.

Overstreet, Mark M. "Fruitful Labor: Assessment and Global Implications for Theological Education in Oral Contexts." A Paper Presented at the ION Global Theological Education Consultation, Hong Kong, People's Republic of China, 2013.

Tuggy, John C. "Test My Own Translation?" *Notes on Translation* 81 (1980) 14–21.

Part 4
Expanding the Horizons

10

Is it Time for The Return of Oral Hermeneutics?

Tom Steffen

WHILE SOME MISSION THEORIES and models enjoy a long self-life, such as the "3-selfs," others fade fast—think Church Growth. While some may be hesitant to recognize hermeneutics as theoretical models[1] of Bible interpretation, I propose we should. In so doing, some long overdue critique becomes possible, paving the way for other potential hermeneutic models. A question raised by the EMS North Central region is apropos: *How should those models (in this case, hermeneutics) be adjusted or abandoned as we make disciples across cultures into the future?*

Such critique is necessary and often conducted best by missiologists who have access to the frontlines of missions where most *everything formerly assumed about Scripture* becomes challenged. *Why missiologists?* Because, "Missiologists practice, reflect, and evaluate global missions with the purpose of discovering ways to improve the worker and the work."[2] Missions and missiologists have a way of keeping theologians and Bible communicators biblically reliable and culturally relevant. Not only does missions help keep theology[3] from going tribal, it does the same for the means of discovering

---

1. "All models and strategies have theories that drive them whether the practitioner is cognizant of them or not. Models—a grid or framework designed to predict outcomes to accomplish—answer the 'what' question. Strategies—ideas and plans used to accomplish a model—answer the 'how' question. Behind models and strategies lies theories. Theories—the assumptions or principles that drive models and strategies—answer the 'why' question. All three then—theories (why), models (what), strategies (how)—are interrelated and incompatible without each other." Steffen, "Theories Drive Our Ministries," 210–11.

2. Steffen and McKinney-Douglas, *Encountering Missionary Life and Times*, 37. Good missiologists are good theologians and good theologians are good missiologists.

3. "There is no such thing as 'theology'; there is only *contextual* theology." Bevans,

theology—hermeneutic interpretive theories and models. Good theology is sound missiology, and good missiology is sound theology.

Two threads weave Bill Bjoraker and my book *The Return of Oral Hermeneutics* together. The first was watching the Ifugao of central Luzon, Philippines, adjust from a predominately oral society to a more literate one. While the Ifugao deeply appreciated and utilized the literate world willingly, including buying life insurance spelled out on paper and signing their name at the bottom, they were *not* quick to give away their oral-aural sociocultural world; they preferred a both/and rather than an either/or. The change from a predominately oral culture to a more literate one was more like a dimmer switch than an off-on switch.

Nor were the Ifugao enamored with my Dallas Bible College (heavily influenced by Dallas Theological Seminary) hermeneutical credentials or denominational or agency affiliations. Rather, they challenged this Bible teacher's preferred hermeneutic, finding it not only difficult to discern, but awkward to replicate. I credit the Ifugao for causing me to rethink hermeneutics from an oralist perspective, thereby presenting possible new interpretative alternatives I never would have considered coming from my literate-print background.

These events raised a number of questions that would take decades before opportunity arose to adequately research. Centered on the narrative sections of Scripture, among other questions, the authors asked:

- *Does one have to know how to do grammar analysis and diagramming to be able to interpret Scripture?*
- *Does one have to know orality to fully interpret Scripture?*
- *Which is the most natural?*
- *Is there a preferred sequence?*

Grammar analysis was certainly *not* something natural for the Ifugao. In the book, the authors called this approach "textual hermeneutics," (TH) recognizing the multiple variants capable of slicing theology from thick to thin. Representing a communal-relational society, the Ifugao found character analysis much more natural. This the authors called "oral hermeneutics," (OH) also recognizing the many variants in use today.

Other questions arose that required investigation included:

- *What are the limits of TH?*
- *What are the limits of OH?*

Models of Contextual Theology, 3.

- *What is the role of grammar in interpretation?*
- *What is the role of characters in interpretation?*
- *Can one really ascertain the full impact and meaning of a Bible story by using TH?*
- *When does TH become metaphorically Saul's armor that doesn't fit someone else?*
- *How oral influenced is Scripture?*

The central question for our introductory book on the topic of oral hermeneutics (OH) is, *why is it important to know and practice OH in interpreting and communicating biblical meaning?*

A second thread that weaves this book together was a graduate course ("Story in Scripture and Service") I taught at Biola University several summers ago. I had invited Bill Bjoraker of William Carey University to tell a Bible story to the class. As I listened to the questions posed to introduce and review the story, I said to the class at the conclusion, "Dr. Bjoraker just demonstrated oral hermeneutics (OH)." The students of course had no idea what I was talking about, nor was I that much further ahead of them.

Having a strong ministry background among modern-day Jewish people in Tel Aviv for eight years, and now in the greater LA area, Bjoraker made the perfect partner to demonstrate that OH is *not* just for tribal people. In fact, OH is required for around 80 percent of the world who "do not depend on written textual transmission!"[4] *What does OH add that TH misses?*

Capturing the Big Picture

The authors outlined the book as follows:

    Setting the Stage

    Part 1 Demonstrations
    1 Elisha and the Widow's Oil
    2 Reflections on the Elisha Story

    Part 2 Propositions

4. Lausanne Movement, "Orality: An Infographic."

3 Orality's Influence on Text and Teaching

4 Oral Hermeneutics

5 Hebrew Hermeneutics

6 Character Theology

7 Questioning Our Questions

8 Reflections

Part 3 Echoes

9 Elisha and General Naaman

10 Reflections on the Elisha Story

Concluding Reflections

Part 1 *demonstrates* what the authors will later *define*. Did the reader catch the order? The authors model in how the book was constructed with what we argue throughout the book—build from the concrete to the abstract and back to concrete. Yes, there is a sequence[5]—but without one being superior to the other.

The authors begin by setting the stage for making the case for the return of oral hermeneutics (OH) by challenging the long-held comfortable conclusions of textual hermeneutics (TH). Chapter 1 follows, providing a concrete example of the use of OH in an oral inductive Bible study of the story of "Elisha and the Widow's Oil." This chapter foregrounds, embodies, and demonstrates in action what is to follow in the book. Chapter 2 summarizes some key reflections from the Bible story the authors will later develop, explain and expand.

The two oral inductive story presentations in Chapters 1 and 9 serve as bookends of practice that encloses theory. Sandwiching the theory between the two slices of bread of the practice of oral storying gives a place of honor to story as the dominant genre of Scripture, and a primary expression of OH.

Part 2 lays out *propositional proposals* on OH based on the clues partially provided from the story of "Elisha and the Widow's Oil." We define

---

5. "Culturally, humans spoke long before they wrote, and individually, children learn to speak before they learn to read or write. All children learn to speak (barring physical disabilities); many children do not learn to read or write. All cultures make use of spoken communication; many languages do not have a written form. From a historical and developmental perspective, speech is clearly primary." Biber, *Variation Across Speech and Writing*, 8.

orality as the reliance on (whether by choice or circumstance) a natural, universal, living (social), strongly concrete, multisensory (sound, sight) means to receive, reflect upon, implement, relay to others and remember. This is accomplished through relationships (material, spiritual, and human), all of which creates a social identity individually and collectively. With this backdrop the authors review how the canon evolved from voice to text, how the spoken and written Word interfaced, and how these are significant for OH today. Over time, of course, scientific logic, linear thought, theorizing, atomized textual analysis, propositions (as the main product of biblical interpretation)[6] and systematic theology dominated, extending to today. This reality raises a series of questions:

- *Is strong print-based systemization too one-sided for a complex world where the majority are oral-preference learners?*[7]
- *Was the Bible designed for only scientific inquiry?*
- *Was grammatical breakdown of a text always necessary to secure its meaning?*
- *Should systematic theology harken back to its biblical theology roots which captures a deep and comprehensive understanding of the whole unfolding story thereby providing rich, Scripture-wide understanding of God and humans?*

---

6. The "dean" of evangelical theologians in the last century, Carl Henry, claims, "As an achievement of the Holy Spirit's inspiration, Scripture presents us with the remarkable phenomenon of a canon concerned primarily with the propositional disclosure of God . . . By its emphasis that divine revelation is propositional, Christian theology in no way denies that the Bible conveys its message in many literary forms such as letters, poetry and parable, prophecy and history. What it stresses, rather, is that the truth conveyed by God through these various forms has conceptual adequacy, and that in all cases the literary teaching is part of a divinely inspired message that conveys the truth of divine revelation . . . and of course the expression of truth in other forms that the customary prose does not preclude expressing that truth in declarative proposition." Henry, *God, Revelation, and Authority*, 96, 463. Note the emphasis on the conceptual.

7. Grant Lovejoy estimates "5.7 billion people in the world are oral communicators because either they are illiterate, or their reading comprehension is inadequate." Lovejoy, "Extent of Orality," 121. This percentage would no doubt go higher if limited to the Global South.

In regard to literacy in the US, which has remained static in the last decade, "1. 32 million cannot read . . . 14% of the population. 2. 21% of US adults read below the 5th grade level. 3. 19% of high school graduates cannot read. 4. 85% of juveniles who interact with the juvenile court system are considered functionally illiterate." Gaille, "15 US Literacy Rate and Illiteracy Statistics."

- *How does shortcutting, by going from the Bible directly to systematic theology and straight for the categorical and abstract, undermine the deeper, more holistic and human meaning of the text?*

The central question addressed in Chapter 3 asks: *How did orality influence text and teaching?* The authors therefore consider how orality and text interfaced before, during, and postconstruction of the canon,[8] something often overlooked in relation to hermeneutics. In the search for a new way to theologize, we mull over orality, the role of scribes,[9] individual and social or collective memory,[10] and how manuscripts were delivered and discussed.

Chapter 4 offers possible course corrections to what some consider the "settled science" of TH, and the authors do so without jettisoning it. Rather, it seeks dialogue between proponents of OH and TH. This chapter calls for a new (actually an old) hermeneutic that specifically addresses the literary portions of Scripture, making Scripture more accessible, meaningful and reproducible to a large and growing audience of oralist (by choice or circumstance) worldwide. It lays out the need for, and the definition of OH.

Interestingly, what the authors discussed and called for in the former chapter—"Oral Hermeneutics"—existed centuries prior. Chapter 5 reviews Hebrew hermeneutics that highlights the distinctives between TH and OH, taking some cues from the first custodians of Scripture, the rabbis, scholars, and teachers of the Jewish people. As a wise man once said, "There is nothing new under the sun" (Eccl 1:9 NIV).

In our frailty, humans are continually vulnerable to the biases and emphases of current times, thereby giving each generation opportunity to make adjustments, additions, and/or deletions, even as they build on the strong shoulders of their predecessors. Perhaps our generation has

---

8. Bjoraker and I agree with Vanhoozer when he writes, "The goal of both script and direction is too serve the drama: 'script and performance are equally necessary, though not equally authoritative. Biblical script without ecclesial performance is empty; ecclesial performance without biblical script is blind.'" Vanhoozer, *Drama of Doctrine*, 362.

9. "[s]cribes in antiquity were not just secretaries copying documents; they were the scholars of their world" Witherington, *What's in the Word*, 35. These scholar scribes in ancient Israel were known to "take on components of creativity and composition" Hess, "Scribes," 718.

10. It should be noted that "by memory" does not mean word-for-word recall. Rather, as Ong notes, "Hearing a new story [the singer] does not try to memorize it by rote. He digests it in terms of its themes . . . he then verbalized it in formulas or formulaic elements he has in stock." Ong, *Presence of the Word*, 25.

Collective memory is composed of narratives that function as "[collective] frames which rhetorically serve as communicative vehicles that do not require elaboration, and function as an argumentative axiom that does not require further illustration" Gitay, "History, Literature, and Memory," 282–83.

an opportunity, now, to recognize the over-emphasis embraced by some biblical scholars under the influence of the Enlightenment and science (later), correcting them by incorporating some of the powerful modes of an OH, thereby resulting in a more robust understanding of Scripture.[11] This chapter spotlights the need for another, different type of hermeneutic, theologizing and theology.

Chapter 6 proposes a different type of theologizing and theology that goes beyond, but does not discard systematic, biblical, missional, or narrative theology. We call it *theologizing* as the verbal form fits the dynamic and in-practice process that happens in OH. We call it *theology* as the noun form fits the results—Bible characters who *demonstrate* and *display* (rather than define and explain) various aspects of theology. We call this *character theology*. This chapter addresses how OH, driven by narrative logic (in contrast to propositional logic), relies on character theologizing (process) that takes us to the foothills of character theology (product) so that we can build an initial and ongoing relationship with the Chief Character—Jesus. Characters create revised relationships (Titus 2) that lead to and celebrate the Chief Character.

All hermeneutics find their base steadied on the answers to sets of questions. Chapter 7 delves into the questions used in many prominent Bible storying models today, such as, Discovery Bible Study (DBS), T4T (Training for Trainers), OT4T (Orality Training for Trainers), S-T4T (Storying Training for Trainers), DMM (Disciple-Making Movements), STS (Simply the Story), Any3, and Simple Church.

Often the questions used today for drawing out transcendent truths (realities as seen by God) of a Bible story find their foundational base burrowed deeply in the textual hermeneutic (TH) tradition. As well, they tend to evoke and promote strongly Western legal moral values, such as innocence and guilt (justice and injustice), often neglecting those found in relational communities—honor and shame. They also tend to seek individual application (in contrast to group or communal). Building on

---

11. No one comes to Scripture absent of perspective. To highlight this reality, Justo Gonzàlez in *Santa Biblica: The Bible through Hispanic Eyes* asks readers to imagine they are looking at the *same landscape* and asked to describe what they see. Perspective, of course, influences observations and descriptions—proximity of viewers, elevation (hilltop to valley), angles, and so forth. While different visuals often result, such do not necessarily denote incorrectness or insignificance. Often, they are just *different perspectives* of the *same landscape*. And these additions can actually enhance one's perspective if one is willing to move beyond his/her present viewing post. Perceptions become, not just mine (a Western, Latin, African, Asian perspective), but ours—the global community of faith. Gonzalez, *Santa Biblica*, 17–20. Such enrichment demonstrates the creativity of the Creator who deserves our highest honor.

such leading lights as Meir Sternberg, Leland Ryken, Grant Osborne, Kevin Vanhoozer, and a host of others[12]—who recognized the interpretive questions used for the Epistles are inappropriate for the narrative and poetic sections of Scripture—the authors questioned some of the anchor questions currently in use in Bible studies and propose more suitable substitutes from an oral perspective.

The authors advocate more *character-centric questions* that promote emotive, experiential dialogue. Rather than, what do you believe? we prefer, who do you follow? The questions also highlight other moral values (beyond the *legal language* of innocence and guilt dominant in the West) consistent within the biblical texts, and the host culture(s), such as the *relational language* of honor and shame (dominant among Asians, Middle Easterners, Africans, Latinos, and growing fast among Westerners),[13] the *control language* of power and fear (dominant among animists and Catholics) and the *hygienic language* of purity and pollution (dominant among Buddhists, Hindus, Muslims, Jews, First Nations). The storyteller can expect the moral values to influence interpretation and communication of Scripture.

Part 2 concludes with Chapter 8 by reviewing and reflecting on the challenges and contributions of OH highlighted throughout Chapters 4–7. It attempts to add a more concrete culture to the cerebral culture that currently dominates the hermeneutic guild.

Part 3 offers a second opportunity to demonstrate what the authors discussed in the previous chapters, this time to dedicated readers who have a clearer vision and better hearing in relation to our intent. Chapter 9 conveys the story of "Elisha and General Naaman" found in Second Kings 5. As in the former parts, the authors conclude Part 3 by again offering reflections (Chapter 10). The authors then tender concluding reflections, summarizing echoes of threads and ideas heard throughout the journey of the entire book, as we built the case for the return of OH at home and abroad.

Assumptions Behind Oral Hermeneutics

Every theory and model, including hermeneutic theoretical models, are driven by assumptions whether one is cognizant of them of not. These assumptions, however, are often difficult to recognize or isolate because they are like the water in which fish swim. Five OH assumptions follow. In sum, OH weds philosophy (narrative logic) and practice through the

---

12. There are over 650 footnotes in the book. One of the authors' goals was readable scholarship.

13. See Crouch, "Return of Shame."

words and works of characters that results in relational theology that is memorable and modellable.

1. **The spoken Word preceded the written Word**

For the most part, the *spoken Word, God's Voice, was heard and lived long before it became the written Word.* "Before time itself was measured, the Voice was speaking. The Voice was and is God" (John 1:2 VOICE). And both the spoken and written were inspired.[14]

2. **Literacy has blinded many to the oral features of Scripture**

In *The Return to Oral Hermeneutics,* the authors recognize the effects of centuries of literacy socialization that produced a blind spot in the Western Christian world—the neglect by most in the academies, agencies, and assemblies[15] of the foundational and forceful role *orality* had on the text and teaching.

Werner Kelber correctly implores, "If [only] we can wean ourselves from the notion that texts constitute the center of gravity in tradition."[16] Loubser offers two reasons for the necessity of some unlearning, "Almost by default, most people living in modern literate cultures are 'media blind' . . . it [oral poetics] goes against the grain of our deep-seated literate inclinations."[17] C. S. Lewis concurs, "the greatest barrier between us and our ancestors is the categorical barrier between oral and literary structures."[18] Alter adds, "As modern readers of the Bible, we need to relearn something of this mode of perception that was second nature to the original audience."[19] Bible communicators often talk about knowing the context of antiquity. Part of that context includes knowing how oralists (due to circumstances or choice) interpret and communicate narratives.

3. **The spoken Word influenced the written Word**

The spoken word influenced the written word because Scripture was written primarily for the ear. Richard Horsely calls Scripture "oral-derived

---

14. God-inspired voice (Deut 18:18–20; 1 Kgs 17:24; 2 Sam 32:2; Ezek 3:27, 30; Acts 28:25; 1 Thess 2:13; 2 Pet 1:20–21) and God-inspired script (2 Tim 3:16–17) co-existed. No "Great Divide" then, nor should there be today.

15. I use this order to represent theological and hermeneutic influence, not significance.

16. Kelber, "Jesus and Tradition," 163.

17. Loubser, *Oral and Manuscript Culture in the Bible,* 4, 74.

18. C. S. Lewis quoted in Wuellner, "Where is Rhetorical Criticism Taking Us," 457.

19. Alter, *Art of Biblical Narrative,* 62.

texts."[20] Jan Assmann adds, "Text is speech in the status of a mnemonic mark."[21] David Carr summarizes, a copied text "stood as a permanent reference point for an ongoing process of largely oral recitation."[22] Scripture became a "sound print" hybrid as rhetoric (art of persuasion) influenced the written and the written influenced the rhetoric. Even so, rhetoric reigned in texts, presentations and interpretations.

"Thus *says* the Lord" (emphasis added) is repeated over 400 times. Jesus often repeated the phrase, "you have heard it *said*." (emphasis added) Loubser goes so far as to call Paul an "oral theologian"[23] because he generously mixed the oral within his written letters. Dean Flemming tells us why, "Paul's writings are less a collection of doctrinal studies than a series of theological conversations between the apostle and his diverse audiences with their life circumstances."[24]

Scripture is strongly speech-sourced writing where personalities integrate with propositions. Influenced predominately by oral audiences,

---

20. Horsley, *Whoever Hears You Hears Me*, 60. Such texts also aided retention: "The compositions were structured to facilitate the retention for the oral performer as well as for the hearing audience. Written text can be understood as memory aids." Maxey, "New Testament and African Orality," 112.

21. Assmann, "Form as a Mnemonic Device," 72. Wendland notes, "a variety of stylistic devices within such ancient written compositions that were utilized for macro-structural design purposes and also to orally shape the text; among them are these: the recycling of major, culturally-relevant themes, concepts, key terms, and images; cohesive and strategic (boundary-marking) repetition, restatement, and paraphrase; the use of standard opening and closing transitional formulas; much parallelism and patterning in doublets/triads, or in terraced and chiastic arrangements; a preference for graphic, 'memorable' imagery, figures of speech, sayings, epithets, catch-words, familiar symbols, acrostic-alphabetic arrangements; citations of, and allusions to information that is already well-known; frequent dramatic, interactive discourse (real and rhetorical questions, interjections, imperatives, vocatives, etc.); periodic poetic or rhythmic, euphonic, sound-sensitive sequences of utterances; and as a general rule, the inclusion of as much direct 'character' speech as possible." Wendland, *Orality and its Implications*, 42–43.

22. Carr, *Writing on the Tablet of the Heart*, 4. Ben Witherington insightfully argues, "It is thus quite the wrong way around to talk about figuring out how rhetoric could be used in an epistolary mode. The issue was how letters could be written in a predominately oral and rhetorical culture that might faithfully reflect the rhetorical nature of discourse, and especially the various forms of public discourse." Witherington, "Why Ignoring the Rhetorical Shape of Oral Texts," para 3.

23. Loubser, "Orality and Literacy in the Pauline Epistles," 67.

24. Flemming, *Contextualization in the New Testament*, 105. Dunn adds, "One cannot hope to write a theology of Paul except by listening to his letters as dialogue, over-hearing, as it were, a great theological mind and spirit as it grappled with diversely challenging situations and questions . . . Rather, in the letters we see and are privileged to overhear *theology in the making*, theology coming to expression, Paul theologizing." Dunn, *New Testament Theology*, 15–16 (emphasis original).

Bible authors adjusted the texts for the ear (heart and memory), not just the eye (mind and documents). The ear interplayed with and complemented the eye, and vice versa.

4. Not only did voice precede text, it also followed text

For centuries after the written text, voice still played a major role in interpretation and communication. Stock synthesizes, "the rules of oratorical discourse invaded the world of texts."[25] Hearon expands:

> Alongside this perception of the text as 'written,' however, is the experience of the written text as, principally, a spoken word that is read aloud, heard, and remembered. This is also how the text is most often employed: it is quoted in discourse and appealed to in debate. Equally strong is both the perception and encounter of the text as a living voice that continues to speak to the present . . . The Hebrew Scriptures, therefore, are representative of the complex relationship between written and spoken word. They are perceived of as both written word and spoken word (as having 'voice'), yet they are most often encountered and employed as spoken word.[26]

The spoken Voice never detached or distanced itself from the written Voice.[27] The written script speaks because it is spoken script![28] Written scripts are living, speaking scripts. The sacred Script speaks! *Has our literate background caused us to undervalue speaking and listening?*

Because most ancients assumed sound to be superior to script,[29] they therefore believed respectable teachers when teaching relied on their memory, *not* written text. They also assumed reading should *not* be conducted silently or in solitude. Reading required the power of voice;

---

25. Stock, "Chiastic Awareness," 26. See also Winger, "Spoken Word," 133–51.

26. Hearon, "Interplay," 65.

27. The Bible ends not just with the written word, but also the spoken word from the throne: ("I, Jesus, have sent My messenger *to show you and guide you* so that you in turn would share this testimony with the churches, I am the Root and Descendant of David, the Bright Morning Star" (Rev 22:16 VOICE [emphasis original]).

28. Jousse provides some nuance to the spoken and oral, "Spoken style is the style of everyday conversation. Oral style is designed to be heard, remembered, and transmitted by memory." Quoted in Harvey, *Listening to the Text*, 56.

29. Third century Christian, Papias, claimed oral tradition to be superior to the printed page: "I did not suppose that information from books would help me so much as the word of a living and surviving voice." (In Irenaeus, *Against Heresies* 3.39.3–4. See also Winger, "Spoken Word."

reading required the script *be read out loud* (Acts 8:30) *and in community* (Col 4:16; 1 Tim 4:13).

Nor did the change from oral to literate happen overnight. As Ong explains, "even after the development of writing, the pristine oral-aural modes of knowledge storage and retrievals still dominate . . . Only during the last half of the second century did a scribal culture . . . begin to dominate the transmission of early Christian literature."[30] Even then, "literacy was used to enhance and facilitate orality."[31]

5. **The narrative sections of Scripture cannot be understood to their fullest without an understanding of orality**

   What perishes in print? Bible authors wrote not just for *cerebral meaning*, but also for *emotional and imaginative impact!* Stories speak, offering a surplus of emotional-imaginative-based transcendent truths that come in a rainbow of colors without bypassing the mind.[32] Grounded in orality, stories are inherently relational in nature.

   Few on the literacy side of spoken-written Scripture have been taught to engage the cinematic nature of Bible *characters* to discover the sense and significance of a story, rather they search for *theological headlines*. Ryken and Longman wave this warning flag: "[L]iterary texts are irreducible to propositional statements and single meanings. A propositional statement of a theme can never be a substitute or even the appointed goal of experiencing a literary text."[33] It is time to reconsider the role of concrete characters in Bible interpretation.

   Theology is conveyed most strongly and completely when demonstrated through *living relationships*. Until an event becomes storied characters where relationships reign within events, theology tends to remain naked ideas having minimal emotional, imaginative impact. *Focusing exclusively or even minimally on theological ideas deplatforms, demystifies, denarratizes, deevents, deenfleshes, and decharacherizes the dominate literary genre of Scripture—narrative. Worse yet, it deincarnates the Chief Character—Jesus—making Him an Idea.*[34] Robust theology revealed through relationships focuses on formation rather than information.

---

30. Ong, *Interfaces of the Word*, 214.

31. Dewey, *Orality and Textuality in Early Christian Literature*, 45.

32. "Spirit-led imagination, an imagination converted by the Word, is an essential faculty for the work of theological exegesis" Hays, *Reading with a Grain of Scripture*, 39.

33. Ryken and Longman, *Complete Literary Guide to the Bible*, 17.

34. "The Voice took on flesh *and became human* and chose to live alongside us." (John 1:14 VOICE).

Theology acquired through reasoning about God is at its strongest when it intersects with others, including Bible characters and the Revealed One. This is because knowledge is most often discovered through relationships rather than reason alone. And this is why OH, intimately and intricately based on relationships, matters.

Life-changing theology has an inherently relational reflection. If Scripture is driven by a missionary God (*missio Dei*), one would expect theology to be missional as well. Theology that deserves respect will express itself to the nations through seeking and serving others, especially strangers.

Viable theology is relational theology that goes beyond the interaction between human and spiritual characters. One way this happens is by tying people's encounters with their Creator to places. Walter Brueggemann captures this concept when he comments on "the preoccupation of the Bible for placement."[35] Such placement encounters begin in the Garden of Eden, moves to the Promised Land, the Exile, the Incarnation in Bethlehem,[36] culminating in the New Jerusalem. Each of these geographical placements could be associated with central Bible characters. God's story is often tied to our story theologically through geography associated with Bible characters.

Viable theology is relational theology that expresses the living voice of the Liberating King. Such theology is engineered to challenge our and our acquaintances daily relationship with the Eternal One. Amos Yong summarizes, "The church is measured by how well it embodies the life of Christ, how extensively it welcomes and is constituted by the weak, and how prophetically it holds up the mirror of the gospel to an unbelieving world."[37] Tasked by the Trinity[38] to guard and advance transcendent truth that transforms and liberates, the global community of Faith (not just professionals), the recipients of grace, offer that same grace (*missio Dei* in action) through daily examples and explanations of "the Way" so that spiritual maturation (wisdom) and numerical multiplication ensues. Viable theology of "the Way" is relationally expressed on the way as the called call out others through works and words.

In sum, orality connects not just people through stories, but hearts and places as well. And it opens the door for *all* to interpret Bible stories, not just those formally trained in biblical and theological studies! The

35. Brueggemann, *Land*, 10.

36. "It is clear from the incarnation that places are the seat of relations or the place of meeting and activity in the interaction between God and the world" Inge, *Christian Theology of Place*, 52. Italics original.

37. Yong, *Theology and Down Syndrome*, 199.

38. "The formula of the Trinity is the shorthand symbol that encodes the story of the Christian community." Haight, *Spiritualty Seeking Theology*, 178.

spoken-written hybrid Word (not just the written[39]) is foundational to a full-orbed, more robust understanding of the narrative sections of Scripture, including her Author.

Capturing the Chapters

Chapter 3 addresses the question, *what was the influence of orality on the text and teaching?* One of the many books I scoured was Werner Kelber's *The Oral and the Written Gospel: The Hermeneutics of Speaking and Writing in the Synoptic Tradition, Mark, Paul, and Q*. Drawing from the classicists, linguists, and cultural anthropologists, this book became a watershed in New Testament studies in the 1970s and 1980s highlighting orality's *missing role* in textual construction and interpretation.

While reading the book, I immediately recognized the close connections between orality and text in first-century Christianity and the Ifugao as they transitioned from a predominantly oral society to a more literate one.[40] Kelber's "text-bound minds"[41] immediately rang true. I later read *Jesus the Voice and the Text: Beyond the Oral and the Written Gospel* that celebrated and challenged twenty-five years of Kelber's ground-breaking volume in New Testament studies, where years of clarity introduced helpful insights both positively and negatively.

Textual Construction

Interestingly, we tend to reinterpret Revelation 2:7 as, "Let the person who is able to *read* . . ." (emphasis added) rather than "Let the person who is able to *hear*" (VOICE, emphasis added). While we read the following words in Scripture, due to our oral blindness, little attention is often given to the implications of the oral background that influenced meaning, motivation and memory.

---

39. God has chosen to build relationships with His highest creation through verbal and visual means. He accomplishes this through word-based relationships (the spoken Word), image-based relationships (symbols), print-based relationships (the written Word). All these find their center and core in an Incarnation-based relationship—Jesus Christ, the Chief Character. The Eternal One utilizes multiple types of relationships to address the various types of learning styles around the globe.

40. Parents will note a similar journey as their oral taught children learn to read and write.

41. Ong, *Orality and Literacy*, 153.

Words such as, "hear," "heard," "said," "say," "speak," "announce," "proclaim," "listen," "teach," "exhort," "sing," and "ear," dominate the landscapes of the Old and New Testaments as authors intuitively chose oral categories to communicate the "Word of God" for listeners. Voiced writing resulted.[42]

Gerhardsson summarizes, "In antiquity words were written down to be read out. Even the written word was formulated for the ear."[43] That is because "All, including literate elites, were steeped in oral culture."[44] Literacy has blinded many of us to the oral inferences of the written text.

In the New Testament, textual construction relied on eyewitnesses who *heard and saw* Jesus in everyday life, thereby providing the written text legitimacy.[45]

> This testimony is true. In fact it is an eyewitness account; and he has reported what he saw so that you also may believe. (John 19:35 VOICE)

> We want to tell you about the One who was from the beginning. We have seen Him with our own eyes, heard Him with our own ears, and touched Him with our own hands. This One is *the manifestation of* the life-giving Voice . . . What we saw and heard we pass on to you so that you, too, will be connected with us intimately *and become family.* (1 Jn 1:1, 3 VOICE emphasis original)

> For those who love God, several other people have already written accounts of what God has been bringing to completion among us, using the reports of the original eyewitnesses, those who were there from the start to witness the fulfillment of prophecy. Like those other servants who have recorded the messages, I present to you my carefully researched, orderly account of these new teachings. (Acts 1:1–3 VOICE)

Some questions often overlooked in relation to eyewitnesses, are:

- *Did Jesus communicate the same message more than once?*
- *Was the message heard differently in rural and urban settings?*
- *In which language was it presented?*
- *When is the "original" the "original" in the oral world?*

42. Steffen, "Saving the Locals from Our Theologies, Part 1," 14.
43. Gerhardsson, "Gospel Tradition," 519.
44. Rhoads and Dewey, "Performance Criticism," 12.
45. See Witherington, *What's in the Word*, 122–42.

- *Have our literate backgrounds placed an overemphasis on words rather than meaning?*

I offer this possible answer to the last question:

> the 'Word' was not thought of as certain unchangeable words (in contrast to meaning), 'word studies,' 'proof-texting,' or word dissections to their minutest fragment. Rather, it was considered as a living event that carried 'deliberate ambiguity' in time and space expressed and sensed through emotive words, inflections, facial expressions, gestures, and so forth. All this demanded dialogue to discover its mysterious meaning.[46]

Volume of Oral Literature in Scripture

A pastor once informed me, "Truth is too important to leave to story." Fortunately, someone had forgotten to inform the Holy Spirit. As Eugene Peterson proposes, "The Holy Spirit's literary genre of choice is story."[47] That is because around 55 percent of Scripture is presented in story format. Add the six books of poetry,[48] another subset of orality, and the percentage jumps to around 85–90 percent of Scripture. The Author seems to assume that emotions and imagination[49] are central to gaining spiritual truths. James K. A. Smith concurs, "It is not primarily our minds that are captivated but rather our *imaginations* that are captured, and when our imagination is hooked, *we're* hooked" (emphasis original).[50] Orality exploits the senses without sidelining reason.

Delivery and Dialogue

When a new manuscript showed up at a community of faith's gathering place, a number of assumptions were generally understood:

---

46. Steffen, "Saving Locals from Our Theologies, Part 1," 14–15.

47. Peterson, *Leap Over A Wall*, 3.

48. Song books (Job, Proverbs, Ecclesiastes) and wisdom literature (Psalms, Song of Solomon, Lamentations). See https://overviewbible.com/poetry/.

49. "Imagination is a necessary component of all profound knowing and celebration; all remembering, realizing, and anticipating; all faith, hope, and love. When imagination fails doctrines become ossified, witness and proclamation wooden, doxologies and litanies empty, consolations hollow, and ethics legalistic. It is at the level of the imagination that any full engagement with life takes place." Wilder, *Theopoetic*, 2.

50. Smith, *Desiring the Kingdom*, 54.

- The individual who delivered the document would intimately know the message the author wished to convey.
- The whole text would be read publicly.
- Emotional exclamations could punctuate the presentation followed by discussion at conclusion.
- As oralists, they focused on meaning rather than words.
- The honor of the one who delivered the text was on the line to guard the author's message, as was the honor of the specific community of faith to guard transcendent truths once internalized. Each entity became responsible patrons.
- Texts were tedious to read, having no punctuation, paragraph markers, and so forth.
- All participants could be involved in interpretation.[51]

Oral Hermeneutics

By oral hermeneutics (OH) the authors mean a communal experiential interpretation method to understand more fully Scripture's narrative genre. It accomplishes this by focusing on the conversations, actions, and interactions of characters found in the biblical text. This ancient-modern art ponders passages of Scripture characterologically, considers the era, event(s), setting and surroundings, plot, attire, gestures, posture, direct and inward speech, symbols, rituals, conduct, conflicts, choices, consequences of choices, among others, as characters embody and demonstrate (rather than define and explain) meaning. To discover the transcendent truths the author wished to convey, OH conducts character analysis through primarily character-centric questions. Multiple versions are presently in use, such as Firm Foundations, Simply the Story, OneStory, StoryTogether, Oral Bible Storytelling, BibleTelling, StoryFire.

The word "oral" tips readers off that its operational mode uses oral skills and is therefore relational oriented—reading out loud, vocal telling that is always accompanied by body language, group discussion, and the exchange of insights. The dynamic of relational chemistry produces a surplus of meaning (including motivation and memory). The mutual honing of observations and applications as group members discuss, complement

---

51. Interpretation included may more non-scholars than scholars. "All interpretation is a risk . . . But it is a risk that no interpreter can avoid taking." Loubser, *Oral and Manuscript Culture in the Bible*, 226, 238.

and correct each other facilitates relevance, accuracy and applications to daily life. This is in contrast to a hermeneutic that can be done alone by an individual sitting in a library with a stack of books.

OH requires an honest review of some of the accepted assumptions in the present hermeneutic world. These could include:

1. orality has little to do with textual construction,
2. propositions dominate Scripture,
3. textual-based hermeneutic theories are sufficient,
4. a narrative text always has a single meaning,
5. propositional logic is superior to all other forms of logic, including narrative logic,
6. rational theology is superior to relational theology, and
7. Scripture is best read when done individually, privately and piece-meal.[52]

The biggest issue most readers will face, as did the authors, is number four—a narrative text always has a single author-intended meaning. Enlightenment-based textual hermeneutic models later influenced by science has argued this for centuries. *But should parts of the Bible be limited to science that allows for only one answer when it was never designed for scrutiny by such a hermeneutic? Does story provide its own set of literary boundaries to serve as guiderails and guardrails of interpretation for the more ambiguous nature of orality?*

A number of terms have been used by various authors to express how transcendent truth is captured in an ambiguous oral-aural sociocultural setting. These include: "creative-correct theology,"[53] "fixed-fluidity," "creative fidelity" and "ruled spontaneity."[54] Dunn depicts it as, "a stable core and substance with variation."[55] Narrative finds itself constricted but not corralled by boundaried fluidity.

---

52. "Gutenberg printing press, because it put information into the hands of everyday people, is credited with the rise of individualism, literacy, complex language, private contemplation, the literary tradition, and the advent of Protestantism. By 1500, just fifty years after its invention, more than twelve million books were in print in Europe (and people were already complaining that there were too many books." Wheatley, "Living in the Age of Distraction," 64.

53. Autry, "Dimensions," 37, 49.

54. Vanhoozer, *Drama of Doctrine*, 129.

55. Dunn, *Oral Gospel Tradition*, 359.

No Bible story, however, is open to *any* interpretation. Rather, all interpretation is *internally* corralled by literary boundaries (e.g., chiasm, verbal echoes, parallelism, repetition of sounds), the grand narrative of Scripture,[56] and *externally* protected through the *individual shame* of the Bible communicator, the *collective shame*[57] of the local hermeneutic faith community, the international hermeneutic faith community through all ages, and of course the guiding hand of the Holy Spirit (Chapter 3).

The circumference of biblical truth, concludes Ivor Poobalan, "must be both rooted [in the Word] and responsive [culturally contextual]."[58] OH operates within the confines of literary boundaries, individual and collective shame, the grand narrative of Scripture,[59] and the universal priesthood of the believers over the centuries to help ensure minimal interpretive distortions.[60]

Interestingly, when talking about the return of OH, the authors are *not* talking about something new. The "people of the Voice" who became "people of the Book" and served as a light to the nations utilized OH for centuries to interpret Jesus' Bible—the Hebrew Bible (Chapter 5). Marvin Wilson quotes George Adam Smith as saying:

> Hebrew may be called primarily a language of the senses. The words originally expressed concrete or material things and movements or actions which struck the senses or started the emotions. Only secondarily and *in metaphor* could they be used to denote abstract or metaphysical ideas.[61]

---

56. "Correct interpretations of Scripture are most often surrounded by correct understandings and practices of God's mission (Gen 41–50; Dan 3–7; Acts 10:44–48; 11:15–18), while obscured interpretation occurs precisely when mission is obscured (Jonah 1–4; Matt 8–1)." Redman, *Missiological Hermeneutics*, 8.

57. Understanding how honor and shame works in a society will help grasp how meaning is protected.

58. Poobalan, "Christology in Asia," 84. Just as Bible authors borrowed and adapted relevant elements from various cultures outside of Israel (covenants, circumcision, kingship), so must today's Bible communicators.

59. "But the fact is that the Bible itself is the grandest of grand stories, yet it prizes truth and reason without being modernist, and it prizes countless stories within its overall story without being postmodern" Guiness, *Fool's Talk*, 33. Some will perceive the grand narrative as linear while others will perceive it as circular. See Steffen, "Clothesline Theology for the World," 37–56.

60. "We can never approach the Bible as though we are the first ones to read it—or the first to read it appropriately. We know that we have much to learn from the wisdom of the people who have reflected deeply on these texts before us. Consequently, *theological exegesis will find hermeneutical aim not hindrance in the church's doctrinal traditions*." Hays, *Reading with a Grain of Scripture*, 39. emphasis original

61. Wilson, *Our Father Abraham*, 137.

The OH that the authors argue for is *not* a new fad, nor is it anti-intellectual, nor is it just storytelling for children's ministry, nor is it just for tribal people. OH is the retrieval and adaptation to our current age and audiences of an ancient and venerable Hebrew hermeneutic. Winston Churchill correctly claimed, "The further back you can look, the farther forward you are likely to see."[62] How far back do you look?

Character Theology

The authors define *characters* as humans, animals (donkeys, horses, cows, birds, roosters, whales), spiritual beings (angels, demons), individuals (Paul, Rahab) or groups (Pharisees and Sadducees), real (Mary) or fictional (Good Samaritan), marginalized (poor blind Bartimaeus) or prominent (Pilate), good (Moses) or evil (Pharaoh) who participate in a story. "Theology" breaks down into two parts, *theos* and *ology* or *logos*. *Theos* is Greek for God while *ology* (words) or *logos* (events)—words as events.[63] *Theology*[64] is defined simply as humans attempt to understand God as revealed through characters and events documented in Scripture. In *Worldview-based Storying* I provided a summative overview of CT:

> By character theology I mean utilizing some of the more than 2900 human characters in the Bible, including groups, such as the Pharisees or Sadducees, along with those associated with the spirit world, such as the Holy Spirit, Satan, angels and demons, to teach abstract doctrines, morals, and ethics. Character theology relies on earthy, concrete characters to frame abstract truths and concepts, thereby providing ideas a home. It does so even as it retains God as the center of the story, and the individual story's place within the broader sweep of Scripture . . . For example, rather than teach the abstract doctrine of justification by faith, let the earthy lives of Abraham and David define this abstract

---

62. https://www.goodreads.com/quotes/535242-the-farther-back-you-can-look-the-farther-forward-you.

63. Kelber notes, "Gerhard Kittel has stressed the activist character of *logos* with a seriousness rarely encountered in Pauline scholarship: 'In all this the *logos* is always genuine *legein,* or spoken word in all concreteness. One of the most serious errors of which one could be guilty would be to make this *logos tou theou* a concept or abstraction.' As a rule, the Pauline reference to *logos* or *logos tou theou* is to the living, preached word of the gospel." Kelber, *Oral and Written Gospel,* 144. For a tidy summary, see also Walton and Sandy, *Lost World of Scripture,* 121–27.

64. Kosuke Koyama points out the life-sustaining abilities of "theology" which he defines as "an exciting report on our having rice with Jesus." Koyama, "We had Rice with Jesus," 19.

doctrine (Romans 4). Dogma without spiritual and human characters defining it is on the fast track to coldness. Bringing Bible characters out of the closet will heat up the conversation.[65]

The Bible's "compelling immediacy"[66] makes Character Theology human, natural, earthy, visceral, immediate. This is brought about in part through "participatory history," i.e., the human experience the listener/reader/viewer encounters in a story. Harry Stout explains, "history stories are neither past nor present but both simultaneously."[67] The past is simultaneously the present, and vice versa, thereby making relational connection possible, often instantaneously with a character in the story. *Bible characters easily enter our lives through familiar pedagogical paths and leave their footprints forever imprinted on our hearts, thereby challenging and even changing present practices and postures.* Recognizing the contrastive role of characters in scriptural stories helps create clarity in our lives.

In character theology, *personalities precede propositions*. This principle should extend to how we learn about the Eternal One. In many passages of Scripture, the First and the Last revealed His character through characters. This is because Bible stories show rather than tell, enact rather than explain, illuminate rather than spell out, demonstrate rather than define, embody rather than conceptualize, encounter rather than detail, present rather than assert, thereby leaving much mystery to the imagination, emotions, and conversation to the listening-examining audience.

Questioning Our Questions

Jesus was not only the quintessential Storyteller, He was also the quintessential Questioner. His 300 plus[68] penetrating questions made people not only think, but rethink. His piercing questions were focused, open-ended, caught listeners off guard, ripped off fake masks, captured the big picture, drilled down to bedrock assumptions, providing storytellers a model to emulate.

Engaging a new type of theology (character theology [CT]) requires a new set of handles for how we grasp Scripture. To review a previous Bible story, introduce a new one, interpret it, tie it to previous stories, and apply (unite doctrine and duty) it, all in a way that contributes to a more robust character theology, *what type of questions should the storyteller ask?*

65. Steffen, *Worldview-based Storying:* 211; Steffen, *Facilitator Era,* 149.
66. Alter, *World of Biblical Literature,* 210.
67. Stout, "Theological Commitment," 48.
68. Tiede, *339 Questions Jesus Asked.*

The authors suggest that these handles come in the form of character-centric questions.

As the authors investigated the questions presently used by a number of organizations, some commonalities emerged:

1. generalized, generic questions;
2. strong focus on guilt and innocence (obedience);
3. strong focus on individuals;
4. systematic questioning; and a
5. limited number of questions.

Limiting the number of questions in Bible discussions raises the following questions:

- *Does the small number of questions actually do a disservice to the story? To the recipients?*
- *Should the number of questions be increased? more free-flowing? more conversational?*
- *Do story-listeners, many having exceptional people intuition skills and phenomenal memories, have difficulty handling more than six to eight questions, especially when focused on what people say and do?*
- *Are questions few in number something Westerners, coming from a highly textual society where print-dependent memories tend to be weak, project on their audiences?*
- *Should the questions be more culturally sensitive?*
- *Do the questions focus mostly on the cognitive? on characters? on actionizing godly wisdom? on value systems such as innocence-guilt, honor and shame, power and fear, purity and pollution?*

Rather than the storyteller relying on a limited number of formulaic questions, the dialogue should determine the number, flow, focus, framing (safe, closed, open ended, rhetorical), and to whom directed.[69] Generally, questions related to OH focus on characters, circumstances, contexts, conversations, comparisons, constraints, clarifications, controversies, critiques, correctives, chances, conclusions, choices, and consequences of those

---

69. "Questions that allow the learner to reflect in a holistic way on a picture or a story may help him or her gain confidence in answering, again because the questions do not imply a right answer." Lingenfelter and Lingenfelter, *Teaching Cross-Culturally*, 54. This is especially true where honor-shame reigns strong in a culture.

choices within said story. *Should Westerners rethink how they use questions when storying the Bible at home and abroad?*

The authors then propose questions designed for oralists on two levels. The ground (micro) level introduces questions for a single Bible story (from ties to previous stories, background of present story, the story itself, walk-the-talk (application) and heresy buster questions). These questions are semi-spontaneous, assymetrical, character-centric. They also ask the same type of questions from a second level– 30,000 feet—the macro level. Such "big picture" questions tie a single story to other stories in a story set *and* previous Bible stories heard, developing a growing grasp of the metanarrative of Scripture (which serves as the foundational hermeneutic to *all* parts of the Bible). Driven by orality and narrative logic, OH theologizes through character-centric questions to 1) discover character theology in each story (and surrounding stories in the same text), 2) detect the metanarrative of Scripture that ties all the characters together and serves as a hermeneutic tool in discovering (or limiting) transendent truth, and 3) as we marinate in the metanarrative, determine our personal/communal identity (mirrored reality) with those characters and our specific role (motivation for spiritual formation and missional service) in the metanarrative.[70]

Concluding Reflections

The central question that drives this introductory book on OH is, *why is it important to know and practice OH in interpreting and communicating biblical meaning?* The proposals offered will be a noisy lightning bolt to some, a light bulb moment to others. One's grasp of orality will most likely be the distinguishing and defining factor.

A metaphorical wagon wheel could summarize this book (Figure 10.1). The hub, which connects the entire wheel to the axle, constitutes symbolically the breadth and depth of orality that drives OH. The axle that turns the entire wheel (often unseen and assumed) symbolizes narrative logic that guides and galvanizes OH. The multiple spokes that connect the hub to the rim represent the controlling characters within said story, including the Chief Character. Guided by text discussion-driven, character-centric questions, communal character-theologizing begins, eventually emerging into character theology. Transcendent truths discerned are then displayed on the outer rim where abstract values, morals, and theology are

---

70. "commitment to preserve the story arc of the entire Bible at all times will protect preachers and storytellers from misrepresentation of particular events." Short, "Formed by Story," 121.

constantly in touch with *terra firma* in life's journey (or "where the rubber [steel] meets the road").

OH Offers A Relational Theology

Given that most Global North[71] Bible communicators of the past who went to the Global South[72] did not pack OH, and it still remains a dubious if not dangerous proposal in the Global North today, this time-tested, Hebrew-based hermeneutic that seeks connections (in contrast to TH that seeks contradictions) offers an attractive global alternative to TH. OH advances a meaningful construct for a global audience who will appreciate it as they discover from the spoken-written Sacred Storybook the demonstrated rather than the defined, a relational Hero rather than an abstract Idea, a person rather than a principle. *Could OH be the mother of relational theology?*

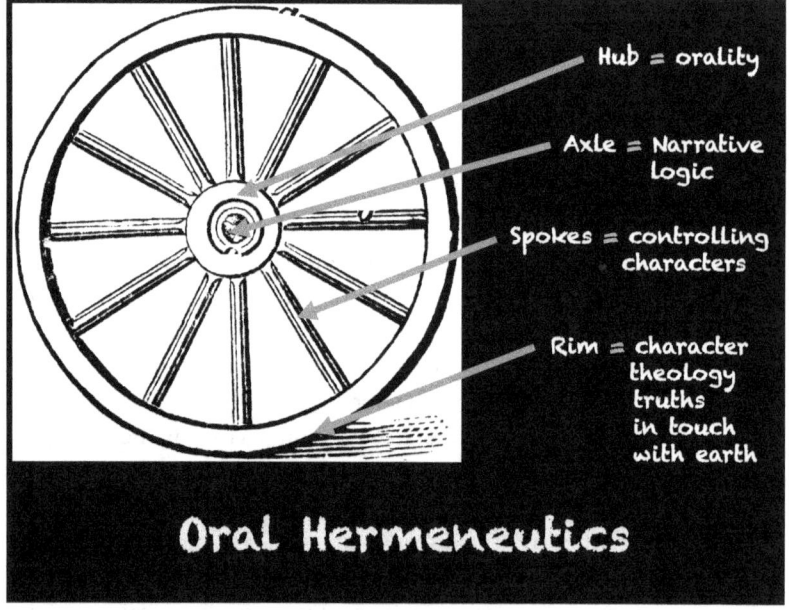

Figure 10.1. The Oral Hermeneutic Wheel

If so, some major adjustments will be required in the present hermeneutic world. This does not mean it has to be an either/or hermeneutic; it can be a complementary both/and continuum evidencing overlap and

---

71. Includes North America, Europe, Australasia, and developed areas of East Asia.
72. Includes Asia, much of the Middle East, Africa, Latin American, the Caribbean.

interplay.[73] But such a continuum requires an initial sequence to respect and protect the narrative genre—from the relational concrete (OH) to the propositional abstract (TH). Table 10.1 summarizes the OH-TH continuum. The authors do not advocate a hostile hermeneutic takeover.

Table 10.1 Oral-Textual Hermeneutic Continuum

Bible is a case book		Bible is a code book
Bible discussions	⟷	Bible studies
Narrative logic	⟷	Propositional logic
Meaning is central	⟷	Words are central
Whole	⟷	Fragments
Heart hermeneutic	⟷	Head hermeneutic
Experiential apologetics	⟷	Evidential apologetics
Character thinking	⟷	Critical thinking
Character-centric questions	⟷	Content-centric questions
Character analysis	⟷	Textual analysis
Character historical	⟷	Grammatical-historical
Character-centric meaning	⟷	Text-centric meaning
Demonstrations	⟷	Definitions
Relational	⟷	Rational
Character theology	⟷	Categorical theology
Relational theology	⟷	Abstract theology
Big character	⟷	"Big idea"
Multiple truths	⟷	"One main point"
Proof chants	⟷	Proof texts

Does OH offer the potential to unleash the proclaimed, published and performed Scripture to the majority of God's current and future Jesus-followers around the globe? While TH hopefully will continue to succeed in what it is scientifically designed to do, the authors believe Bible

---

73. Orality resolves modernity's dualism of "fact-value, intellect-imagination, reason-emotion, and so on." Fisher, *Human Communication as Narration*, 68.

communicators will fail to get people into the Bible and get the Bible into people to the greater extent all would hope for if we fail to invite OH to the banquet table.

Just as orality preceded literacy, so OH preceded TH. Just as the spoken and the written Word were eventually perceived as a continuum, so must OH and TH. Why? Because TH keeps OH on target through fragments while OH keeps TH full of life without sacrificing Scripture's grand narrative. Carr offers another caveat, "Orality and writing technology are joint means for accomplishing a common goal: accurate recall of the treasured tradition."[74] For an audience to discover a more in-depth and sweeping understanding of the mysteries of stories in Scripture, the "treasured traditions," Bible communicators must learn to respect not just the written side of Scripture, but also the rhetorical. While OH is *not the final word* for analysis of the narrative sections of Scripture, it should be the *first*.

Like Ella, contemptuously called Cinderella, has OH been neglected, undervalued, and excluded from the Hermeneutic Palace? Can a female scullery maid and cinder cleaner (in the minds of her stepmother and stepsisters) become a sought out beautiful princess at the Hermeneutic Palace Ball? Will Prince Charming ever be able to find someone who perfectly fits the lost glass slipper, marry her, and live happily ever after in the Hermeneutic Palace—discovered, valued and accepted? The authors hope so.

Whatever the model or methodology, there are always proponents who take it too far. The wise, however, never allow the excesses or romanticizing of some oralist proponents to jettison a legitimate methodology. If the goal is to discover transcendent truth, however, dissenting voices are required. *The Return of Oral Hermeneutics* will be successful if it can initiate an *in-depth reflection and discussion of OH* between professors, pastors and practitioners.

The daring declarations made in *The Return of Oral Hermeneutic* deserve dialogue. This book will be a success if a spirited, mature, in-depth, and ongoing discussion in the academies, agencies and assemblies about the philosophical-cultural underpinnings and implications of TH and OH takes place.[75] *Which hermeneutic model is acultural?* Only when such crucial conversations transpire will a *fuller, deeper, richer* interpretation of narrative texts be possible. Only when this happens will a more *complete* picture of the face of Chief Character be drawn.

---

74. Carr, *Writing on the Tablet of the Heart*, 7. In the New Testament, this would include the "apostle's teaching" (oral tradition) that was memorized (Acts 2:42).

75. OH would be a critical topic for EMS and ASM to take up.

These claims and conclusions, however, are certainly not new. After outlining the interest in orality by secular scholars in the 1920s *to* Christian scholars applying oral theory primarily on the Old Testament in the 1960s *to* Kelber's writings on the relationship between orality and New Testament documents in the late 1970s *to* a proliferation of publications by the 1990s, Columbia Biblical Seminary of Columbia International University's John Harvey wrote almost two decades ago, "Nevertheless, most biblical scholars continue to examine the NT documents using presuppositions that apply more to the nineteenth and twentieth-century literary/print culture than to the culture in which those documents were originally produced."[76] Note any changes?

Does OH offer Bible interpreters from Sunday schools to seminaries a model that renews and restores meaning that respects the narrative genre of Scripture and the pedagogical practices of audiences around the world, resulting in growing wisdom, a different identity and added reverence for the King of kings? Harvey correctly concludes, "It is time we give closer attention to the techniques of communication which existed—and continue to exist—in strongly oral cultures. It is time we recapture the ancient paradigm of orality as one of our hermeneutic tools for biblical studies."[77] Maxwell adds, a "print culture mindset affects the way we view the biblical text and should at least to some extent, be set aside in favor of the hermeneutic of a rhetorical culture."[78] The authors wholeheartedly agree.

Fortunately for the majority of humanity, the orality drumbeats continue to escalate, yet still with little response from an oft skeptical professional hermeneutic community. And this in spite of

1. a growing understanding of orality in antiquity in relation to text and teaching,
2. a deeper understanding of orality in the sacred writings of the major religions outside of Christianity,[79]
3. a highly relational (personal and communal) theology that results,
4. an inherent framework that vividly enhances comprehension, engagement, enlightenment, reproducibility and memorability,

---

76. Harvey, "Orality and Its Implications," 99.
77. Harvey, "Orality and Its Implications," 109.
78. Maxwell, "From Performance to Text to Performance," 161.
79. See Graham, *Beyond the Written Word*.

5. a clearer understanding of the West's cultural limitations, including the limits of the Enlightenment and science in interpretation that are "bound by the categories of western rationality,"[80] and

6. knowing that around 80 percent of the present world are high oral-reliant learners and communicators.[81]

Among others, theologians and/or missiologists continued the charge on the theoretical and practical levels of hermeneutics, such as Vanhoozer in 1998 with *Is There Meaning in the Text?*, Walton and Sandy in 2013 with *The Lost World of Scripture: Ancient Literary Culture and Biblical Authority* and Larry Caldwell with *Doing Bible Interpretation* in 2016. And there are a number of books and dissertations on OH currently in the making. Stay tuned.

Back to the question tied to this year's EMS theme: *How should those models (in this case hermeneutic) be adjusted or abandoned as we make disciples across cultures into the future?* The answer is *neither!* Rather, an *addition* is needed—a hermeneutic that respects and does justice to the narrative genre of Scripture influenced by orality. Maxey correctly concludes, "Issues of orality can transform exegetical methods."[82] *Could yesterday's ridiculousness be today's sensibleness? Could what some perceived as Death Valley (OH) be a blossoming spring desert?* The authors hope they have cultivated curiosity. Let the dialogues and debates begin between those within the academies, agencies and assemblies.

Bibliography

Alter, Robert. *The Art of Biblical Narrative*. New York: Basic, 1981.
———. *The World of Biblical Literature*. New York: Basic, 1992.
Assmann, Jan. "Form as a Mnemonic Device: Cultural Texts and Cultural Memory." In *Performing the Gospel: Orality, Memory, and Mark*, edited by Richard A. Horsley et al., 67–82. Augsburg: Fortress, 2011.
Autry, Arden C. "Dimensions of Hermeneutics in Pentecostal Focus." *Journal of Pentecostal Theology* 3 (1993) 29–50.
Bevans, Stephen B. *Models of Contextual Theology*. New York: Orbis, 2002.
Brueggemann, Walter. *The Land: Place as Gift, Promise and Challenge in Biblical Faith*. London: SPCK, 1978.
Carr, David M. *Writing on the Tablet of the Heart: Origins of Scripture and Literature*. Oxford: Oxford University, 2005.

---

80. Shenk, "Recasting Theology of Mission," 102.

81. "Oral cultures, along with the postmodern world, bias story over propositions. Just as the Enlightenment denarrativized the Bible, so postmodernism depropositionalized it, bowing to the altar of any and all stories." Steffen, *Facilitator Era*, 130.

82. Maxey, "New Testament and African Orality," 19.

Crouch, Andy. "The Return of Shame." *Christianity Today* 59 (2015) 32–41.
Dewey, Joanna, ed. *Orality and Textuality in Early Christian Literature.* Semeia Studies. Atlanta: Scholars, 1995.
Dunn, James D. *New Testament Theology: An Introduction.* Nashville: Abingdon, 2009.
———. *The Oral Gospel Tradition.* Grand Rapids: Eerdmans, 2013.
Fisher, Walter R. *Human Communication as Narration: Toward a Philosophy of Reason, Values, and Action.* Columbia, SC: University of South Carolina, 1987.
Flemming, Dean. *Contextualization in the New Testament: Patterns for Theology and Mission.* Downers Grove, IL: InterVarsity, 2005.
Gaille, Brandon. "15 US Literacy Rate and Illiteracy Statistics." May 22, 2017. https://brandongaille.com/us-literacy-rate-and-illiteracy-statistics/.
Gerhardsson, Biger. "The Gospel Tradition." In *The Interrelationships of the Gospels,* edited by David L Dungan, 495–45. Leuven: University, 1990.
Gitay, Yehoshua. "History, Literature, and Memory." *Journal of Semitics* 18 (2009) 275–300.
Gonzàlez, Justo L. *Santa Biblica: The Bible through Hispanic Eyes.* Nashville: Abingdon, 1996.
Graham, William A. *Beyond the Written Word: Oral Aspects of Scripture in the History of Religion.* Cambridge: Cambridge University, 1987.
Guiness, Os. *Fool's Talk: Rediscovering the Art of Christian Persuasion.* Downers Grove, IL: InterVarsity, 2015.
Haight, Roger. *Spiritualty Seeking Theology.* Maryknoll, NY: Orbis, 2014.
Harvey, John D. *Listening to the Text: Oral Patterning in Paul's Letters.* Grand Rapids: Baker, 1998.
———. "Orality and Its Implications for Biblical Studies: Recapturing an Ancient Paradigm." *JETS* 45 (2002) 99–109.
Hays, Richard B. *Reading with a Grain of Scripture.* Grand Rapids: Eerdmans, 2020.
Hearon, Holly. "The Interplay Between Written and Spoken Word in the Second Testament as Background to the Emergence of Written Gospels." *Oral Tradition Journal* 25 (2010) 57–74.
Henry, Carl F. H. *God, Revelation, and Authority, Volume III: God Who Speaks and Shows.* Carlisle, UK: Paternoster, 1999.
Hess, Richard S. "Scribes." In *Dictionary of the Old Testament: Wisdom, Poetry and Writings* edited by Tremper Longman III and Peter E. Enns, 717–20. Downers Grove, IL: InterVarsity Academic, 2008.
Horsley, Richard A. *Whoever Hears You Hears Me: Prophets, Performance, and Tradition in Q.* Harrisburg, PA: Trinity Press International, 1999.
Inge, John. *A Christian Theology of Place.* New York: Routledge, 2003.
Kelber, Werner H. "Jesus and Tradition: Words in Time, Words in Space." In *Orality and Textuality in Early Christian Literature,* edited by Joanna Dewey, 139–67. Semeia Studies. Atlanta: Scholars, 1995.
———. *The Oral and Written Gospel: The Hermeneutics of Speaking and Writing in the Synoptic Tradition, Mark, Paul, and Q.* Minneapolis: Fortress, 1983.
Koyama, Kosuke. "We had Rice with Jesus." In *Theology in Action: Papers and Extracts on Doing Theology in Today's World,* edited by Jae Shik Oh and John C. England, 19–32. Manila: East Asian Christian Conference, 1972.
Lausanne Movement, "Orality: An Infographic." May 1, 2019. https://www.lausanne.org/content/orality-an-infographic.

Lewis, C. S. Quoted in Wuellner, Wilhelm. "Where is Rhetorical Criticism Taking Us," 457. *Catholic Biblical Quarterly* 49 (1987) 448–63.

Lingenfelter, Judith E., and Sherwood G. Lingenfelter, *Teaching Cross-Culturally: An Incarnational Model for Learning and Teaching*. Grand Rapids: Baker Academic, 2003.

Loubser, J. A. (Bobby) "Orality and Literacy in the Pauline Epistles. Some New Hermeneutical Implications." *Neotestamentica* 29 (1995) 61–74.

———. *Oral and Manuscript Culture in the Bible: Studies on the Media Texture of the New Testament—Explorative Hermeneutics*. Biblical Performance Criticism 7. Eugene, OR: Cascade, 2013.

Lovejoy, Grant. "The Extent of Orality." *JBTM* 5 (2008) 121–33. https://orality.imb.org/files/1/1255/Lovejoy—Extent%20of%20Orality%202012.pdf.

Maxey, James A. *From Orality to Orality: A New Paradigm for Contextual Translation of the Bible*. Eugene: Cascade, 2009.

———. "New Testament and African Orality: Implications for Exegesis and Translation." Paper presented at the OTSSA Conference on Bible Translation, University of KwaZulu-Natal, Pietermaritzburg, South Africa, 2005, 1–23.

Maxwell, Kathy. "From Performance to Text to Performance: The New Testament's Use of the Hebrew Bible in Rhetorical Culture." In *From Text to Performance: Narrative and Performance Criticisms in Dialogue and Debate*, edited by Kelly R. Iverson, 158–81. Biblical Performance Criticism 10. Eugene, OR: Cascade, 2014.

McGeever, Ally. "Fame-Shame Culture and Social Media." *HonorShame*. March 25, 2020. http://honorshame.com/fame-shame-culture-and-social-media/.

Ong, Walter. *Interfaces of the Word: Studies in the Evolution of Consciousness and Culture*. Ithaca, NY: Cornell University, 1977.

———. *Orality and Literacy: The Technologizing of the Word*. New York: Methuen & Co., 1982.

———. *The Presence of the Word*. New Haven, CT: Yale University, 1967.

Peterson, Eugene H. *Leap Over a Wall: Earthy Spirituality for Everyday Christians*. New York: HarperCollins, 1997.

Poobalan, Ivor. "Christology in Asia: Rooted and Responsive." In *Asian Christian Theology: Evangelical Perspectives*, edited by Timoteo D. Gener and Stephen T. Pardue, 83–100. UK: Langham Global Library, 2019.

Redman, Shawn. *Missiological Hermeneutics: Biblical Interpretation for the Global Church*. Eugene, OR: Wipf & Stock, 2012.

Rhoads, David, and Joanna Dewey. "Performance Criticism: A Paradigm Shift in New Testament Studies." In *From Text to Performance: Narrative and Performance Criticisms in Dialogue and Debate*, edited by Kelly R. Iverson, 1–26. Biblical Performance Criticism 10. Eugene, OR: Cascade, 2014.

Ryken, Leland, and Tremper Longman III, eds. *A Complete Literary Guide to the Bible*. Grand Rapids: Zondervan, 1993.

Shenk, Wilbert R. "Recasting Theology of Mission: Impulses from the Non-Western World." *International Bulletin of Missionary Research* 25 (2001) 98–107.

Short, Sharon Warkentin. "Formed by Story: The Metanarrative of the Bible as Doctrine." *Christian Education Journal* 3 (2012) Supplement 110–23.

Smith, James K. A. *Desiring the Kingdom: Worship, Worldview, and Cultural Formation*. Grand Rapids: Baker Academic, 2009.

Steffen, Tom. "A Clothesline Theology for the World." In *Honor, Shame, and the Gospel: Reframing Our Message and Ministry*, edited by Christopher Flanders and Werner Mischke, 37–56. Littleton, CO: William Carey, 2020. https://www.youtube.com/watch?v=1XBlm9HgqyU&list=PLg_VzVwXw5LP57Qpa7Kyde4rIa4viUTmq&index=30.

———. *The Facilitator Era: Beyond Pioneer Church Multiplication*. Eugene: Wipf & Stock, 2011.

———. "Saving the Locals from Our Theologies," Part 1. *JAM* 19 (2018) 3–33.

———. "Theories Drive Our Ministries Whether We Know Them or Not." *Reformed Life Theology and Mission* 1 (2011) 191–239.

———. *Worldview-based Storying: The Integration of Symbol, Story, and Ritual in the Orality Movement*. Richmond: Orality Resources International, 2018.

Steffen, Tom, and Lois McKinney Douglas. *Encountering Missionary Life and Times: Preparing for Intercultural Ministry*. Grand Rapids: Baker Academic, 2008.

Stock, Augustine. "Chiastic Awareness and Education in Antiquity." *Biblical Theology Bulletin* 14 (1984) 23–27.

Stout, Harry S. "Theological Commitment and American Religious History." *Theological Education* 25 (1989) 44–59.

Stringer, Stephen, ed. *S-T4T: Intentional Evangelism Utilizing Stories from God's Word Resulting in Multiplying House Churches*. Monument, CO: WigTake, 2008.

Tiede, Bob. *339 Questions Jesus Asked*. LeadingWithQuestions.com, n.d.

Vanhoozer, Kevin J. *The Drama of Doctrine: A Canonical Linguistic Approach to Christian Theology*. Louisville: Westminster John Knox, 2005.

Walton, John H., and D. Brent Sandy. *The Lost World of Scripture: Ancient Literary Culture and Biblical Authority*. Downers Grove, IL: InterVarsity Academic, 2013.

Wendland, Ernst R. *Orality and its Implications for the Analysis, Translation, and Transmission of Scripture*. Dallas: SIL International, 2013.

Wheatley, Margaret J. "Living in An Age of Distraction." *Shambala Sun*. May 2013, 63–67. https://www.margaretwheatley.com/articles/Wheatley-LivingInTheAgeOfDistraction.pdf.

Wilder, Amos. *Theopoetic: Theology and the Religious Imagination*. Philadelphia: Fortress, 1976.

Wilson, Marvin R. *Our Father Abraham: Jewish Roots of the Christian Faith*. Grand Rapids: Eerdmans, 1989.

Winger, Thomas M. "The Spoken Word: What's Up with Orality." *Concordia Journal* 29 (2003) 133–51.

Witherington, Ben, III. *What's in the Word: Rethinking the Socio-Rhetorical Character of the New Testament*. Waco, TX: Baylor University, 2009.

———. "Why Ignoring the Rhetorical Shape of Oral Texts Including NT Letters Won't Do." *Patheos*, December 2, 2020.

Yong, Amos. *Theology and Down Syndrome: Reimaging Disability in Late Modernity*. Waco, TX: Baylor University, 2007.

11

New Hope

A Theodramatic Approach to Trauma Healing

Tricia and Stephen Stringer

When the first man and woman disobeyed God in the garden, the perfect unity that existed was destroyed. Gaps formed between our heart (emotions), mind (thinking), body (physical life), and soul (spiritual life). The resulting discord affects all the relationships around us—causing gaps in the relationships we have with each other, with nature, and with God. Under normal circumstances, we learn to function in life more or less effectively despite these gaps, but additional trauma fractures us to the point that those gaps in our lives may seem impossible.

We inhabit a world in a particular time that includes our fellow human beings, our community, and our nation. God's words and actions throughout history purpose to bring God's Kingdom on earth, as it is in Heaven, in perfect unity (God's theodrama). God's plan has always been that we participate fully and perfectly in his theodrama. In a perfect world, our hearts, souls, minds, and bodies work together in harmony, enabling us to participate fully in the theodrama. In order for us to experience unity within ourselves, we need to bridge the gaps that have formed between the parts of ourselves that no longer function well together. This inward unity facilitates restored relationships we have with each other, with nature, and with God. This restoration finds its consummation in God's eternal kingdom.

New Hope is designed to help close the gaps and equip people who have experienced trauma find their purpose by participating fittingly in God's theodrama. New Hope combines biblical narrative with personal narratives and healing activities in a healing community to bring unity to those broken inner parts of us.

Why is Narrative, and Narrative in Community, Important in Trauma Work?

Cognitive scientists and psychologists have laid the groundwork for the importance of using narrative in trauma work.

Trauma

Trauma definitions are varied. Although the Diagnostic and Statistical Manual has required the definition of trauma to include "actual or threatened death, serious injury, or sexual violence," some mental health professionals broaden that definition.[1] New Hope uses a broad definition of trauma: any highly stressful experience that causes negative consequences mentally, emotionally, physically, or spiritually. In this way we do not 1) give the impression that we are training trauma counselors, and 2) do not turn away those who are carrying any kind of hurt that affects them daily. In some cases, especially in those of complex trauma,[2] mental health professionals need to be involved in the trauma healing process. However, some psychologists working among refugees agree that the majority of refugee children and their families will "manifest resilience and not need specialized psychiatric services."[3] New Hope does not attempt to offer a replacement of good mental health practices for those who need professional care. It does offer a structure for an on-going healing community. This is important because in the last stages of recovery, participants benefit from on-going interpersonal groups to help them reintegrate into the broader world.[4]

> *New Hope does not train counselors nor replace professional mental health care.*

Trauma widens the gaps that already exist between heart, soul, mind, and body to the point that normal coping mechanisms are no longer sufficient. In trauma our emotions take over and we no longer feel in control of

---

1. American Psychiatric Association, *Diagnostic*, 271. Francine Shapiro states that "small t" events such as childhood humiliations and disappointments can also leave lasting negative effects on emotions, cognition, and physical well-being. Shapiro, *Eye Movement*, 4.

2. The traumatic stress field has adopted the term "complex trauma" to describe the experience of multiple, chronic and prolonged, developmentally adverse traumatic events, most often of an interpersonal nature (e.g. sexual or physical abuse, war, community violence) and early-life onset.

3. Brymer et al., "Acute Interventions," 627.

4. Herman, *Trauma and Recovery*, 234–35.

our reactions. When we experience trauma or high stress, the logical and the emotional parts of our brain no longer communicate well with each other. The emotional part of our brain is made up of the "reptilian brain" (coordinates the functioning of the life-sustaining systems of our body) and the limbic system (the seat of emotions, monitors what is important to survival). Although the limbic system develops the most in the first six years of life, it continues to be shaped by its environment and is greatly impacted by trauma. Senses enter our brains through one part of the limbic system (the thalamus) which then sends them to the amygdala controlling fundamental survival and emotion senses.

The information is also relayed to our frontal lobes (our "rational brain"), but it takes a few milliseconds longer. The rational brain attaches meaning to information and helps rebalance our bodies, telling us if the senses coming in do or do not actually pose a threat to our life. The more intense the senses coming in, the more overwhelmed the limbic system becomes. Our rational brains become less able to process the information in order to rebalance us. In fact, our rational brains effectively go "off-line." When these parts of our brain become unbalanced, we may get 'stuck' in emotional responses to stress or the perception/memory of that stress, and no amount of understanding or logic can rebalance us because the amygdala does not respond to logic. Stress hormones continue to propagate, and we continue to react in a certain way. Over time, those neural connections form deeper and deeper pathways until our unhealthy stress responses become entrenched.[5] However, it is the rational part of our brain that makes sense of our memories and emotions. It enables us to understand how the past relates to the present and the future (integration of memories). Processing of trauma must include both the emotional and rational parts of our brain.[6] How do we do this when trauma has effectively destroyed the connections between the two? Recent and on-going neuropsychological research suggests that narratives may help.

Narrative in Trauma

The most basic definition of narrative is that it is a series of actions and events that unfold over time, according to causal principles.[7] The causation, or discourse, of the narrative demands that events occur in a logically coherent order. Because trauma creates chaos, the skill of being

---

5. Van Der Kolk, *Body Keeps the Score*, 56–60.
6. Van Der Kolk, *Body Keeps the Score*, 247.
7. Mar, "Neuropsychology of Narrative," 1415.

able to organize personal narratives into a cohesive structure contributes significantly to healing of past trauma.[8] Therefore it may also be possible to understand where someone is in their healing journey by the coherence of the personal narrative they tell.[9] The prefrontal cortex is where narratives are processed, comprehended, and produced. This area helps us understand the narrative characters' mental states. The processing of narratives, both the comprehension of them and the production of them, tend to center around the prefrontal cortex, our "rational brain."[10] These are somewhat the same areas of the brain responsible for episodic and autobiographical memories—the record of a person's experience of everyday events including time, feelings, and context.[11]

Research about the use of narrative in trauma has largely centered around people telling their personal trauma narrative. However, narratives in general, unlike expository material, stimulate the emotions as well as provide cognitive stimulation.[12] We know that when listeners hear a story, especially one about a character with whom they can relate well, they experience the same emotions as that character. When a character runs in the story, the same neurons are activated as when we physically run. When a character is afraid or lonely or happy, the listener experiences similar brain activity—this is why certain movies make us sad or happy.[13]

A recent Princeton University experiment may help explain that phenomenon; it showed that when a storyteller told a story to a listener who understands it, the same parts of the brain in the listener were activated as in the storyteller, specifically the frontal cortex which controls analytical and logical functions.[14] Narrative may not be the only oral form in which this happens; certain traditional rituals, drama, and other fictional forms were developed because they were found to have value for helping us integrate autobiographical memories into our present. These rituals "achieve their principal therapeutic value for emotions that have been too overwhelming for people to assimilate in ordinary life. These narrative forms prompt individuals to recall such devastating emotional circumstances

---

8. Mar, "Neuropsychology of Narrative," 1414.
9. Frank, *Wounded Storyteller*, 102.
10. Mar, "Neuropsychology of Narrative," 1418; 1422.
11. Mar, "Neuropsychology of Narrative," 1430.
12. Oatley, "Why Fiction," 101–2.
13. Heffernan, "Power of Storytelling."
14. Stephens et al., "Speaker-Listener."

and come to terms with them.[15] Oatley postulates that "fictional"[16] stories offer a kind of "laboratory" that enables the hearer to explore emotions in a safe environment.[17] People vicariously "embody" them in the narrative as they fully experience it.

Although Oatley was speaking primarily about literary forms (whether plays, movies, or written literature), the Princeton experiment mentioned above would suggest that similar reactions would exist in more conversational stories communicated in person. People recall emotional circumstances in these safe "fictional" environments and then consistently work through them using drama, ritual, discussion, and retelling. They learn over time that it is possible to safely address these emotions and work through them. Although genetics do contribute to how our brains work, Daniel Siegel hypothesizes that new neural connections can be formed as we experience new things over time.[18] Perhaps as people experience these narrative forms safely over and over, new neural pathways can be formed as the same neural connections are made repeatedly.

The Princeton research found that at times the listeners' neurons fired, appropriately, slightly *ahead* of the action in the story because they anticipated the outcome.[19] We tell biblical stories chronologically, revealing repeating patterns of actions and reactions. Our listeners begin to see patterns in the outcomes of characters' lives as God works in them. In addition, the participants participate in kinesthetic activities such as drama that help them more effectively enter into the emotions of the story. Is it possible that through this repetition they can begin to *anticipate* the outcome for the characters? As they anticipate the outcome for the characters, perhaps they can imagine themselves in similar outcomes. As they imagine similar outcomes for themselves, could outward behaviors also change, strengthening new neural pathways?

---

15. Scheff, *Catharsis in Healing*.

16. Oatley argues that "fiction" has "effects that are personal and often emotional. There is perhaps no sharp dividing line between fiction and nonfiction." Oatley, "Why Fiction," 112.

17. Oatley, "Why Fiction," 112.

18. Siegel and Solomon, *Healing Trauma*, 5.

19. Stephens et al., "Speaker-Listener."

Narrative in Community

Judith Hermann reminds us that "The core experiences of psychological trauma are disempowerment and disconnection from others."[20] This is what makes embodied narrative experienced *in community* effective for long-lasting transformation. Diane Langberg says that those living with ongoing trauma need community even before they tell their individual stories.[21] In fact, "ongoing connection and community" is one of "three things [which] are vital in the midst of trauma."[22] Therefore, recovery involves a community, but not just any community—one that develops cohesion, intimacy, and generosity of compassion. When groups have that, "a complex mirroring process comes into play. As each participant extends herself to others, she becomes more capable of receiving the gifts that others have to offer. The tolerance, compassion, and love she grants to others begin to rebound upon herself . . . [this] occurs most powerfully in the context of a group."[23] Perhaps even here, in healing community, new neural pathways are being formed as safe interactions occur again and again.

As we repeatedly listen to and encourage production of both personal and biblical stories in the midst of an ongoing and safe community, it may be that both our rational and emotional brains are being activated. Building new and healthier neural pathways allows us to process trauma more effectively.

Can a theodramatic approach to trauma help us accomplish this task of forging new neural pathways in the brain so that people are released to rightly understand their own stories and set them within the framework of God's larger story?

Why is Theodrama Important in Trauma Work?

Theologian Hans Urs Balthasar coined the term *theo-drama* in his five-volume treatise *Theo-Drama: Theological Dramatic Theory*.[24] For Balthasar, God is the ultimate protagonist who has initiated a great redemption story. This theodrama of the Bible is a matter of what God, *theos*, has said and done, *draō*. It is the story of God's interaction with this world and humanity. God is revealed through this theodrama as recorded in Scripture. God speaks to

---

20. Herman, *Trauma and Recovery*, 133.
21. Langberg, *Suffering and the Heart of God*, loc. 2509.
22. Langberg, *Suffering and the Heart of God*, loc. 2552.
23. Herman, *Trauma and Recovery*, 215–16.
24. von Balthasar, *Theo-Drama*.

us through Scripture to enable us to seek him, find him, be restored, and be in community. God acted and continues to act through the theodrama to communicate his love for us and his desire for relationship with us. As such, the goal of theodrama is our participation in God's communicative action, his word-deeds and deed-words.[25] Theodrama moves beyond narrative in that it enables participation and invites relationship with the Triune God. It encourages community with the other players on the theodramatic stage. Theodrama is therefore a particularly helpful model for trauma work in that it initiates healing communities, instills faith by bringing us into communion with the Triune God, and imbues us with purpose as we embody the theodrama through fitting participation.

Initiating Community through Theodrama

Humanity takes its place on the stage of the theodrama: in acting out the theodrama, we no longer simply indwell the world of the story, but we are conformed to the story, thereby being transformed by it.[26] This performance is not done in isolation. Just as the theodrama invites participation in the divine communion, it also creates a holy community of believers (John 17:21–23). Theodramatic communities operate much like theatrical companies who work together using both past traditions and present communities to understand a script. In the case of theodrama, the theodrama is represented by the biblical text; the biblical text is faithfully performed by the church in community.[27] New Hope takes an oral approach in sharing carefully crafted biblical stories in healing communities.

Instilling Faith through Theodrama

> We all live story-shaped lives. The issue is not whether we will do so; the issue is rather which are the stories that will shape our lives? . . . the story that most decisively shapes our lives must be the biblical story.[28]

The use of theodrama in trauma work avoids the pitfalls of Hegelian epic and lyric categories. Objectivist epic narrativists view narrative as historical accounts told by a detached, objective observer. The lyric narrativists view

---

25. Vanhoozer, *Remythologizing*, 282–83.
26. Wolterstorff, "Living Within a Text."
27. Craigo-Snell, "Command Performance," 479.
28. Wolterstorff, *Divine Discourse*, 212.

narrative as highly expressive and personal. For the lyricist, stories that count are personal and subjective. Hegel describes drama as an appropriate approach for combining the two. A theodramatic approach to narrative is also particularly helpful in theology. In his manifesto on *The Future of Christian Theology*, Ford considers Hegel's typology in light of theology and identifies drama as the future of theology, "At its best, drama is able to embrace the objective and the subjective, to maintain a sense of plot and purpose without suppressing individuality, diversity, and the complexity of levels, perspectives, motivations, and ideas. It can have epic detachment and lyric intensity and enable a coherence without assuming one overview."[29]

Theodrama brings the discursive nature of the biblical narrative to center-stage. The triune God is the author and primary actor in the drama. People are not only the audience for the story/theodrama, but they embody the drama by becoming a part of the theodrama. These actors understand and trust the biblical narrative as the theodrama is performed.[30] The subject of theodrama is the Triune God in communicative action. The triune union of God is progressively revealed through the theodrama, and the *telos* of this emplotted narrative is that, through the gospel, humankind is invited to enter into this communion.[31] As people who have experienced trauma live the theodrama, they engage the author and primary actor in the theodrama. Entering into eternal relationship with the Triune God is the foundation of our faith and is an essential component of trauma work.

Imbuing Purpose through Theodrama

The task of drama is to build worlds and indwell them. The world most worthy of indwelling is the world created by God's theodrama as revealed through the Bible. The theodrama is the emplotted story of the Bible, and the hero of the theodrama is the Triune God in communicative action. Embodying this story then involves theodramatic participation in communion within the Trinity. The indwelling of the biblical story becomes the interpretive key to life and godliness. The fundamental form of Scripture interpretation is the ongoing faithful performance of the theodrama. Scripture is in fact "rendered" through the lived performance of the church.[32]

Theodrama relies upon logical coherence and consistency but cannot be reduced to it. Its primary concern is helping disciples better understand

---

29. Ford, *Future of Christian Theology*, 26.
30. Vander Lugt, *Living Theodrama*, 19.
31. Vanhoozer, *Drama of Doctrine*, 41–43.
32. Lash, *Theology*, 42.

the theodramatic plot: how God's plan conceived before the foundation of the world is now being worked out through the incarnation and the disciples' fitting participation in the theodrama. Christian disciples are to embody the message of the Christian theodrama: through Christ and his salvation we are brought into eternal communion with the Triune God. Just as the stage becomes a new reality for the actors walking upon it, so too does the new life in Christ. When we see ourselves as participants in this eternal theodrama, we are given a renewed sense of meaning and purpose in life. To be sure, life is fraught with complexities, tragedies, and seemingly catastrophic plot twists.[33] Despite this the Christian theodrama is always, ever moving towards a glorious end, and we are called to perform our roles in it.[34] This is our theodramatic, thus Christocentric, *hope* as well as our eschatological *purpose*.

New Hope as a Theodramatic Framework to Address Trauma

A Healing Environment: Community, Faith, and Purpose

"A cord of three strands is not quickly broken" (Eccl 4:12 NIV). The writer of Ecclesiastes knew that three strands of anything is much stronger than just two. Three principles are vital for healing environments to exist: community, faith, and purpose.[35] A trilogy of stories woven together in this healing environment—our story, God's Story, and God's stories shared—is the tripart cord that makes New Hope sessions powerful.

Each session structures these three principles by dividing the sessions into *Looking Back, Looking Up, and Looking Forward*. In the *Looking Back* portion of the session, participants share how their week went when they shared the previous Bible story, and they share part of their personal stories with each other. Because the metanarrative of New Hope is grounded in Joseph's story from Genesis, the participants learn his story in Session 1 and revisit it each session, journeying through different parts of his life in conjunction with similar situations in their own. In the *Looking Up* section of the session, participants interact with a Bible story set within the overarching metanarrative. In the *Looking Forward* section of the session, participants articulate the vision statement together in agreed hope:

---

33. Quash, *Theology and the Drama of History*, 3–5.
34. Wright, *New Testament*, 121.
35. Langberg, *Suffering and the Heart of God*, loc. 2552.

> *Is it possible that we could come to see things the way Joseph did when he said to those who had hurt him, "Do not be afraid. You meant to harm me, but God used what has happened for good—not just for me—but so that many other people could be saved."* (based on Gen 50:20 NLT)

Purpose becomes "real" when participants realize that this is about more than just hearing, but about passing on the comfort they have received. The following week in the *Looking Back* section, the community celebrates the multiplied healing brought through the participants sharing the Bible stories with others, strengthening their sense of purpose both individually and as a group.

Our Story (*Looking Back*): Building Community

Sharing one's personal story of pain in a safe environment is integral to healing. Storytelling (one's own story) is a way of "restoring a sense of efficacy and power" and reverses the "helplessness that constitutes the essential insult of trauma."[36] One New Hope participant confirmed that learning biblical stories in a traditional Bible study is not enough for healing. She said, "Even believers . . . are serving the Lord and maybe they know the [Bible] story but they didn't be healed inside. But in this training you share your pain with others."[37] However, "Bad storytelling [personal stories] or unregulated telling replicates trauma."[38] Safe environments for sharing are necessary so that participants are not retraumatized by sharing their stories too early, before they are ready, or by other participants who try to give advice or judge. Sometimes people do not know where to start telling their stories, are afraid to share with someone they do not know or telling their entire story in one sitting is too overwhelming. Pushing people to share before they are ready makes people uncomfortable or even may bring back traumatic memories to the point that they are retraumatized as past negative feelings resurface.

The first goal of New Hope is to create an open, safe environment for every participant. New Hope does not create a classroom-like environment in which participants feel they need to give "correct" answers. To begin,

---

36. Batchelor, "Orality," 193; Batchelor comments on Herman, *Trauma and Recovery*, 41.

37. Quotes are direct translations from non-native English speakers. Subsequent quotes are similar in nature; therefore, we will not utilize [sic] each time. Interview with New Hope participant in North Africa, January 2020.

38. Langberg, *Suffering and the Heart of God*, loc. 2545.

facilitators guide participants through a "healing journey" role-play. In each stage of the healing journey,[39] participants are asked how they tend to feel in that stage. For example, when something difficult happens, we ask, "How do you typically feel immediately after something difficult happens?" We use the analogy of picking up a heavy burden. As each person states their own experiences, they are validated. Then we move on to the next stage by saying something like, "After about one month, how does the heavy burden feel?" As participants talk about being tired and wanting to put down the burden but not being able to, they begin to realize for themselves how these physical reactions often mirror their emotional reactions. They consider for themselves the kinds of things people may do in this stage of healing. Their emotions are validated as they see that everyone walks a similar emotional journey. Even from the first few minutes of Session 1, participants reconstruct and discover for themselves what it looks like to heal from trauma, rather than being taught information about trauma.

The second session continues similarly—participants learn a simple method of listening, and they are asked to share a good story from their lives—whatever story they want to tell and including whatever details they want to include.

It is not until the third session that participants are asked to begin sharing past stories of hurt. By this time, they have experienced several activities together. Even then, when participants share a story about when things began to go badly, they are not asked to share the entire story, and they are given a time limit (this varies from culture to culture as appropriate). Participants promise each other two things before they start listening to each other

1. I will not share this story outside of the group, and
2. I will not give advice! Each participant promises this in front of the entire group—the community continues to strengthen as they fulfill the promises together.

As the sessions progress, different parts of participants' personal stories are highlighted. Each listening prompt is vague enough that participants can share as little or as much as they would like. No listener is permitted to ask more than the basic three listening questions:

1. What happened?

---

39. The healing journey is loosely based on the stages of grief in Kubler-Ross, *On Death and Dying*. We thank Hill, *Healing the Wounds*, for the analogy of the "Three Villages" as a way to walk participants through New Hope's healing journey.

2. How did you/do you feel?

3. What was the hardest/worst/best part of that for you?[40]

In most New Hope groups, participants begin to feel more comfortable after the third or fourth session. The listening pairs often become friends and keep in touch between sessions. Participants seem to enjoy the uninterrupted time of talking to someone else about what worries them. And even in this section of the session, participants begin to help others just by listening, just as they are listened to for the first half of the listening time, they will then listen to their partner in the second half.

It is this dialogue in New Hope groups that builds confidence and true community. One participant said:

> Before I took this training, I didn't have confidence by myself . . . when I saw the trainers I was praying and crying because . . . I think they are really holy people. All the time, I cry to God, "I just want to be like these people—please help me." And God showed me . . . all of [these people] have the same problems like [me] . . . [Now] I am new—I am not counting who I [was] before because now I have confidence to talk to other people. I am not the only one who has a problem—everyone has a problem. Jesus he makes me free.[41]

Building community happens throughout the entire session: Participants work together in the *Looking Up* section to reconstruct the Bible story together. They act out the story and discuss it with each other. They actively engage in a healing activity that engages them either individually or as a community "team." Even the individual activities are debriefed in the group creating a sense that, in the group, everyone journeys together towards healing. For example, in the first session, participants draw a picture of their journey of healing and share together what it is like to think about their personal journeys.

---

40. Hill et al., *Healing the Wounds*, 28. These questions have been taken directly from Hill's materials, but the third question has been altered to include settings in which it is more appropriate to ask: "What was the best part of that for you?" We have also specified that it is important to ask, "How did you feel?" as opposed to "How did that make you feel?" so that the participant is not encouraged to place themselves into the role of a victim.

41. Interview with New Hope participant in North Africa, January 2020.

God's Story (*Looking Up*): Building Faith

Does a loving, listening community alone engender healing? Participants regularly say things like, "I have been released from my problems after sharing them with others." Release is just the first step, however, in full healing. Just as we know simply telling Bible stories is not enough, neither is simply telling our own stories. As participants consistently experience a safe listening environment, they begin to trust. This gives space for them to experience truth at a deeper level, hopefully leading to new neural connections and truly transformed thinking and behavior.

Advice provides only a band-aid for the wound. Embodying the theodrama changes the way we think and live. After participants tell personal stories, are listened to, and then listen to others' stories, they hear a biblical story that relates to the subject they have just discussed with each other. They hear it twice, reconstruct it by retelling it as a group, and then act it out twice. These dramas are not just child's-play. As people act out a story, they become the characters, experiencing the emotions of the characters in a safe way."[42] "When we act it out, we feel in our heart what the story says. We like the dramas because we feel it—what Joseph is passing."[43]

The second time the participants act out the story they do not use words, and the actors are forced to show emotion in order to convey the action well. At significant points in the story, we stop the action and ask each character how they are feeling. The dramas in the New Hope session provide the "practice sessions" needed for participants to understand how these situations in God's theodrama really work, and how they might respond in similar situations in their own lives. Faith becomes faith in the fullest sense of the word; not just a thought process, but a thought process that results in action based upon it. As participants begin to engage with the author and primary actor—the triune God—their relationship is restored, and they can fittingly participate in the theodrama.

Participants have the opportunity to discuss the story using five questions that lead them through a process of discovering *for themselves* truths in the story:

- What did you like in this story?
- What did you find difficult to accept in this story?
- What does this story show us about God/Jesus/Holy Spirit?
- What does this story show us about people?

---

42. Oatley, "Why Fiction," 112.
43. Interview with New Hope participant in North Africa, January 2020.

- If this story is true, how does it change your thinking, your behavior, or your attitude?

The fifth question asked in this way, along with the acting out of the stories, allows the participants to "try on" the truth of the story for the moment, even if they do not think they want to accept the truth long-term.

We see that the five questions helped this woman "become" Ruth and accept the truths in Ruth's life as her own.

> So, I said when we discussed about the five questions, . . . oh, okey, now I believe God he will help me. You see, Ruth . . . was not from that country. . . We discussed about . . . how the people [feel about this kind of woman in our area]. I was the same with that woman. So now God he put her, Ruth, he put her in that top place, so I say, even God he's today even he's the same. He can do for me.[44]

One participant 'tried on' the truth of the Bleeding Woman story (session 4, New Hope). She decided to accept it!

> That acting, that acting, the story acting, still now comes in front of me. I am human being so sometimes I did mistake, sometimes I will sin, but God still he's looking for me. But God still he's looking for me, and he want me to say, "God I am here." So, he wants to hear that from me so I learn that thing the biggest thing for me so that helps me to be strong with God.[45]

God's Story Shared (*Looking Forward*): Building Purpose

In the *Looking Forward* section of a New Hope session, participants are asked who they might share the story with that week, and they are challenged to perform an act of kindness. They see that they have purpose in God's theodrama. The act of articulating the story, in community, is an important physiological and emotional benchmark for participants to prove to themselves that they can do it. Just as psychologists tell us that telling a personal story is healing for the participants, so is telling a biblical story that has been embodied as a sort of personal story. We have found that the verbal "performance" of the biblical story in community contributes to the healing of the participants.

---

44. Interview with New Hope participant in North Africa, January 2020.
45. Interview with New Hope participant in North Africa, January 2020.

Sharing with others then becomes a natural outpouring of renewed hope and purpose. One man who lived in a refugee camp in North Africa for fourteen years had become a depressed, desperate alcoholic. He participated in a New Hope healing group, and said:

> I was not this kind of person before... Now I have heart to help the others, the people like me. After that day I am looking for those kind of people and I will bring them and I will tell them how God helped me, what I did, he helped me. Now I have big heart for lost people and to tell them this way... What I get now also my friends they been healed. Because the first thing I have been healed and God gave me burden for these kind of people and most of them they've been healed so we are the same now.[46]

Misery may love company, but so does joy. In sharing joy, an individual's confidence and the group's community are strengthened. In the same camp another refugee says:

> The first time what we teach, for example, what I teach that person, he learn, and now he's leading the church. So now when I see that guy, God, he's using us, so we feel we are important and we like each other to give our testimony for each other.[47]

A Reconstructed Narrative

Our story, God's story, and God's-story-shared become a strongly woven tripart cord. Our personal story finds purpose in the theodrama which shapes and guides our personal stories moving forward. God's story becomes the consistent thread that holds together our lives' tapestry. God himself becomes the weaver. In the last session of the initial New Hope healing group, participants are asked to imagine how God could use their pain to help others. As each of the seven previous sessions have given them more space to internalize truths, they begin to reconstruct a life narrative fully engaged in God's theodrama. This is only the beginning—these groups now have the needed structure to continue meeting together.

The below participant does not differentiate between her story and the biblical narrative. In her mind, she lives in the theodrama, and its truths are just as real to her as to the biblical characters. She refers to the Bleeding

---

46. Interview with New Hope participant in North Africa, January 2020.
47. Interview with New Hope participant in North Africa, January 2020.

Woman story in Session 4 of New Hope and the Lost Son story in Session 1 of the Forgiveness Journey (a sequel to the New Hope material).

> But now God himself he came to look for the lost one and when we did the lost son I feel how God he loves us. He is the one who came to look for us. From that one I feel really God is my father. With the healing activities [story visualization][48] with bleeding woman and lost son at that time I feel that he is the real father. And even we feel we have many brothers, but they didn't come to look for us, but when we came back how he run to us and how he run to us and respect us and I feel he is a really good father. Still he is looking for me still he loves me. I feel I like the most that part. After this training God completely he changed my heart and now I have to forgive the others and love the others. God, he changed my life to love the others and to live even they don't like me or want me I have to love them.[49]

As participants embody the theodrama, they can *anticipate* their own next actions.

> Those people [who] hurt me if they came now how do I will act, I ask myself? Maybe if they [come] maybe they will say something more and they will go. But God still he's with me. He's taking who I am and what I'm doing inside. So, I ask myself if they came just like Joseph's brothers, when they came [I think of] the way he act. If they came, how . . . will I react, I ask myself. About Jesus—what he [said] on the cross because he forgive people. So, after I learn that one, I will never think about these people [who] hurt me. So, I compare with Jesus his forgiveness and these people what they did to me. But Jesus he forgive us. He forgive me more. So, you know all the time after we learn what Jesus say, ok, even what Joseph say, you [intended] to harm me, but God he change for good. Even Jesus he said in the cross, please forgive them they don't know what they doing. So that thing he heals me. Now everything is gone. Now my heart is really clean. Everything is gone now.[50]

---

48. In story visualizations, participants imagine themselves as a character in the story, immersing themselves in the sensory experiences of that character. In the sessions, a facilitator walks the group through the experience, but participants can do this on their own with any bible story.

49. Interview with New Hope participant in North Africa, January 2020.

50. Interview with New Hope participant in North Africa, January 2020.

Healing continues as participants enter into God's theodrama *themselves*, ready to live the next chapters of their lives within the overarching redemptive story.

> This Ruth and my story, it's the same, it looks the same. When we discuss . . . the Ruth story, I used to see myself and I say for myself, oh God, he give to Ruth all this chance, now you see how she is, so I decide for myself, ok, God, if you use Ruth to be a mother for this, God he will use me. And I decide for myself and I start talking to the people. And now even the churches they choose me and they give me chance to serve the others, and now I'm not scared, and I will stand before anybody, and I start serving.[51]

None of this happens as a result of one magical trauma healing session or one "silver bullet" story. A trilogy of stories—ours, God's, and the stories shared—turn like a wheel. And then the next trilogy of stories turns the wheel a bit more, moving forward inch by inch. Our lives are so complex, full of interwoven and overlapping stories, that we must be re-narrated into an equally complex narrative. This takes time and repetition. Oral audiences need repetition to believe a thing is true—and repeated practice is required for traumatized participants to change entrenched patterns of relationships.[52] New neural pathways are formed, and age-old truths are fully appropriated and embodied.

Just as healing from trauma is an on-going, iterative process, so are the methods used to address trauma. Theodrama may be a powerful and effective theological foundation for trauma work. It may also provide the appropriate framework for a healing environment in which our brains can heal physiologically also. More research and assessment are needed in theodramatic approaches to trauma work to measure its effectiveness on reducing post-traumatic consequences as well as its contribution to resilience in trauma survivors. As a theodramatic approach to trauma, New Hope has shown potential in that it initiates community, instills faith, and imbues purpose for people who have experienced trauma.

Bibliography

American Psychiatric Association. *Diagnostic and Statistical Manual of Mental Disorders, Fifth Edition*. Arlington, VA: American Psychiatric Association, 2013.

---

51. Interview with New Hope participant in North Africa, January 2020.
52. Herman, *Trauma and Recovery*, 234.

Balthasar, Hans Urs von. *Theo-Drama: Theological Dramatic Theory, Vol. 2 The Dramatis Personae: Man in God*. San Francisco: Ignatius, 1988. Kindle.

Batchelor, Kathryn. "Orality, Trauma Theory and Interlingual Translation: A Study of Repetition in Ahmadou Kourouma's Allah n'est pas oblige." *Translation Studies* 8 (2015) 191–208.

Brymer, Melissa J., et al. "Acute Interventions for Refugee Children and Families." *Child Adolescent Psychiatric Clinic North America* 107 (2008) 625–40.

Craigo-Snell, Shannon. "Command Performance: Rethinking Performance Interpretation in the Context of Divine Discourse." *Modern Theology* 16 (2000) 475–94.

Ford, David. *The Future of Christian Theology*. Blackwell Manifestos. Oxford; Malden, MA: Wiley-Blackwell, 2011.

Frank, Arthur W. *The Wounded Storyteller*. Chicago: University of Chicago, 2013.

Heffernan, Micheal. "The Power of Storytelling and How it Affects Your Brain." February 23, 2017. https://talesfortadpoles.ie/blogs/news/the-power-of-storytelling-and-how-it-affects-your- brain.

Herman, Judith, M. D. *Trauma and Recovery*. New York: Basic, 2015.

Hill, Harriet, et.al. *Healing the Wounds of Trauma: How the Church Can Help*. New York: American Bible Society, 2013.

Kim, Kyu Bo. *Embracing Trauma in Theodrama: Embodying Christiformity*. PhD diss., The Southern Baptist Theological Seminary, 2016.

Kubler-Ross, Elisabeth. *On Death and Dying*. New York: Macmillan, 1969.

Langberg, Diane. *Suffering and the Heart of God: How Trauma Destroys and Christ Restores*. Greensboro, NC: New Growth, 2015. Kindle.

Lash, Nicholas. *Theology on the Way to Emmaus*. London: SCM, 1986.

Mar, Raymond. "The Neuropsychology of Narrative: Story Comprehension, Story Production and their Interrelation." *Neuropsychologia* 42 (2004) 1414–34. https://www.sciencedirect.com/journal/neuropsychologia/vol/42/issue/10.

Oatley, Keith. "Why Fiction May Be Twice as True as Fact: Fiction as Cognitive and Emotional Simulation." *Review of General Psychology* 3 (1999) 101–17.

Quash, Ben. *Theology and the Drama of History*. Cambridge: Cambridge University, 2005.

Scheff, T. J. *Catharsis in Healing, Ritual, and Drama*. Berkeley: University of California, 1979.

Shapiro, Francine. *Eye Movement Desensitization and Reprocessing (EMDR) Therapy, Third Edition*. New York: The Guilford, 2018.

Siegel, Daniel J., and Marion Solomon, ed. *Healing Trauma: Attachment, Mind, Body, and Brain*. New York: W. W. Norton, 2003.

Stephens, Greg J., et al. "Speaker-Listener Neural Coupling Underlies Successful Communication." *Proceedings of the National Academy of Sciences of the United States of America* 107 (2010) 14425–30. https://www.ncbi.nlm.nih.gov/pmc/articles/PMC2922522/.

Stringer, Stephen, et. al., *Storying Training for Trainers*. WigTake Resources, 2014.

Van Der Kolk, Bessel. *The Body Keeps the Score: Mind, Brain and Body in the Transformation of Trauma*. Great Britain: Penguin, 2015.

Vander Lugt, Wesley. *Living Theodrama: Reimagining Theological Ethics*. Ashgate Studies in Theology, Imagination and the Arts. Burlington: Ashgate, 2014.

Vanhoozer, Kevin J. *The Drama of Doctrine: A Canonical-Linguistic Approach to Christian Theology*. Louisville: Westminster John Knox, 2005.

———. *Remythologizing Theology Divine Action, Passion, and Authorship*. Cambridge, UK; New York: Cambridge University, 2010.

Wolterstorff, Nicholas. *Divine Discourse: Philosophical Reflections on the Claim That God Speaks*. Cambridge; New York: Cambridge University, 1995.

———. "Living within a Text." In *Faith and Narrative*, edited by Keith E. Yandell. Oxford; New York: Oxford University, 2001.

Wright, N. T. *The New Testament and the People of God*. London: Society for Promoting Christian Knowledge, 1992.

12

What's Patronage Got to Do with It?

Beyond Storying in Oral Learning[1]

Lynn Thigpen

A LONG-TERM MISSIONAY, AVERY Willis, lamented his ignorance of orality while serving in Indonesia. He wrote,

> An estimated 90 percent of the world's Christian workers present the gospel and do discipleship using highly literate communication styles. 90 percent. Throw that up against the 67 percent who are oral learners and what do you have? A strategic problem ... The fact that we, as literate, print oriented, missionaries from the west, have missed this oral storying method for so long may be one of the single most serious tactical mistakes we have made in the last 200 years.[2]

Since Willis's days and partly due to his efforts, missiology has embraced orality—but only to a point. Certainly, storying exploded, and work blossomed in the field of applied orality, but we have yet to see Bible schools, colleges, seminaries, and universities offer multiple courses, majors, or minors in this critical field. Additionally, in moving beyond storying with persons who do not read, how do we teach the whole Bible, including the non-narrative portions?

Over the course of 20 years of missionary service, I observed cross-cultural workers doing discovery Bible studies, attempting inductive Bible

---

1. This chapter should be read after exploring the chapter entitled "Deconstructing Oral Learning: The Latest Research." The title of this chapter comes from the song, "What's Love Got to Do with It" written by Terry Britten and Graham Lyle and performed by Tina Turner.

2. Willis and Greeneish, "What Do You Think, Mr. Gutenberg?"

study, and working through lists of questions with little lasting fruit or reproduction of those tools. Some of those methods might work with the minority of highly literate learners, but they exclude many non-readers from the conversation and leave them barely able to remember the content of the story or passage.

For some time, I have remained dissatisfied in my quest to teach the whole Bible to such holistic learners. Finally, another personal research project outside the field refined by understanding of oral learning theory. In working through an animistic practice in Cambodia, I realized my friends were not just oral or animistic/folk religionists, but a combination of both, profoundly oral and deeply animistic, with the two worldview elements tightly intertwined. This chapter investigates the question of how to teach Scripture to oral animists by consulting principles from a classic model of education, along with researched oral learning theory and ethnographic and emic exploration of the worldview of these learners.

In considering pedagogies beyond storying to use with these learners, I consulted a classic schematic created by the educational philosopher Frankena. Depicted in Figure 12.1, the first step in developing any course involves the teacher (who in this case would be a missionary) ascertaining the ultimate goal(s), the ends or *telos* of a particular educational endeavor (A).[3] Secondly, he/she explores the context of the students involved, which in this case would be the worldview or cultural *milieu* of the people (B). The teacher then considers the skills or qualities to be produced or outcomes required (C), all of which influence the final stages of how to produce the desired outcomes in the form of an appropriate teaching methodology (D and E). In other words, teaching methodologies derive from an understanding of the students, their context or worldview, from how the students learn best in order to produce the desired ends, fulfilling the end goal or *telos*.[4] In this chapter, I combine these elements into three, considering the *telos* of Bible study or missions, the situation encountered (a mixture of orality and animism), and the solution for effectively teaching oral animists beyond storying in ways they prefer.

---

3. Frankena, *Philosophy of Education*, 9.
4. Frankena, *Philosophy of Education*, 7–9.

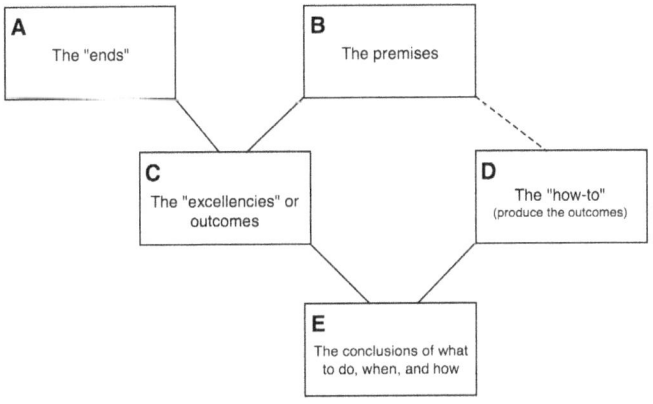

Figure 12.1. Frankena's Reasoning in Evaluating a Philosophy of Education[5]

The *Telos*: "What Business Are We Really In?"[6]

In the case of missions in intercultural settings, what, then, should be the aim, the ends, the *telos*? When examining old notions with new eyes, Keller proposed: "Each institution needs to see itself as if for the first time and ask, 'What business are we really in?.'"[7] What "business," then, are missionaries in? Since Willis and Greeneish feel we have a strategic problem, this question is critical. Whether we call our efforts "missions," "discipleship," "Christian education," "Bible study," or "spiritual formation," in settings with oral animists what should be our ultimate aim? If we observe many efforts, we might assume our aim should be producing highly intelligent, literate exegetes, or hermeneutical and homiletical giants. Is this God's will for the peoples of the world? Should our focus be the parsing of verbs or knowing every setting, every author, and every date of every book in the Bible? Should it be knowing how to do inductive Bible study? Is it Scripture memory? Over the years as I pondered presenting every oral animist "mature in Christ" (Col 1:28), I struggled with this question. This section is my humble attempt at answering that question by exploring Frankena's first priority question through Scripture and the words of a few experts.[8]

5. Frankena, *Philosophy of Education*, 9.
6. A question posed by Keller in *Academic Strategy*, 121.
7. Keller in *Academic Strategy*, 121.
8. The reader will note the impossible task of adequately addressing this crucial question in a brief section of one chapter in one book and realize this is only a cursory

First, in a brief examination of the overarching story of the Old Testament, we note God chose a man, created a nation, but then judged and exiled His people. That people and many of her kings deeply and repeatedly displeased God. How? Samuel told Saul, with whom the Lord was displeased: "To obey is better than sacrifice, and to listen than the fat of rams" (1 Sam 15:22). Many years later when one of the exiles, Daniel, prayed for his nation, he admitted they had "sinned, done wrong, acted wickedly, rebelled, and turned away from" God's laws, that they had been disloyal, and had not obeyed God's voice (Dan 5–9 HCSB).[9] In regard to Israel, God Himself lamented: "She has rebelled against My ordinances . . . rejected My ordinances and have not walked in My statutes" (Ezek 4:6). Later in that chapter, God called them insubordinate (verse 7) and promiscuous (verse 9). Why? Unfortunately, the people who saw God's provision and glory turned to pagan practices and idolatry.

Throughout the Old Testament, God seemed to long for a certain kind of follower. Second Chronicles 16:9 pronounced, "The eyes of Yahweh roam throughout the earth to show Himself strong for those whose hearts are completely His." In that context, a fearful Asa, king of Judah, made an alliance with a foreign king even though God urged him toward total trust in Him. He and so many other Israelites failed this trust test. When Nehemiah recounted the history of his people, he lamented they had not listened to God; that they had been stiff-necked; that they were disobedient, rebellious, and did evil; and had "flung Your law behind their backs" (Neh 9). These passages suggest God seeks people who are committed, obedient, trusting, and loyal.

Continuing to search for an appropriate *telos*, we might also explore what God rewards. Psalm 19 tells us there is "great reward in keeping" God's precepts (Ps 19:11 HCSB). He rewards those who do not mistreat their enemies (Ps 25:21–22). God rewards justice (Isa 61:8), hidden righteousness, prayerfulness, giving, and fasting (Matt 6:1–6, 16–18). He has created a "book of remembrance . . . for those who feared Yahweh and had high regard for His name" (Mal 3:16). At the end of all time, he will "repay each person according to what he has done" (Rev 22:12). Evidently, obedience and reverence are important.

In the New Testament, some of Jesus' final words to His disciples instructed them to "make disciples of all nations . . . teaching them to observe everything I have commanded" (Matt 28:19–20). Additionally, Jesus told a

---

glance at the question from an honest heart. The conclusion, however, does come from much study and prayer.

9. Unless otherwise noted, all biblical passages come from the *Holman Christian Standard Bible* (Nashville: Holman Bible, 2016).

parable of two houses. The one who "hears these words of Mine and acts on them" weathered life's storms (Matt 7:24). Evidently, God values obedience.

Later in the New Testament, Paul told Timothy: "Now the goal of our instruction is love that comes from a pure heart, a good conscience, and a sincere faith" (1 Tim 1:5). John wrote: "If you love me, you will keep my commandments . . . This is my commandment, that you love one another as I have loved you . . . You did not choose me, but I chose you and appointed you that you should go and bear fruit . . . (John 14:15; 15:12, 16 ESV). He also wrote in 1 John 2:3 HCSB: "This is how we are sure that we have come to know Him: by keeping His commands." The marks of a person belonging to God include love and obedience.

Based on a cursory examination of these verses, I would suggest the *telos* of Bible study and our mission efforts closely aligns with obedience. Others agree. The early church reportedly trained for martyrdom, a process which "was by no means confined to the mastering of the contents of a small collection of carefully prepared treatises, or to the listening to eloquent and burning exhortations of devoted teachers, or even to the constant dwelling on the words of the Divine Master."[10] That training emphasized self-denial and suffering, fasting and prayer.[11] The passages bringing most comfort came from Matthew: "If anyone wants to come with Me, he must deny himself, take up his cross, and follow Me" (Matt 16:24).

Considering a few expert voices, we find James K. A. Smith also explored the *telos* of Christian education. He posits,

> Being a disciple of Jesus is not primarily a matter of getting the right ideas and doctrines and beliefs into your head in order to guarantee proper behavior; rather, it's a matter of being the kind of person who *loves* rightly.[12]

Another scholar, Dietrich Bonhoeffer, one who made the ultimate sacrifice in serving God, wrote,

> Who stands fast? Only the man whose final standard is not his reason, his principles, his conscience, his freedom, or his virtue, but who is ready to sacrifice all this when he is called to obedient and responsible action in faith and in exclusive allegiance to God–the responsible man who tries to make his whole life an answer to the question and call of God.[13]

10. Spence-Jones, *Early Christians in Rome*, 201.
11. Spence-Jones, *Early Christians in Rome*, 203.
12. Smith, *Desiring the Kingdom*, 32.
13. Bonhoeffer, *Letters*, 5.

In *The Cost of Discipleship*, Bonhoeffer also wrote: "When he called men to follow him, Jesus was summoning them to a *visible act of obedience*."[14] It would seem Bonhoeffer concurs.

Willard explained, "Spiritual formation could and should be the process by which those who are Jesus' apprentices or disciples come easily to 'do all things whatsoever I have commanded you.'"[15] Willard also urged believers toward spiritual maturity or "soul transformation" and an obedient life of Christlikeness, stating: "Routine, easy obedience to Christ *with reference to specific actions*, then, is the natural outcome of the transformation of the essential dimensions of our personality into Christlikeness."[16] According to him, "The abundance of life realized through apprenticeship to Jesus, 'continuing in his word,' naturally leads to *obedience*."[17] In conclusion, Willard seems to say the noble end of Bible study should be soul reformation and maturity, becoming like Jesus and walking in loving obedience.

In Frankena's model, the *telos* drives the educational endeavor. Having briefly examined Scripture and some literature, we find God greatly values love, obedience, trust, allegiance and loyalty. God found those characteristics lacking in many of the Israelites in the Old Testament. For those who forgot Him, who followed other gods, who did not keep His law and covenant, He reserved judgment and exile. In teaching oral animists, it would seem our focus, our *telos*, and our outcomes or excellencies (C in Figure 12.1) all need to point toward cultivating obedience, trust, and allegiance in our learners. Whatever methods, then, the situation of our learners demands, our ultimate aim does not seem to be centered around inductive Bible study or Scripture memory or even memorization of stories, but on these ends God has chosen—an intertwined aim of love, obedience, trust, and fidelity–all of which in combination quite closely resemble something I choose to call spiritual monogamy. Of this notion, Raj and Harmon explained:

> Western monotheistic traditions are accustomed to the idea . . . that a person must participate in only one religious tradition at a time . . . We have treated religious affiliation as a form of monogamy . . . But the common folk among South Asian Hindus, Buddhists, Muslims, Jains, and Christians don't understand religious adherence in such exclusive terms.[18]

God desires a relationship of fidelity, so how might we teach this?

14. Bonhoeffer, *Cost of Discipleship*, 233.
15. Willard, "Spiritual Formation: What it is."
16. Willard, "Spiritual Formation and the Warfare," 2–3.
17. Willard, *Divine Conspiracy*, 368.
18. Raj and Harmon, *Dealing with Deities*, 7.

The Situation: Where Orality and Animism Meet

After choosing the appropriate *telos*, Frankena advises considering the context or worldview of the learners involved. In the scenario I am presenting, what is the situation or the worldview? In the country of Cambodia in which I ministered for 20 years, there was not just orality, there was also folk Buddhism. However, most of my friends knew very little about Buddhism. Usually, they could not tell me the Four Noble Truths or the Eightfold Path; but they understood the spirit world. Those two complicated constructs of orality and animism were strangers to me when I arrived in Cambodia days before Y2K, but they quickly became familiar neighbors.

Orality[19] or Connected Learning

After spending our first year or so in language learning, our family escaped the bustle of the capital city for Kampong Cham province to begin evangelism, church planting, and NGO work. From the moment we sat with Christian leaders, we quickly realized Bible study would be different than we expected. We implemented a well-known curriculum of studying small booklets, complete with questions and blanks for answers. That effort failed. Then I truly met orality and realized quite a few people do not prefer to read. Twenty years ago, however, few workers majored on orality, so we traveled to learn from experienced colleagues in the Philippines.

Afterward, we began chronological Bible storying, training national storytellers, and creating something we called "The Oral Bible School." We quickly realized stories engaged people more deeply, but listeners also needed a "text" to "ruminate over," just as readers consult books. As a result, we made recordings and visuals as teaching and memory aids for our Cambodian learners.

Still, I felt there was more to learn in the field of orality and began doctoral studies. Through my research, I discovered many of my friends were adults with limited formal education (ALFE) who really preferred to learn by means of people rather than by means of print. The foundational issue was not Ong's dichotomy of orality versus literacy, but rather one of people versus print.[20] Those I previously labeled as "oral learners" really preferred to gather information by more than listening. They watched. They related.

---

19. Orality is a large field of study and could not be adequately addressed in this brief section. Please see my earlier chapter on deconstructing orality in this work, as well as my book *Connected Learning* for an extensive discussion of the literature surrounding this field.

20. Ong, *Orality and Literacy*.

They used all their senses to learn; but most of all, they learned from others. As a result of researching and discovering their true preference, I called my friends "connected learners" or "relational learners" instead of using the confusing misnomer of "oral learners."

I discovered connected learners have different ways of gathering information, different ways of knowing, a different epistemology; but ontologically, their identity, their very worldview involves connection and relationship. Any oral learning theory, then, must include connected learning. What is it? In one respect, Ong was correct when he called orality "the primary modeling system."[21] Connected learners learn in the ways we all used from infancy onward. They observe and mimic. Connected learning is relational, reflexive, redemptive, and relevant, a process needing repackaging through "accessible technologies and other portable vehicles of connection."[22]

Animism or Spiritual Patronage[23]

Just as I met orality early in my missionary career, I was summarily accosted by animism. A constant, ubiquitous companion in Southeast Asia, animism presented me with the smell of incense, with altars, and a plethora of unfamiliar objects and symbols at every turn, on nearly every wrist or around every neck or waist. The culmination of meeting animism and my entrance into a greater understanding came through a relationship with one special family. They introduced me to an object indwelled with a spirit entity, one that had protected them and their extended family through turbulent times in Cambodia's history. Initially, my friend wondered whether he should abandon the object to worship Christ. I felt certain he must, being quite puzzled by the object, I embarked on ethnographic research to unearth the meanings tied to my friend's *kru gom-night-ut* ("birth teacher").

---

21. Ong, *Orality and Literacy*, 12.

22. Thigpen, "Connected Learning," 125.

23. The research for this concept was conducted during doctoral studies at Biola University. A version of that research was awarded the Hiebert Scholarship through the Hiebert Global Center at Trinity Evangelical Divinity School. The paper entitled *An Emic Understanding of the "Excluded Middle": Spiritual Patronage in Cambodia* was also presented at the 2015 EMS North Central Missiology Conference and can be found at http://www.hiebertglobalcenter.org/1103-2/lynn-thigpen-an-emic-understanding-of-the-excluded-middle-spiritual-patronage-in-cambodia/. Another version, "The Excluded Middle, Spiritual Patronage, and a Refined Missiological Response," will be published as a chapter in the forthcoming book *Practicing Mission: From Theory to Practice and Back Again*.

As I interviewed person after person, I discovered following a *kru* had benefits—provision, protection, health, safety, etc. Some people had even been given a *kru* by a shaman when they were desperately ill. People told me they knew when they should leave their homes and when they should not, what foods they should and should not eat, when to make offerings, etc. They knew both the benefits and the obligations of following their *kru*.

As I listened and pondered, transcribed and analyzed, searching for themes in these conversations, I finally realized such a situation of benefits and obligations with a powerful entity resembled patronage.[24] I had already met patronage in personal relationships in Cambodia and avoided becoming a patron as much as possible; but in researching the meanings ascribed to the *kru gom-nigh-ut*, the one providing benefits was not a physical being, but a spiritual one. Even though the patron was unseen, the client knew exactly what was expected and welcomed the relationship. "The participants viewed spiritual patronage as something like 'being under grandpa's watchful eye.'"[25]

Originally in dialogue with my friend, I had called the object an "it" (*vee-ah*), while he used a personal pronoun "he/she" (*goe-aht*). When I first saw the object in which the *kru* dwelt, a mass of paper and string with a coconut base, I felt certain my friend could easily throw it into a fire, renounce animism, and turn to follow Jesus. Fortunately, I researched first and came to understand his worldview better. I discovered I was not asking my friend to burn an object. Rather, I was asking him to divorce from an important relationship, to renounce a trusted friend. The spirit associated with the object held a real and precious place in the lives of my national friends. It was a guardian spirit.

In the end, I realized the whole seemingly complicated construct was actually very simple. It was merely another form of patronage I call "spiritual patronage." For the most part, the literature did not discuss folk religion in such familiar terms like those who espoused it. Their emic perspective and daily life existed in close communion with the spirit world, highly relational, like their learning style.

This worship of a fetish housing a tutelary deity or guardian spirit was not commonplace in Cambodia, but such belief in the spirit world was. In this case, a representation of Hanuman, the monkey god, inhabited the center of the fetish, a powerful "theriomorphic deity."[26] Hiebert, Shaw, and

24. For a more thorough discussion of patronage, see works such as de Silva's *Honor, Patronage, Kinship and Purity*; Eisenstadt and Roniger's *Patrons, Clients, and Friends*; and Georges' *Ministering in Patronage Cultures*.

25. Thigpen, "Emic Understanding," 9.

26. Lutgendorf, *Hanuman's Tale*.

Tienou taught that studying such "sacred symbols, in particular, provides a window on a people's understanding of ultimate reality."[27] The foundational ultimate reality of my friends was spiritual patronage.

Now that I have introduced the situation of connected learners involved in spiritual patronage, in order to avoid their unwieldy description or the less specific term "animistic oral learners," or "oral folk religionists," I will refer to them as "connected clients," combining terminology from both aspects of their worldview. Connected learners desire to become clients of those with knowledge, those who can be trusted, and learn from them; and the same folks who espouse spiritual patronage prefer the comfort of being a client in a relationship with a trusted spiritual entity.

"What's patronage got to do with" this discussion? Orality/connected learning is a social identity set in a worldview. In order to adequately address their learning needs, we must also explore the deep foundational worldview(s) on which orality rests. Figure 12.2 depicts this reality. Social patronage operates as a foundational element in the Cambodian worldview, along with pillars of spiritual patronage undergirding the whole belief system. On top of all this, connected clients learn by means of relationship and connection. Addressing this situation requires more than understanding connected learning. It requires understanding the foundational worldview(s) involved.

---

27. Hiebert et al., *Understanding Folk Religion*, 252.

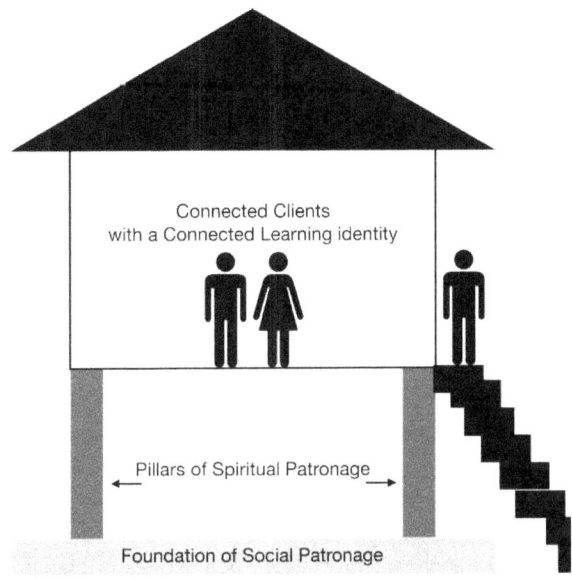

Figure 12.2. A Depiction of the World of Connected Clients[28]

The Solution: "A Whole New World"

FOLK BUDDHISM IN CAMBODIA unfolds with symbols and color, concrete examples appealing to the senses—peaceful monks in saffron robes, colorful paintings adorning temple walls, the heavy smell of burning incense, and the haunting sound of chanting. Families gather for social festivals at the local temple. Into this milieu comes Christianity, with no pungent odors, no colors, no ornateness, and no familiar chords to bind the Asian to itself. When Cambodians leave their colorful worlds and step into a Christian one, they often leave the simplicity of observation and relationships for a world akin to formal schooling, one with books, teachers, and information targeted at the cerebral cortex instead of the heart.

What sort of Christian education, discipleship, or training might be needed for connected clients moving away from folk religion toward Christian maturity and spiritual monogamy? How do we teach the whole Word of God to holistic learners often too busy living to learn? Given our overarching *telos*, how do we reach our Father's goals?

28. Figure 12.2 depicts a foundation of social patronage, pillars of spiritual patronage, and learning through others (connected learning).

In this section, I examine the learning needs of connected clients and the discipleship they need. I studied both on separate occasions—how oral learners or ALFE preferred to learn and what those who embrace spiritual patronage needed—and only now realize the intertwined nature of these two. What answered the need for one similarly answered the foundation of the other. The central piece was relationship and a whole new world.

How Connected Clients Prefer to Learn

An education researcher, Shulman, observed, "If you wish to understand why professions develop as they do, study their nurseries, in this case, their forms of professional preparation. When you do, you will generally detect the characteristic forms of teaching and learning that I have come to call *signature pedagogies*."[29] In the research that followed Shulman's work, Foster et al. discovered four pedagogies involved in "forming a pastoral, priestly, or rabbinic imagination": pedagogies of information and interpretation, pedagogies of contextualization, pedagogies of transformation or performance, and pedagogies of formation.[30] Additionally, the researchers found three pedagogies of interpretation in clergy education: "interpreting as continuous dialogue," "interpreting as appropriating tradition," and "interpreting by choosing 'right methods.'"[31]

I worked with ALFE (Adults with Limited Formal Education) for a decade and a half before I explored their learning experiences and how they really preferred to learn. What I discovered in researching the question was so simple it was surprising. Connected learners prefer a "simple, ubiquitous kind of learning," "a natural, self-directed process that resembles socialization, learning by connecting, observing, trying, repeating without the pain or shame associated with the formal learning in a school environment"[32]– quite opposite to the way I learned to study God's Word.

An African scholar concurred with my findings: "African orality must be seen as socialisation [sic]."[33] I found connected learning "to be a relational process, one that involved known, trusted, and/or successful people."[34] Jousse called these people "the living press."[35] Connected learners' funds of

29. Shulman, "Signature Pedagogies," 52.
30. Foster et al., *Educating Clergy*, 68.
31. Foster et al., "Pedagogies," 207–11.
32. Thigpen, "Connected Learning," 154–55.
33. Mazamisa, "Reading From This Place," 71.
34. Thigpen, "Connected Learning," 127.
35. Jousse, *Oral Style*, 135.

knowledge lie not in experts or journals, but in trusted people, warm bodies, as opposed to a dead corpus of knowledge. Einstein explained it this way: "Knowledge exists in two forms–stored in books, and alive in the consciousness of men. The second form of existence is after all the essential one; the first indispensable as it may be, occupies only an inferior position."[36]

What does patronage have to do with this discussion? Whereas my research with ALFE showed they valued connection and relationship in their learning, my exploration of spiritual pedagogy showed similar findings. In both instances, they valued connection. Connected clients valued relating to a strong, powerful force. They needed refuge, protection. Indeed, Ledgerwood found of social patronage in Cambodia: "The only way to get something that is beyond your capacity is to attach yourself to a superior."[37] Mazlish called the informal system "an economy of power" and titled his article "Invisible Ties."[38] Whether social or spiritual, patronage involves connection. For many in Cambodia and around the world, social patronage is foundational. Spiritual patronage was equally espoused, like the pillars supporting a traditional Khmer dwelling (see Figure 12.2).

Returning to sharing the Gospel in a way my friend with the *kru gom-nigh-ut* might understand, I compared his relationship with his guardian spirit as finding refuge from the hot sun under the shade of a vine. However, where he had found refuge under a vine, I had found refuge in a different place. I drew a sprawling tree with expansive branches towering over his vine and taught him about a Patron large enough for every person of all time to dwell under His branches. I then retold the Gospel story with this theme of patronage.

I found my friend needed to understand God in this way, as a refuge, a Protector. He needed to understand exchanging his trust in a guardian spirit for trust in the Almighty God. That process required a transfer of allegiance. Indeed, Crook saw conversion as "a change in patronal relationship."[39] My friend understood that language which had been unfamiliar to my worldview.

After his conversion, how could he learn and grow in the same ways he learned to follow his guardian spirit? He needed a visible community with new relationships. He needed to be resocialized into a new world by watching God's people worship and serve Him. We do not think this way when we think of discipleship. We tend to think of books and pens and paper.

36. Einstein and Calaprice, *Ultimate Quotable Einstein*, 439.
37. Ledgerwood, "Understanding Cambodia."
38. Mazlish, "Invisible Ties," 3.
39. Crook, *Reconceptualizing Conversion*, 333.

What if connected learners value "interpreting as dialogue" or "appropriating tradition," pedagogies of interpretation mentioned earlier instead of our own preference for right methods?[40] What if they prefer formation to information? That is definitely the case. Seminary emphasizes homiletics and hermeneutics, but as one philosopher wisely observed, "Hermeneutics begins where dialogue ends."[41] What our connected client friends need is not hermeneutics, but dialogue—with the community of faith and the Author of that faith.

What Discipleship Needs to Look Like for Connected Clients

My friends learned by means of people, with a preference for observation. Connected learning was revealed to be a relational process, one that involved known, trusted, and/or successful people. As I explored their desired way of learning, I noticed it resembled the natural process of socialization. I had never thought of people as being central to the learning process. Cambodian ALFE preferred learning from people instead of learning from print.[42]

Simple and natural, connected learning is a holistic form of socialization. I depicted connected learning as a wheel,

> an integration of learning by experience, by observation, through discussion, even in the midst of the need to solve problems, all revolving around deep and central spiritual needs, and driven by social, relational, cultural, and affective elements . . . Connected learning seemed to be a holistic inclusion of all these forms of learning with an emphasis on relationship or connection.[43]

Among the pedagogies listed earlier, connected clients need pedagogies of formation and transformation, while many of those who teach overseas tend to employ pedagogies of information. By and large, missions' signature pedagogies are not the signature pedagogies embraced by connected clients. According to Bacher, "the difficulty is to shift from a text you study to a text that is staged."[44]

---

40. Foster et al., "Pedagogies," 207–11.
41. Ricœur, *Interpretation Theory*, 32.
42. Thigpen, "Connected Learning," 127.
43. Thigpen, "Connected Learning," 127.
44. Bacher, "Bible in the Future."

How had my friends learned to serve their *kru*? They had been socialized into the process. They had watched family members burn incense, make offerings. No books existed to walk them through the process. It was one of relationship and mutual understanding. Patronage ran like a river through their society and they instinctively understood finding protection and provision from an outside source.

So, how would such people learn a new religion, learn to follow the Creator God, and follow a new *telos*? By inference, they need to observe someone following Him. They need to begin a new relationship. They need to watch trusted others. They would need stories of faithfulness and hope in this newfound patronage journey. What they cannot fathom is learning all these things from a book or to be left alone with print on a page. They need others. They need the Teacher.

Connected clients need a curriculum directed at their foundation and pillars, a curriculum for changing their "rock," their allegiance. For some folk religionists/animists venturing toward Christ this never happens and syncretism lies deep in their bedrock. Tienou saw this issue when Bobo Christians reverted back to their former ways and explained:

> As older Bobo Christians sense the end of their life approaching, they feel more and more distant from Christ and they feel closer to their ancestors. They return to the religions of their ancestors because they know the ancestors through kinship bonds. They do not know Jesus that way.[45]

Stories can help change worldview, but alone they are not a complete strategy in the business of changing allegiance, teaching obedience, and promoting love and trust. Teaching for transformation differs from teaching information. Somehow, the Israelites who knew the stories of God's power and faithfulness and knew God's law, turned away from Him, forgot Him, and worshiped idols. The opposite heart after God proclaims, "The Lord is my rock, my fortress, and my deliverer, my God, my mountain where I seek refuge, my shield and the 'horn of my salvation,' my stronghold" (Ps 18:2).

Bonhoeffer faced a similar dilemma but with highly literate students. In response, he instituted a community seminary, "an unorthodox experiment in communal Christian living," a place "where one aimed to live in the way Jesus commanded his followers to live . . . where one lived not merely as a theological student, but as a disciple of Christ."[46] Finkenwalde

---

45. Tienou, "Christian Response," 214.
46. Metaxas, *Bonhoeffer*, 270–71.

was a place of "life together," the antidote for signature pedagogies that failed.[47] Bonhoeffer also wrote:

> I am firmly convinced that in view of what the young theologians bring with them from the university and in view of the independent work which will be demanded of them in the parishes . . . they need a completely different kind of training which life together in a seminary like this unquestionably gives . . . . The questions that are seriously put to us today by young theologians are: How do I learn to pray? How do I learn to read the Bible? If we cannot help them there, we cannot help them at all.[48]

Connected clients need the same kind of communal learning Bonhoeffer's Finkenwalde offered. For the one espousing spiritual patronage, the aim, the *telos* must be a change of patron with all that entails–new allegiance and firm spiritual monogamy. All this looks different than traditional Bible study and requires different pedagogy, moving connected clients from dependency on people, spirits, and shamans to dependency on God alone. Crook maintained, "Loyalty is what made the patron-client relationship a *relationship*."[49] While one might change earthly patrons, the expectation in Christianity is that God alone is worthy of exclusive loyalty. If we return to a verse we explored earlier, 2 Chronicles 16:9, we find God shows Himself strong for those whose hearts are *shalem*, especially friendly or loyal. How do you educate for loyalty and fidelity?

Crook expounded, "Conversion, a change in patronal relationship, would have involved simultaneous acts of disloyalty and loyalty—disloyalty to a former patron, loyalty to a new patron," a process that also involves honor and dishonor.[50] After conversion, this process entails cultivating a continual loyalty. Nurturing a lifelong loyalty and honor to God, nurturing obedience and relationship takes a different kind of discipleship, the kind that Jesus undertook with His disciples, a "life together" which Bonhoeffer advocated.

A connected client, then, by definition could not be a "lone ranger" believer. Connected clients need the Body. Why? They need people who will be their living books, with living exegesis, including the "life together" of

---

47. Bonhoeffer, *Communion of Saints*.
48. Metaxas, *Bonhoeffer*, 270–71.
49. Crook, "BTB Readers Guide," 167.
50. Crook, *Reconceptualizing Conversion*, 250.

Bonoeffer,[51] the curriculum for Christlikeness of Willard,[52] Smith's embodied learning,[53] and connected learning.

In addition to the idea of community, Paul interjected habit. Some believe he taught by means of "traditioning."[54] In 1 Corinthians 5:3, he stated, "For I passed on to you [*paradidomi*] as most important what I also received: that Christ died for our sins according to the Scriptures." Connected clients learn their first religion by observing traditions, rituals, and liturgies, through dialogue with trusted funds of knowledge. They need to relearn a new faith by the same means—traditioning, resocialization, observation, and dialogue. One early church elder noted of this kind of relational learning, "The word of God existed less as scratchings on a piece of parchment or papyrus, to be studied and puzzled over in solitude, than as a living response to a question."[55]

This kind of teaching as Jesus taught differs from the signature pedagogies of modern seminary. Willard explained:

> Jesus teaches contextually and concretely, from the immediate surroundings, if possible, or at least from events of ordinary life ... This "concrete" or contextual method of teaching is obviously very different from how we attempt to teach and learn today, and the difference makes it difficult for us to grasp *what* precisely it is that Jesus is teaching. What he is saying cannot be understood unless we appreciate how he teaches, and we cannot appreciate how he teaches unless we take into account something of the world within which his teaching occurred. We must recognize, first of all, that the aim of the popular teacher in Jesus' time was not to impart information, but to make a significant change in the lives of the hearers.[56]

The aim? Significant change. Johnson-Miller and Espinoza also promoted this kind of change, a "catechesis that is dynamic, God-centered (in contrast to human-growth centered), and a life-long process of theological spiritual cultivation for the sake of divine attentiveness (communion, meaning, consciousness, virtue, and vocation)."[57] They explained that "for

---

51. Bonhoeffer, *Communion of Saints*.
52. Willard, *Divine Conspiracy*.
53. Smith, *Desiring the Kingdom*, 227.
54. Keener, "Assumptions," 26–58.
55. Christie, "Listening," 219.
56. Willard, *Divine Conspiracy*, 107, 112.
57. Johnson-Miller and Espinoza, "Catechesis," 157.

Luther, the point of catechesis was holy *living*, not merely correct beliefs."[58] They advocate a focus on "shaping the affections, aiming the heart toward the love of God."[59] They explained: "Christian formation in the early Church stood in stark contrast to the didactic intellectualized proposition-centered practices," and instead they promote mystagogy, "the experiential process of leading Christians into the mysteries of faith" which was actually the focus of the early church.[60]

Finally, in this mixture, "rituals are crucially important in managing change in cultures where people value agentive causation."[61] As Song explained,

> By taking the receptor's context seriously, it acknowledges, first of all, the simple and obvious fact that no one comes to Jesus in a spiritual vacuum . . . The truth is that every new idea must be integrated with the existing ideas, sometimes requiring a violent clash and other times necessitating an accommodation to the existing set of beliefs.[62]

Mejudhon called this "power discipling"–a movement "from the familiar to the unfamiliar."[63]

Willard called the process of "soul reformation" one of "reforming the broken soul of humanity in a recovery from its alienation from God."[64] Willard even proposed a "curriculum for Christlikeness,"[65] in which

> the *primary* objectives of any successful course of training for "life on the rock," the life that hears and does, are twofold. The first objective is to bring apprentices to the point where they dearly love and constantly delight in that "heavenly Father" . . . The second primary objective of a curriculum for Christlikeness is to remove our automatic responses against the kingdom of God, to free the apprentices of domination, of "enslavement" to their old habitual patterns of thought, feeling, and action.[66]

---

58. Johnson-Miller and Espinoza, "Catechesis," 161.
59. Johnson-Miller and Espinoza, "Catechesis,"162.
60. Johnson-Miller and Espinoza, "Catechesis," 163.
61. Bradshaw, *Change Across Cultures*, 223.
62. Song, "Contextualization and Discipleship," 251.
63. Mejudhon, "Evangelism in the New Millennium," 102.
64. Willard, "Spiritual Disciplines," 108.
65. Willard, *Divine Conspiracy*, 316.
66. Willard, *Divine Conspiracy*, 321–22.

James K. A. Smith went beyond worldview to worship, emphasizing "formative pedagogy" and proposed "that the primary goal of Christian education is the formation of a peculiar people—a people who desire the kingdom of God."[67] To that end, Smith advised prioritizing "*practices* rather than ideas as the site of challenge and resistance" and understanding "human persons as *embodied actors* rather than merely thinking things."[68] Further, "if Christian education is formation, and such formation happens in the full-bodied practices of worship, then worship is the *sin qua non* of Christian education."[69] He espoused a focus on liturgies and habits, critical for connected clients, as well.

Beside all these elements, connected clients also need self-efficacy, trust, hope, and agency. They especially need hope, "the sum of perceived capabilities to produce routes to desired goals, along with the perceived motivation to use those routes."[70] According to Snyder, hope equals agency plus pathways.[71] "The exercise of agency is necessarily central to the development of lifelong learning abilities,"[72] and "agency reflects the person's perception that he or she can begin movement along the imagined pathways to goals; agency also can reflect one's appraisal of the capability to persevere in the goal journey."[73] Without hope and agency, connected clients feel they have no opportunities, so our pedagogical solutions need to provide pathways for learning apart from reading.

Crabtree and Sapp wrote an article entitled "Your Culture, My Classroom, Whose Pedagogy?"[74] To build a whole new world and worldview, pedagogy must follow the needs of the connected client and the *telos* of Scripture. Beyond storying, drama, and song, what do connected clients need in order to become mature and transformed believers? They need new signature pedagogies that involve non-traditional discipling methods such as:

- Apprenticeship
- Modeling in Christian community
- Liturgies, rituals, and traditioning
- Embodied pedagogies

67. Smith, *Desiring the Kingdom*, 34.
68. Smith, *Desiring the Kingdom*, 35.
69. Smith, *Desiring the Kingdom*, 224.
70. Snyder, "Hypothesis," 8.
71. Snyder, "Hypothesis," 10.
72. Su, "Constitution of Agency," 402.
73. Snyder, "Hypothesis," 10.
74. Crabtree and Sapp, "Your Culture," 105–32.

- Mystagogical catechism
- Memorizing in community
- Communal reading (1 Tim 4:13, Rev 1:3) with dialogue/explanation (Neh 8:1–8)
- Spiritual disciplines implemented in community
- Experiential and observational learning

In agreement, Mejudhon researched "ways of religious discipling" in neighboring Thailand and found the process to be "affective, applicable to felt needs, practical, solving life's problems; emphasizing rituals, ceremonies, and festivals; having integrative functions; concrete, experiential; bonding, and not forcing faith."[75]

Concluding Reflections

The situation in Cambodia involves adults with limited formal education (ALFE) who are oral learners or as my research found—connected or relational learners. When given a choice, they prefer learning from people over learning from print. That situation was true for the majority of the population of Cambodia where I worked; and according to the International Orality Network and the Lausanne Committee for World Evangelization, it is true of much of the world's population.[76] Many simply do not prefer to learn by reading or value print.

This situation is further complicated by the fact that many connected learners around the globe also espouse animistic or folk religion practices. When I researched a particular animistic practice in Cambodia, I discovered the relationship between my friends and their fetish was really a form of patronage, so I began to call this practice of relying on a supposedly powerful unseen entity for provision or protection as spiritual patronage. I called those who espoused both connected learning (orality) and spiritual patronage (animism) "connected clients."

I found connected learning to be a way of gathering information (education), a way of knowing (epistemology), and a social identity (ontology). So, what does patronage have to do with orality in this case? Everything. The existence of patronage steers us toward pedagogies of

---

75. Mejudhon, "Evangelism in the New Millennium," 102.

76. International Orality Network and Lausanne Committee for World Evangelization, *Making Disciples*, 3.

formation, pedagogies promoting relationship and refuge. Connected learning is relational and so is spiritual patronage.

What does patronage have to do with going beyond storying in oral learning theory? It is a hidden foundational worldview that makes it a bridge in teaching connected clients. That worldview provides additional vocabulary and insight into values and beliefs. Patronage is their social understanding of relationship that includes protection and provision, but it is also a foundational spiritual worldview for everything else layered on it.

In the unfortunate occurrence of the US Civil War, many slaves who wanted to learn were forced undercover. Williams explained, "They truly had to 'steal' an education."[77] Slaves hid, bribed, and traded in order to learn. Williams also shared the sad situation of "a young man who learned to read and write in a cave," while others "would dig a pit in the ground way out in the woods, covering the spot with bushes and vines." [78]

Today connected clients suffer a similar situation. Some of my ALFE friends talked about sneaking to watch another person doing their job in order to learn how to do it. Stealing an education still exists. My friends do not dig pits, but some live in pits of despair because they cannot learn to read like others. Oral learners face a shameful situation, not only in their own societies, but in the world at large.[79] I find myself wondering, "Who will truly see them and care on a larger scale?"

Walking through the process of Frankena's schematic, we found a *telos* for training connected clients that focused on spiritual monogamy. The solution for how to deliver this *telos* to connected clients involves different signature pedagogies from those missionaries receive. Connected clients require direct personal relationship, apprenticeship, and resocialization to a new Kingdom worldview, in other words, a discipleship not by traditional Bible study and fill-in-the-blanks, but my means of observation, listening, dialogue, storying, arts, proverbs, ceremonies, symbols, etc., all coupled with believing refuge and obedient hearts submitted to the Holy Spirit as Teacher.

How can this kind of learning be practically applied? First, we need to think in terms of apprenticeships, of mentoring relationships, of learning that is social, experiential, dialogical, practical, and contextual or cultural–all without printed material. Or, if print is used, the concept of proximate literacy comes into play.[80] A famous professor, well acquainted

---

77. Williams, *Self-Taught*, 27.
78. Williams, *Self-Taught*, 28.
79. See Thigpen, "Dark Side of Orality."
80. Proximate literacy means having a literate person at hand for reading purposes.

with oral learners over 1900 years ago, Augustine, told his adults with limited formal education: "We are your books."[81] We can be books for those who cannot or do not read. We can make information more accessible. Sienaert discussed the findings of a researcher famous in the study of orality, Jousse, and stated,

> What Jousse makes us aware of, is of the existence, of the nature of the operation of the Oral Style. This Oral Style is based on anthropological laws and is performed in a multitude of variations by each ethnic milieu in all times and all over the world. It is up to us, belonging as individuals to a particular civilization, to become aware of the tenets and values of other civilizations. And in this we have in the main failed.[82]

Let us not continue that legacy of failure. Willis and Greeneish in the first quote of this chapter lamented the strategic problem and tactical mistake in overlooking orality.[83] We cannot afford to ignore our "business," the *telos* God has given us, to facilitate a full change of loyalty in the worldview of connected clients.

Bibliography

Bacher, Henri. "The Bible in the Future: What Future Is There for the Bible in Our Churches?" *Scripture Engagement*. http://www.scripture-engagement.org/node/372.

Basu, Kaushik, et al. *Isolated and Proximate Illiteracy and Why these Concepts Matter in Measuring Literacy and Designing Education Programs*. Working Paper No. 00-W02. Nashville: Vanderbilt University, 2000. http://www.vanderbilt.edu/econ.

Bonhoeffer, Dietrich. *The Communion of Saints: A Dogmatic Inquiry into the Sociology of the Church*. New York: Harper & Row, 1960.

———. *The Cost of Discipleship*. New York: Touchstone, 1995.

———. *Letters and Papers from Prison*. New York: Macmillan, 1971.

Bradshaw, Bruce. *Change Across Cultures: A Narrative Approach to Social Transformation*. Grand Rapids: Baker Academic, 2002.

Christie, Douglas E. "Listening, Reading, Praying: Orality, Literacy and Early Christian Monastic Spirituality." *Anglican Theological Review* 83 (2001) 5–25. http://digitalcomons.lmu.edu/theo_fac/106.

Crabtree, Robin D., and D. Sapp. "Your Culture, My Classroom, Whose Pedagogy? Negotiating Effective Teaching and Learning in Brazil." *Journal of Studies in International Education* 8 (2004) 105–32.

See Basu et al., *Isolated and Proximate Illiteracy*; Maddox, "World's Apart?"; Maddox, "What Good is Literacy?".

81. McCarthy, "'We are Your Books.'"
82. Sienaert, "Levelling," 53.
83. Willis and Greeneish, "What do You Think, Mr. Gutenberg?"

Crook, Zeba. "BTB Readers Guide: Loyalty." *Biblical Theology Bulletin* 34 (2004) 167–77.
———. *Reconceptualizing Conversion: Patronage, Loyalty, and Conversion in the Religions of the Ancient Mediterranean*. Berlin: Walter de Gruyter, 2004.
Einstein, Albert, and A. Calaprice. *The Ultimate Quotable Einstein*. Princeton: Princeton University, 2011.
Foster, Charles R., et al. "Pedagogies of Interpretation in Educating Clergy." *Teaching Theology and Religion* 8 (2005) 204–17.
———. *Educating Clergy: Teaching Practices and Pastoral Imagination*. San Francisco: Jossey-Bass, 2006.
Frankena, William K. *Philosophy of Education*. New York: Macmillan, 1965.
Hiebert, Paul G., et al. *Understanding Folk Religion: A Christian Response to Popular Beliefs and Practices*. Grand Rapids: Baker, 1999.
International Orality Network and Lausanne Committee for World Evangelization. *Making Disciples of Oral Learners*. Lima, NY: Elim, 2005.
Johnson-Miller, Beverly C., and Benjamin D. Espinoza. "Catechesis, Mystagogy, and Pedagogy: Continuing the Conversation." *Christian Education Journal: Research on Educational Ministry* 15 (2018) 156–70.
Jousse, Marcel. *The Oral Style*. Translated by E. Sienaert and R. Whitaker. New York: Routledge, 2015.
Keener, Craig S. "Assumptions in Historical-Jesus Research: Using Ancient Biographies and Disciples' Traditioning as a Control." *Journal for the Study of the Historical Jesus* 9 (2011) 26–58.
Keller, George. *Academic Strategy: The Management Revolution in American Higher Education*. Baltimore, MD: The Johns Hopkins University, 1983.
Ledgerwood, Judy. "Understanding Cambodia: Social Hierarchy, Patron-Client Relationships and Power." http://www.seasite.niu.edu/khmer/ledgerwood/patrons.htm.
Lutgendorf, Philip. *Hanuman's Tale: The Messages of a Divine Monkey*. New York: Oxford University, 2007.
Maddox, Brian. "What Good is Literacy? Insights and Implications of the Capabilities Approach." *Journal of Human Development* 9 (2008) 185–86.
———. "Worlds Apart? Ethnographic Reflections on 'Effective Literacy' and Intrahousehold Externalities." *World Development* 35 (2007) 532–41.
Mazamisa, Welile. "Reading from This Place: From Orality to Literacy/Textuality and Back." *Scriptura* 9 (1991) 67–72.
Mazlish, Bruce. "Invisible Ties: From Patronage to Networks." *Theory, Culture, Society* 17 (2000) 1–19. http://tcs.sagepub.com/content/17/2/1.
McCarthy, Michael C. "'We Are Your Books': Augustine, the Bible, and the Practice of Authority." *Journal of the American Academy of Religion* 75 (2007) 324–52.
Mejudhon, Ubolwan. "Evangelism in the New Millennium: An Integrated Model of Evangelism to Buddhists Using Theology, Anthropology, and Religious Studies." In *Sharing Jesus in the Buddhist World*, edited by D. Lim and S. Spaulding, 95–120. Pasadena, CA: William Carey Library, 2003.
Metaxas, Eric. *Bonhoeffer: Pastor, Martyr, Prophet, Spy*. Nashville: Thomas Nelson, 2010.
Ong, Walter. *Orality and literacy: The Technologizing of the Word*. New York: Routledge, 1982.
Raj, Selva J., and William P. Harman, eds. *Dealing with Deities: The Ritual Vow in South Asia*. Albany, NY: State University of New York, 2006.

Ricœur, Paul. *Interpretation Theory: Discourse and the Surplus of Meaning.* Fort Worth, TX: Texas Christian University, 1973.

Shulman, Lee S. "Pedagogies of Uncertainty." *Liberal Education* 91 (2005) 18–25.

———. "Signature Pedagogies in the Professions." *Daedalus* Summer (2005) 52–9.

Sienaert, Edgard R. "Levelling the Oral-Literate Playing Field: Marcel Jousse's Laboratory of Awareness." In *Or Words to That Effect: Orality and the Writing of Literacy History*, edited by Daniel F. Chamberlain and J. Edward Chamberlin, 47–62. Amsterdam: John Benjamins, 2016. https://www.academia.edu/27880524/LEVELLING_THE_ORAL_LITERATE_PLAYING_FIELD.

Smith, James K. A. *Desiring the Kingdom: Worship, Worldview, and Cultural Formation.* Grand Rapids: Baker Academic, 2009.

Snyder, C. R. "Hypothesis: There is Hope." In *Handbook of Hope: Theories, Measures, and Applications*, edited by C. R. Snyder, 3–21. San Diego: Academic, 2000.

Song, Minho. "Contextualization and Discipleship: Closing the Gap between Theory and Practice." *Evangelical Review of Theology* 30 (2006) 249–62.

Spence-Jones, H. D. M. *The Early Christians in Rome.* London: Methuen, 1911. https://archive.org/details/theearlychristia00spenuoft.

Su, Ya-Hui. "The Constitution of Agency in Developing Lifelong Learning Ability: The 'Being' Mode." *Higher Education* 62 (2011) 399–412.

Thigpen, Lynn. *Connected Learning: A Grounded Theory Study of How Cambodian Adults with Limited Formal Education Learn.* PhD diss., Biola University, 2016.

———. *Connected Learning: How Adults with Limited Formal Education Learn.* Eugene, OR: Pickwick, 2020.

———. "The Dark Side of Orality." In *Honor, Shame, and the Gospel: Reframing Our Message for 21st Century Ministry*, edited by Christopher Flanders and Werner Mischke, 117–126. Pasadena, CA: William Carey, 2020.

———. "An Emic Understanding of the 'Excluded Middle': Spiritual Patronage in Cambodia." *Hiebert Global Center for Intercultural Studies*, 2015. http://www.hiebertglobalcenter.org/1103-2/lynn-thigpen-an-emic-understanding-of-the-excluded-middle-spiritual-patronage-in-cambodia/.

———. *The Oral Bible School.* 2005. http://theoralbibleschool.com.

Tienou, Tite. "The Christian Response to African Traditional Religion." In *Christian Witness in Pluralistic Contexts in the Twenty-First Century*, edited by E. Wan, 209–20. Pasadena, CA: William Carey, 2004.

Willard, Dallas. *The Divine Conspiracy: Rediscovering Our Hidden Life in God.* San Francisco: HarperSanFrancisco, 1998.

———. "Spiritual Disciplines, Spiritual Formation, and the Restoration of the Soul." *Journal of Psychology and Theology* 26 (1998) 101–9.

———. "Spiritual Formation and the Warfare between the Flesh and the Human Spirit." *Journal of Spiritual Formation and Soul Care* 1 (2008) 2–3.

———. "Spiritual Formation: What It Is, and How It Is Done." https://dwillard.org/articles/spiritual-formation-what-it-is-and-how-it-is-done.

Williams, Heather Andrea. *Self-Taught: African American Education in Slavery and Freedom.* Raleigh, NC: University of North Carolina, 2005.

Willis, Avery, and James Greeneish. "What Do You Think, Mr. Guttenberg? The Challenges Print Evangelism Ministries Face in Meeting the Needs of Oral Cultures." *Lausanne World Pulse Archives.* October 2006. https://www.lausanneworldpulse.com/themedarticles-php/507/10-2006.

Concluding Thoughts

CAMERON D. ARMSTRONG

IN AN ARTICLE CHRONICLING missiology's journey for acceptance as a "proper" educational discipline, Tom Steffen wrote, "Missiology demands informed practice and deliberate participation."[1] Steffen's words ring true because missiology moves ministers from ministry to study and back again. Or, to use the words of David Bosch, missiology acts a "gadfly in the house of theology,"[2] since missiologists are always pushing boundaries and calling for ministerial action among real people in the real world. Missiology is an action discipline at heart.

Orality is an action discipline within missiology, albeit one that deserves further scholarly attention. Grounded in the lived experiences of the majority of the world's peoples, orality takes seriously identity and learning preferences and calls educators to creative action. This volume comprises research from multiple authors who believe that, if the Church is tasked with making disciples of all nations and teaching them to obey Christ (Matt 28:19–20), employing orality strategies is not optional.

We all came to this realization in different ways. For my part, I was months away from graduating with my M.Div. degree from a large seminary in the United States. I needed one more class in order to graduate on time, so my advisor suggested I take a one-week class on Bible Storying. Taught by Don Barger (one of the contributors in this book), I found myself simultaneously challenged and excited by orality. I then chose to study orality further by doing a Th.M., where I explored how orality's implications interact with biblical authority and inerrancy.[3] It was during my

---

1. Steffen, "Missiology's Journey," 137.

2. Bosch, *Transforming Mission*, 596.

3. While my ThM thesis is unpublished, I later published my findings in article form. Armstrong, "Contextualization."

Th.M. research that I kept coming across the name Tom Steffen, who was part of the Orality Movement from the beginning. I vowed that if the Lord ever opened the door for me to do a Ph.D., I would like to study under Steffen. Editing a book on orality with Steffen, then, is something of an academic dream come true.

In order for orality to be taken seriously in both the Church and Academy, authors on orality (there is a certain irony in saying that) take several approaches in persuading gatekeepers. First, the *theological approach* points to God as the Sacred Storyteller whose revelation tells a grand narrative with Jesus as the Hero. If God is himself a storyteller, and we are made in God's likeness, we were also made to tell stories in various ways. Second, the related *anthropological approach* highlights how humans are "wired" for stories. Both biological and social evidences demonstrate how orality is more foundational than literacy. Third, an *historical approach* discusses how the Church has always leaned on orality and storying. Only recently has the Church moved theology away from its oral roots. Fourth, authors advocating a *theoretical approach* tend to connect orality with educational research. Using orality strategies, these writers claim, is helpful for good teaching. Fifth, a *pragmatic approach* holds that orality works. It is tested and proven in the real world.

Each of the contributors to this volume apply all five approaches in their chapters. Certainly, each author tends toward one of these approaches (Figure 13.1). Yet they all make use of findings from the other approaches in making their case.

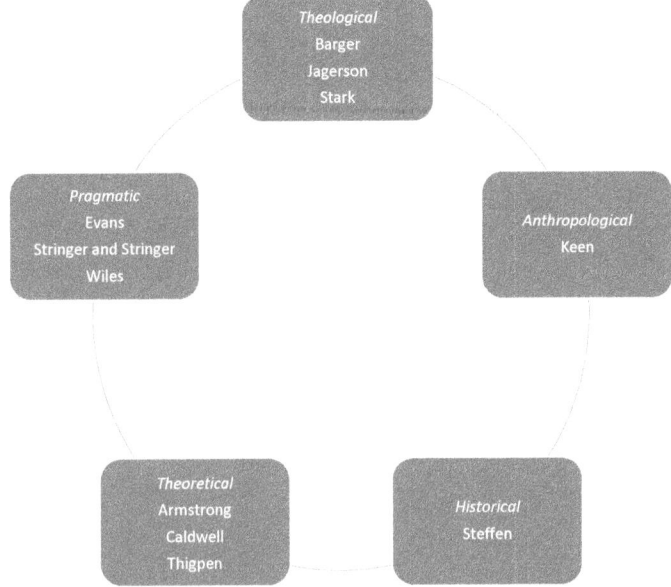

Figure 13.1. Approaches to Orality Research

Of course, the ultimate heartbeat of each author is neither to advance the discipline of orality nor to convince readers to employ orality strategies. Such is our hope, but not our ultimate goal. The ultimate heartbeat of this book is that God might build his global Church with mature and ministering worshipers. In teaching to that end, orality research exposes both a gap and an opportunity for church leaders moving forward.

Bibliography

Armstrong, Cameron D. "Contextualization, Biblical Inerrancy, and the Orality Movement." *Journal of the International Society of Christian Apologetics* 7 (2014) 244–304.
Bosch, David. *Transforming Mission: Paradigm Shifts in Theology of Mission*. American Society of Missiology Series 16. Maryknoll, NY: Orbis, 1991.
Steffen, Tom A. "Missiology's Journey for Acceptance in the Educational World." *Missiology: An International Review* 31 (2003) 131–53.

List of Contributors

Cameron D. Armstrong, PhD, serves with the International Mission Board in Bucharest, Romania. Cameron teaches at the Bucharest Baptist Theological Institute. One of his publications includes *Listening Between the Lines: Thinking Missiologically About Romanian Culture*.

Don Barger, PhD, has served with the International Mission Board since 1997. He has worked with orality projects in Latin America, trained missionaries, and developed strategies for engaging oral people groups. His dissertation topic was *Toward the Development of a Bible Storying Evaluation Model Utilizing a Synthesis of Bible Translation Consultation Models*. He currently lives in Birmingham, Alabama.

Larry Caldwell, PhD, is Academic Dean and Professor of Intercultural Studies and Bible Interpretation at Sioux Falls Seminary in Sioux Falls, SD. In addition, he is Director of Strategy and Senior Missiologist for Converge Worldwide. Prior to this, he and his family were missionaries with Converge for 21 years in Manila, Philippines, where he was Academic Dean and Professor of Missions and Bible Interpretation at Asian Theological Seminary, as well as Director of the Doctor of Missiology program of the Asia Graduate School of Theology—Philippines. Larry teaches regularly on contextualization and cross-cultural Bible interpretation (ethnohermeneutics) at missionary training institutions throughout the world. He has authored dozens of books and articles, and for several years edited the Journal of Asian Mission. His latest book is *Doing Bible Interpretation! Making the Bible Come Alive for Yourself and Your People*.

A. Steven Evans is an IMB missionary communications specialist, focusing on the development and implementation of Orality and Bible Storying projects in southern and central Africa. Several of his projects are in partnership with The Seed Company and WEC Int'l. Among his many articles written and published is "Matters of the Heart: Orality, Storying and Cultural

Transformation–The Critical Role of Storytelling in Affecting Worldview," published by *Missiology*, the journal of the American Society of Missiology.

Jennifer Jagerson, PhD, Prior to becoming an assistant professor at Vanguard University in the Department of Graduate Education, Jennifer served in urban ministry in Los Angeles, as a church planting missionary in New Delhi, India, and as a public school teacher. She had firsthand experience of the effectiveness of Bible storytelling in Delhi, which lead to the privilege of conducting doctoral research on the impact of the Simply the Story Bible storytelling method in rural southwestern Ethiopia. This life transforming experience deeply confirmed the power of the Gospel and the unending riches of God's Word.

Wiley Scot Keen, DMin, is currently pursuing a PhD in Bible Exposition. Scot serves as a trainer for missionary candidates with Ethnos360 (formerly New Tribes Mission). Scot has been teaching at Ethnos360 Bible Institute since 2003, where he currently serves as Academic Dean of Online Education. In addition to his ministry with Ethnos360, Scot also develops cross-cultural training resources for Access Truth.

John Stark, PhD, joined Spoken Worldwide in 2015, where he provides global development and directional insight to deliver training and operational oversight to local language translation teams as they translate the Bible into oral delivery formats. He has taught classes at Houghton University and at Dallas International University, where he continues to serve as adjunct faculty. Previously, he was involved in Bible translation and leadership positions with SIL in Peru and Nigeria.

Tom Steffen, DMiss, is professor emeritus of intercultural studies at the Cook School of Intercultural Studies, Biola University. He specializes in church multiplication, orality, honor and shame, and business as mission. He and his family spent 15 years in the Philippines in church planting and consulting. Semi-retired, he continues to teach courses, advise dissertations, publish, and consult. His latest books include: *The Return of Oral Hermeneutics: As Good Today as It Was for the Hebrew Bible and First-Century Christianity*: *The Facilitator Era: Beyond Pioneer Church Multiplication*; and *Worldview-based Storying: The Integration of Symbol, Story, and Ritual in the Orality Movement*.

LIST OF CONTRIBUTORS

Tricia Stringer and Stephen Stringer have served with the International Mission Board for 22 years in West Africa and South Asia. They are now based in the United Kingdom and travel globally in their roles. In their role as Scripture Resource Specialists, they help field teams develop and strategically implement appropriate Scripture resources in accessible formats. Stephen also serves on the Global Executive Team of the International Orality Network, and Tricia leads New Hope, a trauma healing initiative that helps teams develop trauma-informed church planting and discipleship strategies.

Lynn Thigpen, PhD, is an emeritus missionary with the International Mission Board. Having ministered over 25 years in Southeast Asia in Singapore and Cambodia, she is a passionate advocate for Adults with Limited Formal Education (ALFE) or oral/connected learners. She is an adjunct professor at Liberty University and the director of The Wisdom Project, which plans to offer coursework in orality on a global scale through Gateway Seminary's ADVANCE program.

Jerry Wiles, serves as the North America Regional Director for the International Orality Network, President Emeritus of Living Water International, and Mission Advisor with Missio Nexus for Orality Methods and Strategy. He has more than 40 years of experience in ministry and international mission work. He is an author and radio program producer and has been a frequent guest on radio and television talk shows and traveled extensively as a public speaker. Jerry is a United States Air Force veteran, former pastor, and university administrator. He and his wife, Sheila, have two grown children and seven grandchildren.

www.ingramcontent.com/pod-product-compliance
Lightning Source LLC
Chambersburg PA
CBHW071235230426
43668CB00011B/1444